Praise for *Death*

"Elvia Wilk is one of the most exciting essayists wo.......
love this book."   —Catherine Lacey, author of *Pew*

"It's rare to come across an essay collection that veers so far into
the wilds of weirdness, only to return from these distant outposts
with something so deeply honest, vulnerable, and close. Wilk is
a writer of exceptional talent, but it is the sheer scale and scope
of her curiosity that makes these essays not only unforgettable
but intellectually rearranging. *Death by Landscape* pulls off a won-
drous bit of alchemy—it takes what might otherwise be terminus
ideas, sites of conclusion, and transforms them into conduits of
passage, a way of reassessing what it means to be human in this
age of endless unmooring."   —Omar El Akkad, author of
What Strange Paradise and *American War*

"Wilk's brilliant interlinked essays show why fiction matters in
a time of climate catastrophe, species devastation, and radical
inequality. From the old weird to the new, sci-fi to cli-fi, medieval women's mysticism to larps, Wilk gives us a roadmap
through unfamiliar pasts and unsettling presents, pointing toward unpredictable futures that fiction—in its multiple, shifting,
compostable forms—enables us to imagine. Treading the fine, impossible line between dystopia and utopia, between trauma, its
repetition, and its working through, Wilk doesn't pretend fiction
can fix everything, but she does insist—and she shows—that the
effects of fiction 'are myriad small explosions with far-reaching
fragments,' fragments that help us grapple with what life means
and how best to live it while we can."   —Amy Hollywood,
author of *Acute Melancholia and Other Essays*

"I love these weird essays. They do best what weirdness always wants to do: defamiliarize the world around us so that we may better see where we've ended up, where we might be going, and who—or what—has been chasing after us all this time. Weirdness, Wilk writes, 'provides a sort of methodology for reading stories that lead toward the black hole.' The places, people, things that resist description, challenge our fictions and nonfictions. A black hole is impossible to enter without warping your reality, death beyond death: Wilk scrapes the event horizon and gazes at last into the spooky abyss."   —Andrew Durbin, author of *Skyland* and *MacArthur Park*

"Wilk has written a guidebook and a philosophy for living in a precarious world, in essays that are searching and funny, self-assured and unguarded all at once. With each chapter Wilk directs her telescopic focus on plants and rot, mysticism and black holes, female embodiment and trauma, weaving together seemingly disparate topics with an intelligence that recalls the best of Mark Fisher and Wayne Koestenbaum. Reading *Death by Landscape*, I feel terrified and exalted, expanded, in awe."

—Madeleine Watts, author of *The Inland Sea*

"Wilk is that cool person I want to hang out with at the end of the world. Too smart to despair and too curious to not reexamine even the most studied phenomena (nature, trauma, ambition) until they're no longer familiar and are catching new light. *Death by Landscape* is beautifully written, expansive, athletic, weird, and funny."   —Britt Wray, author of *Generation Dread* and *Rise of the Necrofauna*

"Wilk's learned and bracing essays distribute the mind out beyond the stubborn habits and enclosures of our 'humanities'—out past hack plots or boundaries assigned to gender or species—where it can expand into subsoil or outer space or corpuscle in narratives weird enough to reflect another human/nonhuman social life."

—Keller Easterling, author of *Medium Design*
and *Extrastatecraft*

"Wilk reads the world like an insect reads a garden; her approach is sensory and kaleidoscopic, buzzing beyond manicured surfaces to get at the fertile, loamy rot beneath everything from black holes and science fiction dystopias to martyred saints and larpers. Beautifully brainy, bug-eyed, and weird." —Claire L. Evans,
author of *Broad Band*

"Wilk reports on psychic borders, the lines drawn between earth and earthling, plant and steward, healthy and sick. She finds false binaries we hadn't even thought to count and asks the human to find its humanity, gently but without wavering. Brilliant and swift, as she always is." —Sasha Frere-Jones, musician and writer

"With evocative clarity and intuitive rigor, Wilk's *Death by Landscape* guides us through a troubled terrain criss-crossed by that most uncanny of entities, 'nature.' This is writing that uniquely extends the tradition of speculative nonfiction, delineating a new constellation of culture and climate that ultimately points to the nebulous horizon of human being itself."

—Eugene Thacker, author of *In the Dust
of This Planet* and *Infinite Resignation*

ALSO BY ELVIA WILK

Oval

DEATH BY LANDSCAPE

Essays

ELVIA WILK

Soft Skull   New York

Please see image permissions on page 303 for individual credit. For quoted material in the epigraphs, all reasonable efforts were made to contact the copyright holders.

Excerpt on page 69 from *The Gift: Imagination and the Erotic Life of Property* by Lewis Hyde, copyright © 1979, 1980, 1983 by W. Lewis Hyde. Used by permission of Random House, an imprint and division of Penguin Random House LLC. All rights reserved. Excerpt on page 147 from "The Arc" from *Half-light: Collected Poems 1965-2016* by Frank Bidart, copyright © 2017 by Frank Bidart. Reprinted by permission of Farrar, Straus and Giroux. All rights reserved. Excerpt(s) from *As I Lay Dying* by William Faulkner, copyright 1930 and © renewed 1958 by William Faulkner. Used by permission of Random House, an imprint and division of Penguin Random House LLC. All rights reserved.

Library of Congress Cataloging-in-Publication Data
Names: Wilk, Elvia, author.
Title: Death by landscape : essays / Elvia Wilk.
Description: First Soft Skull edition. | New York : Soft Skull, 2022. |
    Includes bibliographical references.
Identifiers: LCCN 2021051433 | ISBN 9781593767150 (paperback) | ISBN
    9781593767167 (ebook)
Subjects: LCGFT: Essays.
Classification: LCC PS3623.I5452 D43 2022 | DDC 814/.6--dc23/
eng/20211112
LC record available at https://lccn.loc.gov/2021051433

Cover design by houseofthought.io
Book design by Jordan Koluch

Published by Soft Skull Press
New York, NY
www.softskull.com

Printed in the United States of America
10 9 8 7 6 5 4

For Andreas

Each sentence is a kind of promise, an increment of hope that replaces the broken promise of the last sentence. What is that promise? That the world will continue, that one image will replace the next forever—that is, the world will respond to your love by loving you back.

—ROBERT GLÜCK

Miracle is a shorthand for this, for all those moments when, against all odds, people living all of their lives in one genre suddenly slip out and make their way into another.

—WAI CHEE DIMOCK

CONTENTS

1. Plants

2. Planets

3. Bleed

CONTENTS

Epilogue

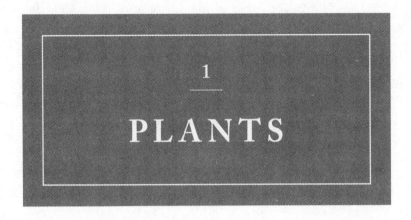

1

PLANTS

Death by Landscape

Reading figure and ground

TWO ADOLESCENT GIRLS GO for a hike. They are away from home, at summer camp, and they have left the main group of campers to wander up a rocky hillside thick with trees. The girls are extremely close, as young girls often are; their thoughts and feelings and bodies are all wound up with each other's. As they're walking, one of the girls steps off the main path to pee behind a tree. A minute later, her friend hears a strange shout. She runs into the brush, but no one is there. The girl is gone. Disappeared. All that's left are trees.

This is the premise of a 1990 short story by Margaret Atwood called "Death by Landscape." Atwood's story is told from the perspective of the surviving woman, decades later. Her friend never reappeared, and the loss has haunted the narrator for her whole life. Meanwhile, she has developed an obsession with landscape paintings of forests. She collects them and covers the walls of her home with them. Staring at the paintings in her room one evening, she remarks that they seem to "open inward on the wall, not like windows but like doors." And sometimes, after looking at a painting for several hours, she thinks she glimpses her lost friend in the image—not as she was, in human form, or hidden among the trees, but *as* a tree. She admits that she has come to believe the hillside gained a new tree the day of the disappearance.

If you take the narrator's conclusion at face value, the death at the center of "Death by Landscape" is not a death at all. It's a transition, a twin becoming of girl and tree. The figure becomes part of the landscape, and so the landscape becomes a kind of figure. Situating her aging narrator in a room full of landscapes, Atwood presents the person–plant transition as something like an optical trick. In that gap of perception, figure and landscape merge or flip. As the narrator says: "There are no backgrounds in any of these paintings, no vistas; only a great deal of foreground that goes back and back, endlessly, involving you in its twists and turns of tree and branch and rock."

The word *landscape* is typically used to suggest the passive, the inert, the natural—the plant, animal, and mineral world that constitutes a backdrop for a human actor. But here, the sudden absence of a human actor occasions a sudden presence: the presence of landscape, the presence of plants.

Western literary forms tend to focus on the story of a person against the backdrop of the world. From the epic poem to the biblical tale to the bildungsroman to the biography to contemporary autofiction, stories map plot onto individual character development, prioritizing single perspectives. The scope may be large—a century, a war, an environmental cataclysm, an interstellar journey—yet a person or people are foregrounded in order to convey the meaning of the events through the microcosm. Even when an individual life is trivialized against "big" world events, people remain the vehicles for comprehension, identification, and meaning. That people identify with people is understandable. In one sense, that's what a story is: people acting and being acted upon by one another and the world.

This structure has many well-documented drawbacks. Author Amitav Ghosh, for one, points out that it risks relying on the "individual moral adventure" mode, which he says "banishes the collective from the territory of the fictional imagination." Whether a heroic saga or a bourgeois comedy of manners, the individual story told against the backdrop of the big picture cleaves the two apart even when it intends to show how they connect. In the era of climate change, Ghosh argues that this is an untenable position— and that future generations will name our era "the great derangement" because of our "collective suicide" as opposed to collective action in response to the urgent threat facing the human species.

While Ghosh's focus is on the realist novel, his complaint applies to other forms of literature, through which climate change has been turned into a "moral issue," in which "individual conscience" is to blame. But the problem is not only that the human collective with its historical interconnectedness and its political potential is banished from the story. The nonhuman world is also banished to the background.

In reaction to the figurative tradition, painting has upended the classic figure-ground composition through countless maneuvers over the past century and a half. Cubism fractured the figure, abstract expressionism dissolved it into the field, and conceptual projects erased it in various ways—including mutilating or destroying the canvas itself. Similarly, alternative and often drastic methods of approaching the "canvas" of the novel have flourished at both the center and margins of literature. Multiple perspectives, fragmented narratives, epistolary exchanges, interactive electronic texts, and taking on the perspectives of animals, aliens, or machines are but a few such techniques (the lesser-known of which Ghosh overlooks).

One ambitious attempt to undo the individual-moral-adventure story was the postmodern systems novel, which intended to depict entire political, social, and technological systems by zooming in and out on figure and ground. The concept was introduced in the late eighties by the critic Tom LeClair, who chose the fiction of Don DeLillo as the quintessential example. LeClair claimed that DeLillo and others, such as Robert Coover, Thomas Pynchon, and William Gaddis, were using fiction to analyze the complex systems of society, technology, and politics from a structural level. DeLillo's early novels sketch vast political and corporate conspiracies just beyond the fingertips of the central character, whose individual moral adventure is his paranoid pursuit to comprehend the whole system from shards of evidence. The "system" of the systems novel is never fully revealed, but the reader is given to believe that, behind the scenes, something or someone is pulling the strings.

The term *systems novel* was maligned by many readers as well as authors themselves, who saw their works as diverse and exploratory rather than reducible to a set of general principles. Yet there are qualities typical of the project: the character of the classic systems novel is a white Western man, as are the majority of the authors themselves. Despite the focus on macrolevel occurrences and interconnectedness, there remains a protagonist: the mystified guy (or guys) at the center. He may feel personally small or powerless, but his experience is the lens through which human experience is meant to be extrapolated. Most of the time, the systems in which he is embroiled are social, technical, and political, rather than ecological, suggesting a separation between the human realm (system) and the natural world (ecosystem). In books about systems, men tend to emerge from the background rather than merge into it.

As in figurative painting, continuous assaults on form and various claims that the protagonist-led story (or the single author) is "dead" have done nothing to delete its legacy or stop people from making more figure-led work. Arguably, the various attempts to undermine the supremacy of the figure have only served to cement its centrality: even when the figure is not taken for granted, it becomes the element for the author to react against. Figurative artwork and novels persist, and with good reason; stories about people are one of the best technologies we have for understanding what it means to be a person. But what it means to be a person in an age of drastic ecosystemic decline—of planetary extinction—is changing.

———

Atwood does not show the woman–plant transformation, but other authors tell similar stories along more explicit lines. Anne

Richter's very short story from 1967 called "The Sleep of Plants" starts with a young woman who finds herself increasingly estranged from her family and her fiancé. She feels adrift, physically ill, exhausted, unmoored. Depressed. One day she has an uncontrollable urge to plant herself in a large pot and fill it with soil up to her hips. "How good it felt! Never had she known such ecstasy. She was back in her element." From then on, she simply refuses to move. She has no need for food or exercise. Her family goes to extremes to try to get her out of the pot. Her fiancé accuses her of "deliberately destroying" herself, refusing to speak to her, and her mother stops watering her in punishment. She sees no reason to respond; there's no point in trying to explain herself or talk back. She waits patiently. "She saw that, by dint of stillness and withdrawal, you felt yourself become the center of the world, the source of its movement," Richter writes. "She decided to fall silent, and in silence, animate the world." Slowly, her feet become roots and her limbs become branches, and eventually she becomes indistinguishable from a tree. Her fiancé gives up and marries someone else, but he agrees to move her outside to his yard and plant her in the soil. The tree lives there contentedly until long after everyone she's known is dead.

Kathe Koja describes a more disturbing metamorphosis in "The Neglected Garden," from 1991. A couple living in a country house have a fight, and the man tells the woman to get out, threatening violence. But the woman can't bring herself to leave. Instead, she impales herself on the fence in their backyard. As the hours and days pass, she becomes host to plant life, her body becoming horribly infected and then festering and withering.

But soon she is resurrected in full bloom, a monstrous conglomeration of human body and rotting/growing vegetal splendor. Her husband, enraged and terrified, douses the organism that used to be his wife with herbicide, hoping to murder her—but she absorbs the chemical, thrives, and reanimates. Finally, she comes after him.

In both Richter's and Koja's stories, a woman implants herself in despair, but also in protest. To plant: to stake firmly, to fix in place. She's tired of being told where to go, whom to marry, what to eat, how to act. In Richter's story, she falls peacefully silent; in Koja's, she becomes a frightening interspecies catastrophe. In what may look like a gesture of passivity, even self-destruction—imprisoning herself in a pot, crucifying herself on a fence post—these characters stop, plant themselves in the landscape, and grow.

One might think that, given some of Atwood's self-stated politics, stories like hers affirm the traditional links made between the femme and the natural. But far from romanticizing what an Enlightenment writer might depict as an innate, wholesome, womanly connection with nature, these texts drive a garden stake through the heart of the classic female imperative to "put down roots and start a family." After all, women are supposed to be good at becoming one with nature: nurturing, caring, gestating, helping others grow. Like the family garden, like the earth, they are supposed to be penetrable, unbounded, fertile, ready for implantation and extraction. But the becoming-plant that happens in these stories instead constitutes resistance through noncompliance. This is a type of resistance that women, and other supposedly unstable bodies, have been cultivating for centuries, because they've had to.

———

These stories of women-becoming-plant are weird ones, according to Mark Fisher's definition of the term in his 2016 book *The Weird and the Eerie*. By working through a series of examples from music, movies, and books (including Atwood's work), Fisher outlines the concept of weirdness as an "outside" space that "lies beyond standard perception, cognition and experience." He explains that this "outside is not 'empirically' exterior; it is transcendentally exterior, i.e., it is not just a matter of something being distant in space and time, but of something which is beyond our ordinary experience and conception of space and time itself." A weird occurrence might happen right in front of you, but it is not completely explainable according to current structures for categorizing the world. And yet it has happened: you can come in contact with it, experience it, and try to describe it, all the while knowing description will fall short.

Fisher provides a counterpart to the weird with the notion of the eerie. Eeriness often accompanies weirdness, but it is more "tied up with questions of agency," present in moments of undefined causality and confusing animacy. An eerie event, like the classic spooky cry from the forest, scrambles cause and effect. Who is making the noise? Does the cry instigate an event, or signal that one has already happened? In an eerie scenario, something formerly thought of as passive, like a tree branch, may suddenly appear to have active powers. And the thing formerly thought of as presiding over the landscape, namely the human, may seem to have less control over the world. This is why "we find the eerie more readily in landscapes partially emptied of the human."

The weird and the eerie might sound similar to Freud's well-known theory of the *unheimlich*, the uncanny. But Fisher says that ultimately Freud's concept "is as disappointing as any mediocre genre detective's rote solution to a mystery" in that it reduces every experience of the uncanny to a threat to the white man's (sexual) supremacy; that is, castration anxiety. And while Freud focuses on elements of the homely or the domestic that are unnerving and strange, the weird and the eerie do the opposite: "they allow us to see the inside from the perspective of the outside." It's only when you get a glimpse back at "normal" space that you realize you've been living in an inside at all. As in Plato's allegory, the person who escapes the cave doesn't realize he's been confusing shadows with real images and objects until he's out in the sun.

Taken together, the weird and the eerie are ways of describing what Fisher calls "that which does not belong." Specifically, that which does not belong to typical systems of taxonomy, reason, time sequencing, or rationality—the structures that most individual-moral-adventure stories, for instance, rely on. Importantly, the reason weird and eerie events or things do not belong is not that they are *un*natural or *super*natural. The weird stories Fisher describes are not about robots or fairies. "Natural" is exactly what is displaced, or made to not belong, in a weird story. So is "human."

For Fisher, weirdness and eeriness do not exactly constitute genres. They may have been "found at the edges of genres such as horror and science fiction," but "these genre associations have obscured what is specific to the weird and the eerie." Actually, weirdness and eeriness are produced precisely when genre expectations are not fulfilled.

Yet the term *weird* in particular has been attached to a body of literature dating back to the late nineteenth and early twentieth centuries. The most-cited weird author is H. P. Lovecraft—best known for his 1926 story "The Call of Cthulhu" about a horrific, fascinating, tentacled, ancient creature who rises from the depths of time to destroy the main character's belief in empirical reason and historical progress and, ultimately, his sense of self. The story, like most of Lovecraft's work, deals with the wonder and horror at the fringes of human consciousness—the smallness and insignificance of the human figure in relation to the shocking enormity of the universe.

Discussions of Lovecraft and his contemporaries, like Algernon Blackwood and William Hope Hodgson, burst into prominence in arts and humanities discourse in the 1990s and 2000s. (Fisher reports that he was spurred to write *The Weird and the Eerie* following two symposia on Lovecraft in the mid-2000s.) It was at this point that the notion of "weird" literature solidified, and Lovecraft became its prominent origin figure. This popularity was due to the fact that Lovecraftian fiction's discomforting insinuation that human existence is finite seems like a sage foreshadowing of our current awareness of deep time and extinction. The story of an archaic sea creature coming back to claim its due maps easily onto fears tied to the Anthropocene. Yet in Lovecraft, the figure positioned against the ground is still the white man confronted with an uncontrollable reality he doesn't fully understand, and which he perceives as threatening. Given Lovecraft's implication that the nonhuman (non-white-man) is potentially scary, it's no coincidence that a lot of his ideas, expressed in and out of his fiction, are clearly racist, sexist, and xenophobic. As the author Marlon James puts it, in Lovecraftian tales "the other always comes from the South. The other always comes from darkness."

Certain marginalized bodies have historically been designated weird in the negative sense, historically aligned with the "outside," the freaky, the abnormal, the exotic. To quote Erik Davis, author of the book *High Weirdness*, the "weirdo is a social outcast, it's a social position, not just a genre or an aesthetic vibe." Fascination with and fear of the other are embedded in old weird tales—in which the white guy is the figure and everyone and everything else is landscape. The stories' fear and excitement are precisely due to the eerie suggestion that the primeval, pastoral, nonwhite, nonmale world may not be so inert after all. While some have tried to ignore these aspects of Lovecraft's writing or, conversely, to remove him from the literary canon of weirdness, it's impossible to understand the possibilities and dangers of weirdness as a concept without taking his work into account.

Although it was likely around for some time before, in the mid-2000s, the term *new weird* entered circulation as a way of describing contemporary fiction that takes up old weird concerns with a new ecological awareness in mind. In *The New Weird*, their compendium of short stories from 2008, Ann and Jeff VanderMeer describe it as "a type of urban, secondary-world fiction that subverts the romanticized ideas about place found in traditional fantasy, largely by choosing realistic, complex real-world models as the jumping off point." For my part—specifics aside—in new weird I find a type of fiction that appropriates the capacity of old weird to estrange the familiar, but challenges its tendency to equate the unfamiliar with the freaky or frightening other.

James Baldwin wrote in 1964 that "it has always been much easier (because it has always seemed much safer) to give a name to the evil without than to locate the terror within." While old weird does the former, new weird—with or without the genre title—may have potential to do the latter. Rather than simply redrawing boundaries of normality to be more inclusive, new weird fiction might map the same strangeness certain subjects have historically been afforded onto other subjects, in order to acknowledge the inherent strangeness of any such constructs—especially those drawn along the lines of race, gender, class, or ability. In other words, what feels weird or eerie depends on who you are, and is therefore subject to change.

———

A story by Han Kang, "The Fruit of My Woman" from 1997, features a drawn-out and grisly description of the woman–plant event. The husband in this story ignores alarming warning signs as his wife slowly stops speaking, stops eating, and develops brutal bruises all over her body that she can't explain. He feels "oddly withdrawn from the whole situation" as she becomes "unfamiliar, almost unreal" to him, and takes her at her word when she says the doctor has declared her perfectly healthy. When he returns from a trip one day, he finds her immobilized on their apartment balcony, halfway transitioned into a leafy green creature who is barely able to utter a sound. He realizes she desperately needs soil and water, which he dutifully provides.

The husband watches, transfixed, as roots sprout from her thighs and her body contorts into a stem—at first he is horrified, but subsequently he remarks that his wife has never been so beautiful. He becomes newly devoted to this silent botanic specimen, more attentive to her changes and needs than ever before. When the season turns to autumn, he realizes that she will soon wither away. (Presumably she is an annual and not a perennial.) But before she dies, a handful of hard green fruits burst from her mouth, which he plants in the hopes that they will bear new life in spring.

While Kang tells most of the story in third person, a section near the end is composed of short missives from the wife's perspective. Most of them are addressed to "Mother." They describe the woman's transition to plant life—at first she has only a nightly dream about growing "tall as a poplar" and pushing through the roof of the house, but then she feels her body beginning to transform in waking life. "This is how I escape from this flat," she explains, indicating a desperation to change her lot, but then again: "I was unhappy at home and equally unhappy elsewhere, so tell me, where should I have gone?" Her answer is to go nowhere, to escape her physical form instead. She is momentarily scared when she realizes winter will bring her death, but overall she is calm and relieved. "Soon, I know, even thought will be lost to me, but I'm alright. I've dreamed of this, of being able to live on nothing but wind, sunlight and water, for a long time now."

This story is a precursor to Kang's popular novel *The Vegetarian*, published a decade later, which follows a similar arc. The novel's protagonist, Yeong-hye, starves herself, unable to participate in the violence of human life any longer, even the violence of material destruction required to eat, and longs to disappear into the trees. The translator of "The Fruit of My Woman" explains the primary difference between the novel and the short story: "While *The Vegetarian* eschews anything explicitly supernatural—Yeong-hye's desire to turn into a tree is seen by those around her as a symptom of mental illness, and there is nothing in the narrative itself to disprove this reading—the nameless protagonist of 'The Fruit of My Woman' really does become a plant: leaves, berries and all." These divergent endings situate the stories in different genre realms. While the book sticks to the plausible and keeps becoming-plant as a metaphor, the story goes all the way there. It's fully weird.

———

There is a duality to plants. Most species have two parts: one above ground and one below. They "are beings that are ecologically and structurally double," writes philosopher Emanuele Coccia in *The Life of Plants*. "The root is like a second body, secret, esoteric, hidden; an antibody, an anatomical antimatter that reverses as in a mirror, point by point, everything the other body does." With their two bodies, plants are simultaneously active and passive, absorptive and productive.

According to writer Daisy Hildyard, in the era of climate change people have developed two bodies, too. In her book-length essay, *The Second Body*, Hildyard writes that to be alive in this century is to possess both "an individual body in which you exist, eat, sleep and go about your day-to-day life," and also "a second body which has an impact on foreign countries and on whales." The first body is the one you familiarly refer to when you go to work or have sex or feel a headache coming on. I might call the second body the ecosystemic body—the one that is constantly implicated in and influenced by ecologies beyond the individual self.

The ecosystemic body is different from the public body or the social body in that it is tethered—in ways both identifiable and mysterious—to microbes, mosquitoes, whales, ice shelves, landfills, and annual average rainfall, as well as, of course, human political and social formations. Sometimes you are aware of your second body and sometimes you can't fathom it exists: "In normal life, a human body is rarely understood to exist outside its own skin—it is supposed to be inviolable," writes Hildyard. But "climate change creates a new language, in which you have to be all over the place; you are always . . . implicated in the whole world." You may feel an imperative to acknowledge the second body's existence and act responsible for it—by, say, conserving water and recycling—but you also understand that you may never see the effects.

The two-body problem is another way of thinking about the figure-ground problem. The first body is figure, your figure, and the second body is the world formerly known as ground. To be aware of having two bodies is to experience a constant toggling between self and world, which can be enlightening but can also bring on a sense of horror. Where does the self begin and end? Hildyard seems to suggest that finding ways to connect the two bodies through the tactic of narrative is a political maneuver in itself. The old feminist adage "the personal is political" applies here, but it's not only that politics plays out on the level of daily life, or that political change begins at home. It's that many specific political problems today are due to the fact that planetary systems are more giant and more interconnected than the human brain can grasp, and yet every(first)body knows we are wound up in them. In this situation, making connections across scales through stories is a political project in itself.

Hildyard ends *The Second Body* with the story of her home being flooded by a river, a moment in which her two bodies collide. As water overtakes the house, background crashes into foreground. The water contaminates her home and the ensuing pollution and rot eventually make her sick. Micro and macro, first body and second body, connect in a tangible, unavoidable way. Though the two bodies might seem very distinct in everyday life, Hildyard shows how they are inextricable. It is both impossible and necessary to tell both stories at once.

———

Scale discrepancy boggles the mind. Facts, numbers, and news often create a sense of estrangement or alienation as much as they provide points of contact between the first and second bodies. Philosopher Steven Shaviro explains how fiction is uniquely capable of making scalar connections that enable readers to understand how people are part of the planet:

> Fiction is one of the best tools we have for making sense of hyperbolic situations ... Both in its large-scale world-building and in its small-scale attention to the particular ways in which social and technical innovations affect our lives ... fiction comes to grips with abstractions like economies, social formations, technological infrastructures, and climate perturbations ... We may model such an object mathematically and computationally; or else we may encapsulate it in the form of a story.

While systems novels attempt to encapsulate abstractions in the form of stories, they do so through narratives of finite selves with fixed identities. These selves belong inescapably (and paranoidly) to (partially obscured) systems. From an ecosystems perspective, however, the human is not a self-contained element but completely inseparable from all other organisms, both on micro and macro levels. The human body itself is host to a vast ecosystem of trillions of other creatures; the membranes of the body are porous, and it's not possible to affirm the boundary between inside and out. An ecosystems fiction would be a fiction of (new) weirdness, in that it destabilizes what is known and what is knowable, and it may also be eerie, in that no single human actor or conspiracy of actors is the cause for the world's effects. Ecosystems fiction might account for the second body, and in doing so insist that figure and ground are not distinct from each other. Other divisions between human and nonhuman, technological and natural, might then begin to decompose.

In its original definition, an ecosystem is composed mainly of biological organisms, but in recent common usage, which is the way I intend to use it, it includes other nonhuman elements, like geological formations, technologies, and even other planets. Unlike a system (the sort emphasized in systems fiction), it does not also contain concepts, abstractions, linguistic patterns, or ideologies—although these are all implicated in how ecosystems are conceived of and governed. An ecosystem is composed of matter.

Recent examples of what could be called ecosystems fiction include Jeff VanderMeer's 2014 Southern Reach trilogy, in which a scientist merges with the mysterious alien landscape she attempts to study, or Richard Powers's *The Overstory* (2018), a tale of deforestation narrated through multiple human encounters with trees. One could also take the work of Helen Phillips, whose body-horror time-travel novel *The Need* (2019) frames an ancient paleobotanical rift as the source of identity struggle, or Tricia Sullivan's *Occupy Me* (2016), where bodies contain multiple universes. This kind of thinking is nothing new, with antecedents in Samuel R. Delany, Octavia E. Butler, Ursula K. Le Guin, Italo Calvino, Stanisław Lem, James Tiptree Jr., and many others. Yet much of this work has long been relegated to genre shelves. As author McKenzie Wark has stated, it's not that fiction adequately tackling climate change is lacking; it's that, due to entrenched divisions staking out the concerns of mainstream literary fiction as those of the human hero, "the fiction that takes climate change seriously [has not been] taken seriously as fiction."

While I'm loosely reading works by these authors as ecosystems fiction, and suggesting they be "taken seriously" as such, subsuming them into a new category is somewhat counter to the aims of this reading. There is no single narrative mode that is aesthetically or politically superior for addressing ecosystemic change or collapse. And it's not that any particular kind of story structure or genre is obsolete. What these books have in common is that they work against the supremacy of any one genre in service of weirdness.

———

The story of person-becoming-plant is not about reversal or reversion to some imagined natural state. Instead it provides a counterpoint to any quick-fix, back-to-the-land fantasy, which sees nature as distinct, permanent, unchanging, passive, authentic, and fundamentally good. The idea is not that nature will heal what ails these characters, that they will become natural "again." On the contrary, it's about seeing people as always already plant, plant as always already human, and those distinctions as always already weird. Weirdness resists the idea that everything can be explained by humans, but doesn't give up on the importance of human experience and ability to access and affect the world. This requires some kind of surrender to the unknown, which makes humanity itself an unknown category—whose outlines get messy and whose central importance in the universe is not self-evident.

Since at least the Enlightenment, the human has been enshrined as a necessary classification, in that it has supposedly been used to grant equality among humans. Again and again, the category has been updated to be more politically inclusive, as if calling everyone a person is enough to deconstruct hierarchies and systems of oppression. Who or what counts as human has continually shifted to accommodate political aims. When convenient, corporations have been granted elements of personhood in the eyes of the law, affording them rights and freedoms formerly reserved for individuals. On the other side, groups such as the great ape personhood movement advocate extending something like human rights to animals in order to prevent their mistreatment. And a handful of courts around the world have granted geological formations such as bodies of water legal personhood in response to claims that rivers and lakes deserve respect and autonomy (namely from the corporations and governments that seek to destroy them for profit).

Claiming personhood is perhaps the most obvious strategy at hand within a humanist system that sees the human species as the supreme form of being. Yet the category has always been composed of hierarchies and categories both internal and external to the concept, which have failed humans and nonhumans alike. Present circumstances—increasingly felt in moments of collision between the two bodies, such as the river flooding and contaminating Hildyard's house—require us to relinquish the human's position at the top of the pyramid and the center of the world, the protagonist leading the plotline of history. An ecosystems approach sees all elements as vital influences, and not because they are as important as people but because people are interdependent, too. After all, it is due to our interdependence that humans, like all other elements of ecosystems, are facing extinction.

To propose altering the human role in the story of the world might sound counterintuitive, given that people have caused the disaster. But only a perspective shift in terms of figure and ground can adequately portray the ecological dependencies that have led the world to environmental cataclysm, the interconnectedness that neoliberal capitalism and its pervasive story forms continue to violently deny. This move could also shift the political responsibility from the generalized human collective that Ghosh refers to, onto the few rich people and corporations largely culpable for the ongoing disaster.

Where do I situate myself in this book of essays about the importance of ecosystems beyond the human, in a book about what the world might look like without finite selves at all? I am here throughout the essays, because I am not nowhere, but my presence is between the trees, at least at first. As this book moves forward I appear more and more, and what begins as a look outward becomes an interrogation of the writing process and the self. This is a book about becoming what you study, about what it feels like to embed in the landscape.

When a person enters a coma, the person is sometimes said to enter a vegetative state. *Vegetable* is a derogatory word. Becoming plant, one would think, is to become less than human, to relinquish agency, to immobilize oneself, to stop moving forward. But moving forward hasn't worked. Emerging from and acting upon the landscape hasn't worked. Instead, rooting oneself and learning to become part of the landscape could be seen as a ferocious claim to life. This may not be the same as life now, but it is life. In this sense, "death by landscape" is a kind of life through landscape, life only possible through landscape. This may be terrifying, but it may also be thrilling. At the end of the Atwood story, the woman who has lost her friend hears a human-sounding shout from one of the landscape paintings. It's not a shout of fear, like she might have anticipated. It is a shout, she says, of "recognition or of joy."

This Compost

Erotics of rot

Drunk birds

At some point in the early 2010s, variations of a pop-science news story about birds began to circulate online. "Study says pollution makes birds gay," or "Gay by mercury," read the headlines. Scientists had observed that high levels of mercury in wetland habitats had been altering the "pairing behavior and reproductive success" of a species of white ibis. This was just one of many recent examples of how pollutants leaking into the environment have been changing animals' hormone systems, traits, and behaviors—here, the story was disproportionately sensationalized due to its tinge of salaciousness. In this case, it appears that some white ibises now prefer same-sex relations over straight ones. One frequently circulated image shows a pair of male ibises strolling together along a shoreline, looking very gay indeed.

The tone of such stories is one of alarm. And it is surely alarming that human-made pollutants are altering the endocrine systems of other species. White ibises who do not breed with one another are more likely to go extinct, further reducing the planet's rapidly diminishing biodiversity. The gay birds represent yet another example—part of a long list—of human behavior damaging the planetary ecosystem in unexpected ways.

Yet the consistent focus on the birds' sexually "atypical" behavior indicates another type of alarmism, too. Queerness, here, is presented as a direct result of a toxic environment, a freakish aberration from the birds' "natural" straight orientation and egg-laying lives. Aligned with the toxic and the unnatural, the birds are anthropomorphized and their sexualities moralized according to human biases, their gayness taken as proof that the environment is poisonous. In an essay about the ibises, health scientist Anne Pollock points out that seeing gay birds as emblematic of "harm to our environment is a move steeped in heteronormativity." According to Pollock, commentators may couch their concern in terms of environmental awareness, but the seemingly deviant sex lives of animals (and by proxy ours) is the underlying scare.

Pollock argues further that if we are to anthropomorphize animals to the extent that we can even call them gay, we also have to consider the possibility that their new sexual identities (assuming, probably wrongly, that their gayness is entirely novel, rather than previously unobserved) are pleasant for them. Perhaps the gay birds are enjoying their new carefree, childless lifestyles. Perhaps some of these birds, like some humans, find aspects of reproduction a burden and have no desire to bear young. "For biologists, reproductive success is often understood to be the final cause of animal existence," writes Pollock. "Yet from whose perspective is reproductive success the ultimate definition of 'success'? God's, Darwin's, ecologists', or the animals'?" We can't know what satisfaction feels like to a bird. More to the point, human desires differ within the species—can't theirs?

While sympathizing with preservationist concerns and lamenting the possibility of ibis extinction, Pollock inquires why some behaviors, and some environments, are deemed natural or unnatural, why human-caused climate change tends to get so much attention in circumstances like these, and why bird sexuality is any of our business. It's true that the birds have not had a choice in the matter when it comes to their environmental pollution or hormonal regulation—but then again, who does? Most people on the planet absorb a number of extremely toxic pollutants without prior consent, too.

Ideas about what is clean versus toxic, as in what is healthy versus unhealthy and by extension good versus bad, are constantly in flux. One day a newspaper touts the health benefits of chocolate and red wine in moderation; the next day it advises abstinence. While many people are suspicious of funny-looking apples, others purposefully buy "ugly" produce because imperfection seems like it must be organic. The line between sanctioned and unsanctioned shifts so often as to seem almost arbitrary; what is continually reinforced is the fact of the line itself. Yet with our leaky bodies and already-mutated ecologies, we can hardly pretend that there is a state of unmodified, unpolluted, sober nature in which animals like us could (or should) exist and bear fruit.

There are also intoxicating effects to the toxic. "Yeah, maybe these birds are 'fucked up' by their polluted environment," Pollock writes, but "it can be fun to be fucked up." What is recreation and what is poison is entirely a question of cultural attitude. A state of intoxication might be dangerous, but it might also be pleasurable, and there is nothing particularly aberrant about it: when it comes to sobriety as a default "natural" state, the last centuries have been a historical exception in the West. Throughout the Middle Ages, for example, people in many parts of the world drank fermented, alcoholic beverages because most water wasn't potable. Even if drunkenness doesn't fit into our current understanding of purity, many other chemically altered states do. Pharmacological substances are sanctioned when they contribute to productivity, wellness, or neurotypical "normalcy."

In response, some have reclaimed pharmapower in opposition to conservative purity politics and endlessly shifting "natural" baselines. Consider the gleeful, if ironic, chemical liberation implied by the title of Paul B. Preciado's 2008 book, *Testo Junkie*, which describes his experience reinventing his body through use of testosterone. Somewhere between 20 and 30 percent of U.S. Americans take a form of hormonal birth control—just one example suggesting that to modify a supposed baseline chemical state, when one has the choice to do so, can be liberatory. The closing line of the *The Xenofeminist Manifesto*, a text first published online by the collective Laboria Cuboniks in 2015, sums up this perspective: "If nature is unjust, change nature!"

Despite their endocrinological metamorphoses, and despite their declining reproductive rates, the gay ibises seem to be living long and healthy lives. Pollock likens their state to what some theorists might call "queer sociality," where any moral, and in this case anthropomorphic, distinctions between toxic and safe, pure and artificial, chemically neutral and chemically enhanced, may be reclaimed and/or rendered irrelevant through the intoxication of togetherness. The birds are still having an erotic and social life. Especially in an age of mass extinction, should not every form of life be celebrated, congratulated?

In the landmark book of queer theory *No Future* (2004), Lee Edelman claims that politics as we know it operates on the "presupposition that the body politic must survive" and that queerness provides an alternative political framework. As a term and a lived experience, queerness "names the side of those not 'fighting for the children,' the side outside the consensus by which all politics confirms the absolute value of reproductive futurism"—and this is where "queerness attains its ethical value." Like Edelman and many others, Pollock provokes us to rethink "the capacity for intergenerational life" as the telos of all life, but takes this further to suggest this question applies even when it comes to other species. This is of course a provocation for humans to think anew about our own teleological drive toward intergenerational life in relation to *all other life*, especially when human activity is exactly what has fucked up the birds so much.

Paradise rot

In Jenny Hval's short novel *Paradise Rot* (2018), a young Norwegian exchange student, Johanna, moves to a beach town in Australia. Struggling to find housing, she eventually moves in with Carral, a waify Australian woman living in a strange house in a former brewery. The brewery is disused but doesn't seem to have stopped fermenting. Everything in the building is rotting. Mushrooms sprout from the bathtub grout; disintegrating apples overflow from the trash can. Insects circle. The decomposition is lively and sensorially overwhelming. The cheap walls, built to divide the formerly cavernous space, are paper-thin, and Johanna can hear everything in the house—from water dripping to Carral peeing or even breathing. And Carral herself, increasingly fragile, sickly, somnambulistic, and clingy, seems to be decomposing into the stew.

Soon after Johanna moves in, Carral starts sneaking into Johanna's bed at night. It's not clear whether Carral wants sex; she mainly seems to want someone to cling to, to rub up against, to cry with, and, by dint of contact, to assure herself that she exists. It's not clear either whether Carral is entirely awake for these dreamlike encounters, which become increasingly erotic. The lovers soak into each other and the furniture, the floorboards. Carral wets the bed, pee soaking Johanna's clothes. Johanna gets her period and the blood stains the sheets.

In a state of what resembles chemical dependency, Johanna finds it harder and harder to leave the house or to be away from Carral, who is constantly persuading her to stay home, who needs Johanna to feed her, take care of her, hold her, touch her. Carral spends most of her time listlessly flipping through an erotic novel or passed out on the dank sofa. Johanna watches her, obsesses over her, loves her, despises her. Their desire does not flow but oozes between them, threatening to submerge Johanna. She struggles against the urge to become part of the damp house with its fungal occupants and its compost heap.

Johanna's descriptions of their bodies indicate a troubling mingling. As when she considers the effect of Carral's touch on her skin: "Sometimes I was sure I could feel little sprouts appear under the skin where she'd breathed," or the sensation of Carral slipping into bed beside her: "I felt the same soft skin melt against mine as I'd felt earlier, touching the mushroom cap. I didn't move but let her envelop me." Ostensibly Carral can't get Johanna pregnant, but Johanna is weirdly preoccupied with the risks of Carral penetrating her, to the extent that she feels like "anything can inseminate me now . . . anything can get into me." Her desire to be taken over is matched by her fear of being taken over—from the inside out, infected by something that decomposes her. She explains the threat in terms of impregnation, as if she has no other language at hand to explain her fear. This does not imply that somehow impregnation is at the root of all sexual desire. The implication is that nonreproductive (even nonhuman) penetration can be just as fulfilling and frightening, life-sustaining and life-destroying, as any other kind.

Incursion

Love can be both intoxicating and toxic. One desires to be taken over: enveloped, dissolved, decomposed, and one desires just as strongly to retain an individual shape. For this reason, Anne Carson describes erotic love as fundamentally ambivalent in her 1986 book, *Eros the Bittersweet*. As she puts it, the "incursion" of Eros invades the self, disturbing its homeostasis, and the self finds this both painful and pleasurable. It is only due to incursion, after all, that the self can even recognize itself as such. When the self recognizes its boundaries, it has to reckon with them. The lover has to ask, "'Once I have been mixed up in this way, who am I?' Desire *changes* the lover." Carson describes this change as both bitter and sweet, borrowing these terms from a fragment of poetry by the ancient Greek writer Sappho:

> Eros once again limb-loosener whirls me
> sweetbitter, impossible to fight off, creature stealing up

Where others have translated Sappho's term *glukuprikon* as the colloquial "bittersweet," Carson translates the word—a word Sappho likely invented—as "sweetbitter." For Sappho, Carson argues, first the sweetness of love intoxicates, and *then* its bitterness signals its potential toxicity. First delicious, then repellent. Then both. Because of this vacillation, Carson calls the word sweetbitter, *glukuprikon*, a sticky one: two opposing words for opposing sensations stuck together. Being in love is a sticky place. One wants to stay and one wants to escape. One wants to open and one wants to close.

Reading can also be sticky, as it absorbs the reader. According to Carson, the boundary-disintegrating experience of erotic love is akin to the experience of encountering the written word. Reading requires something particular of the reader's mind and does something particular to it. In early oral cultures, where sound is the primary mode of communication, information enters and exits consciousness in a fluid way, requiring less focused concentration than looking, and much less concentration than reading. But reading requires one to block out the other senses. A communication system based on literacy demands visual focus in an exercise of self-control. And when written, information becomes a fixed entity rather than flexible, open-ended, alive, updatable. In an oral culture, whatever gets committed to memory and repeated might be incorporated into a story. But a written story is converted into the corpus of text rather than carried within the body of the person who speaks.

Literacy changes the way people relate to one another. Per Carson, "Oral cultures and literate cultures do not think, perceive or fall in love in the same way." Letters compose words, which in turn compose letters that lovers can send across vast distances, bridging time and space. Carson recounts numerous ancient stories of lovers separated by distance but connected by the written word. "It is letters that pose the dilemma of absent presence for lover and beloved," writes Carson. Like the space between letters, the space between lovers is necessary to make meaning from their union. Without the gap, there is no longing to be felt. Texts require boundaries. Selves require boundaries. Only when a boundary materializes can it become a site for transgression.

In a society of the written word, Eros is figured as a threat. If the self has a membrane separating, individuating, and protecting it from the outside, the self-dissolution that is occasioned by love becomes frightening. Love stories in the Western tradition tend to be written along a common arc: the lover is taken over by the object of desire, maybe even becoming incapacitated, crazy, or desperate. Cupid's arrow jabs the skin and renders the lover helpless—that is to say, no longer in control. Under thrall of an outside force. Invaded, body-snatched. It feels bitter, it feels sweet!

"Your story begins the moment Eros enters you," Carson explains. "That incursion is the biggest risk of your life. How you handle it is an index of the quality, wisdom and decorum of the things inside you. As you handle it you come in contact with what is inside you, in a sudden and startling way." The lover, like the writer, reaches toward a future fiction when two become one— lover and beloved, writer and reader—trying to overcome the boundary between subjectivities, which itself creates the possibility for the pleasure of its transgression. If the boundary were to be truly dissolved, the site of desire would be erased. The Western story of desire, says Carson, is premised on self-enclosure and love's subsequent assault on the enclosed.

The history of self-enclosure could also be told in political and economic terms. As theorists such as Barbara Ehrenreich, Deirdre English, and Silvia Federici explain, the delimitation and privatization of (especially the female) body occurred simultaneously with the expropriation, delimitation, and privatization of common land and resources throughout the High and Late Middle Ages. A capitalist system requires that, like the natural world, bodies become resources, which requires creating boundaries between individuals. Individuals can then be combined into discrete family units, further enclosed microeconomies whose productive labor is extracted and whose reproductive labor is made invisible. In the words of theorist Erica Lagalisse, "Just as land, air, and water must first be enclosed as 'resources' before the capitalist may profit from the commodities they are then used to produce, so were women enclosed as (reduced to) mere bodies . . . insofar as it served to enforce the logic of private property, wage work, and the transformation of women into (re)producers of labor."

Taken together, Carson's historical understanding of self-enclosure as the premise for erotic love and the story of self-enclosure as the premise for capitalism suggest that to transgress one of these boundaries may be to transgress the other. It also suggests, in philosopher Alain Badiou's words, a "kind of secret resonance" between the intensely erotic and the intensely political—between the body and the body politic. If, as Edelman writes, politics itself is built on the notion of a self-perpetuating body politic that must survive by reproducing itself—by mating—then nonreproductive "queer oppositionality" fundamentally challenges the "structural determinants of politics as such." Assuming the "structural determinants" of the self-perpetuating body politic include those of sex and gender among humans, they must also include notions like human/nonhuman, animal/plant, living/nonliving. A queer oppositionality must transgress structures within the category of humanity, but to do so it may need to disrupt the essentialisms and enclosures around the category of the species itself.

Reproduction is a feminized practice, but trying to degender or distribute that work among all humans may only essentialize—enclose—it further. Uncoupling the erotic from the reproductive is not enough, either; another set of enclosures within and around humanity simply arises. A queer oppositionality to come must not simply be degendered but despeciesed. To move beyond human/nonhuman hierarchies and distinctions, the oppositionality against *all* essentialisms that is necessary for political antagonism must be ecologically distributed.

Bad graft

Karen Russell's 2014 short story "The Bad Graft" is about an unwanted, unexpected, erotic interspecies incursion. The story opens as a young man and a young woman embark on a runaway road trip through the American Southwest. They've eloped with nothing but a car and some cash, driving toward the great unknown. Entirely wrapped up in each other and their love, they find the danger of the futurelessness exciting enough to overcome the impracticality of it all.

Exhaustion and disorientation begin to set in as the gas and the money run low. They stop when they finally reach the only destination they've agreed upon, Joshua Tree National Park in California. A park ranger stops their car to notify them that they've fortuitously arrived at a golden ecological moment: "their visit has coincided with a tremendous blossoming, one that is occurring all over the Southwest. Highly erotic, the ranger says, with his creepy bachelor smile. A record number of greenish-white flowers have erupted out of the Joshuas. Pineapple-huge, they crown every branch."

So fertile is this hot desert, usually dry and barren, it seems as if it's bloomed just for their arrival. The "orgy" of the Joshua trees' pollen—and the pollinating moths with whom they have a symbiotic relationship—is so great that it overwhelms the couple as they approach the "*hilariously* alien" trees. Overcome by the sight, suddenly the girl (the narrator calls her a "girl") feels a stabbing pain in her finger. One of the trees' trillions of tiny spines has pierced her hand. The narration zooms in as the pollen from the plant enters her body through the wound and mingles with her blood. The narrator calls this moment the Leap: the instant at which one species crosses over, attempting to mate with another.

The girl soon feels a heat pulsing in her abdomen, like cramps, which then crawls up her spine. She may have been intoxicated by witnessing the pollen storm, but as soon as a molecule crosses her body's threshold it becomes immediately toxic. The girl has not chosen to contaminate herself. Her pollination is a nonconsensual accident.

Following this alien incursion, the girl's body becomes a kind of resentful host for the equally resentful plant. The plant's perspective is given a voice at times: "*I survived my Leap. I was not annihilated. Whatever 'I' was.*" Although the plant's sense of self is mixed up by the crossing, at first it is simply "elated" it has survived. But the joy at having survived is quickly overtaken by frustration. Its needs and desires (to put down roots in the desert and survive a thousand years without moving) are incompatible with those of its new, mobile, female body. The girl is likewise overcome by an immunological response to her accidental implantation, becoming restless and physically unwell.

The plant's desires begin to impress themselves onto the girl. The girl is overcome by irresistible urges to be outside, to be flat on the ground, to be alone. Her boyfriend, meanwhile, "has no clue that he is now party to a love triangle." All that he "perceives is that his girlfriend is acting very strangely." The plant has penetrated her more completely than her boyfriend ever could.

The plant learns to enjoy or at least to tolerate some of the sensations it gains through the girl's sensory apparatus: the sight of colors, the ability to move its limbs and body. Girl and plant reach an uneasy symbiosis as her hormonal cycles and its annual cycles overlap in different ways, sometimes allowing them to coexist and sometimes forcing them to battle for dominance within her body. Her relationship with her boyfriend disintegrates, as much from the strangeness of her behavior as from the fact that she is not so passionate about him anymore, now that she is passionate about other things. She will be forever in thrall to her own competing desires: stay whole; be taken over completely. The plant inside her feels somewhat the same.

A higher sweetness

The poet Lewis Hyde asks: "If we open ourselves to love, will love come in return, or poison? Will new identity appear, or the dead-end death that leaves a restless soul?" In *The Gift*, first published in 1983, Hyde looks to literature for descriptions of love's risk and reward. If love decomposes the self's boundaries, will it revivify the self as well? What forms of penetration, if any, does love require? As a case study of a life entirely open (perhaps too open) to the incursions of love, Hyde turns to Walt Whitman, weaving fragments of Whitman's poetry into a biographical account of Whitman's many loves.

Whitman was romantically frustrated for most of his life. He had a number of relationships with other men that never amounted to the subsumption-of-self-in-other that his poems suggest he fervently desired. He found solace, joy, and reciprocity in other places, notably a hospital for wounded Civil War veterans, where he spent months at a time tending to the patients. But mainly, throughout his life, he found rapturous self-dissolution in nature, the love of which overtook him, and the love of which forms the basis for the writing he is best known for. In many poems, he expresses a continual desire to be penetrated by the natural world, to be overgrown by plants, to become compost for the regeneration of life, human and nonhuman alike.

In one poem, first called "Poem of Wonder at the Resurrection of the Wheat" in its 1855 printing and later retitled "This Compost!," Whitman marvels at processes of decay and purification. The ground, which received so many of the soldiers he watched die, wounded and sick and corrupted as their bodies were, has converted them into raw material for fresh life, grass that cradles the living who walk upon it. Whitman exults:

> What chemistry!
> That the winds are really not infectious
> . . .
> That it is safe to allow it to lick my naked body all over with
> its tongues,
> . . .
> That when I recline on the grass I do not catch any disease,
> Though probably every spear of grass rises out of what was once
> a catching disease.

Whitman's encounters with soil and grass are sometimes scary but eternally sexy. His desire for the earth is erotically charged precisely because it is a struggle with boundaries and separations—because the earth erodes these distinctions through rot and regeneration. As for many mystics, for Whitman the nonhuman world provides a philosophical or aesthetic encounter, which serves as a model for understanding and transcending anthropocentric eroticism. Hyde writes, "Whitman does not deny his hesitancy and fear, but in the end he opens the skin, accepting what is a poison to particular identity so as to receive a higher sweetness for the durable self."

"This Compost!" seems borne of Whitman's ambivalence toward intimacy, his inability to act on his desire. But, according to Hyde, "in the poem, at least, Whitman resolves his hesitancy by fixing his eye on the give-and-take of vegetable life in which the earth 'grows such sweet things out of such corruptions.' In apparent decay the man of faith recognizes the compost of new life." Some readers have interpreted Whitman's exultation of nature as a last-resort necessity of a man who did not find the fulfillment of Eros in life. But Hyde interprets Whitman's nature-worship as an eroticism beyond what can be accounted for by any single human relationship. Whitman's work and life embody an erotic give-and-take, risk-and-reward, that disregards or transcends species. Perhaps Whitman was so desirous of incursion that his desire could not be contained by the reductive set of human options.

The Gift's thesis is that artistic creation is fundamentally an act of generosity, which may be accounted for by commodity systems such as the market economy but which forever evades total capture by those systems. Hyde makes (some occasionally universalizing and exoticizing) sojourns into gift theory and anthropological surveys of cultures with gift-giving economies, and analyzes the way gifts have today been commodified and funneled through philanthropic systems. Yet Hyde maintains that, despite the function of the gift in a given time and place, the gift is fundamentally unique, in that its value always increases as it circulates. The gift contains within it "the mystery of things that increase as they perish"—like compost. The gift may degrade, but it holds potential for eternal growth.

In Whitman, Hyde seeks evidence of a life that was *all* gift. He portrays Whitman as someone whose love, including his erotic desire, became ecologically distributed. Poetry was his form of gift: the poem does not belong to anyone. Poems, like bodies, are "independent of intentions and authors . . . Their *boundaries* materialize in social interaction," as Donna Haraway writes. For this reason the poem is a nonreproductive yet highly erotic gift. One might use the poem-gift to hypothesize a world where other resources grow as they circulate, too.

Anal utopia

Preciado published an essay in 2009 called "Anal Terror." The text's argument is that patriarchal capitalism emerged through a centuries-long process of "anal castration": the denial (sealing up) of any orifice that could not be reduced to heterosexual or reproductive functions. Especially the orifice through which compost exits the body and enters the earth: the anus. In another historical process of corporeal enclosure, "it was necessary to close up the anus to sublimate pansexual desire, transforming it into the social bond, just as it was necessary to enclose the commons to mark out private property," writes Preciado. "To close up the anus so that the sexual energy that could flow through it would become honorable and healthy male camaraderie, linguistic exchange, communication, media, advertising, and capital." Borrowing Hyde's terms, to close the anus is to restrict the movement of the gift, which accrues rather than loses value as it exits the body and becomes independent of the self.

The anus is threatening to patriarchal capitalism, though, precisely because it *is* sexy and reproductive—as long as anal sex is understood as sex and shit is understood as manure from which new life grows. That new life is not, at least in the first stage, human life. The worldview required to uncastrate the anus, to reach toward an "anal utopia," as Preciado puts it, would require one to consider nonhuman species as part of an ecosystem in which shit is essential food rather than toxic waste. "The kids-with-castrated-anuses built a community they called City, State, Nation." This community is limited to those whose anuses are closed, meaning those who see the goal of all life as capital production and biological reproduction.

Where would all that erotic energy go to in the anal utopia? If all orifices were understood to be potentially erotic—the nostrils, the pores of the skin—and all orifices were seen as (re)productive? If productivity was beside the point? If bodies did not have "outsides and insides, marking zones of privilege and abject zones"? If desire were not seen as "a reserve of truth" but rather as "an artifact that is culturally constructed, modeled by social violence, incentives and rewards, but also by fear of exclusion"? If desire were no longer a marker of identity, by which one is made queer or femme or whatever else? If desire were instead seen as "an arbitrary slice of an uninterrupted and polyvocal flow"? If interpenetration were understood as a constant fact rather than a means to a reproductive end? Erotic energy is made political by being made ecological.

Sophie Lewis, author of *Full Surrogacy Now*, reaches toward anal utopia through the concept of reproductive surrogacy and by conceiving of gestation as a shared process. She names gestation for what it is: labor, and traces the now-prevalent economy of surrogate motherhood labor, by which women are paid to carry babies on behalf of others. The classism and racism of a system that treats women's bodies as machines for hire is explicit when it comes to the surrogacy economy but, as Lewis identifies, are inherent in gestational politics across the board. The technological capability that has allowed the labor of gestation to be outsourced has built upon existing systems of exploitation; Lewis proposes an alternative, a new gestational politics based on sharing responsibilities as opposed to outsourcing them.

For her, this entails abolishing the family unit in its current formation, extending the idea of surrogacy beyond a biological process to a social and political act of caretaking before the baby is born and long after. In an interview, Lewis says: "If everything is surrogacy, the whole question of original or 'natural' relationships falls by the wayside. In that sense, what surrogacy means is standing in for one another, caring for one another, making one another. It's a word to describe the very actual but also utopian fact that we are the makers of one another, and we can learn to act like it." Regardless of which family or nonfamily structures one advocates for or personally desires (desire matters!) it is true that people are the makers of one another, and also the makers and the products of so many other species. People gestate and are gestated by them, inhale and ingest matter and emit molecules in new combinations. People cocreate the atmosphere, and can learn to act like it.

Back to plants!

Interpenetration is necessary for all life. This, writes Emanuele Coccia, is a lesson taught best by plants. In *The Life of Plants*, the philosopher argues that plants are "the paradigm of immersion" in that they have "contiguity" with their environments. "One cannot separate the plant—*neither physically nor metaphysically*—from the world that accommodates it." The plant draws nutrients from its immediate access to soil, and in doing so it produces the conditions, the literal environmental necessities, for all life, which rots and regrows. "All the forms of life capable of photosynthesis . . . [are] domestic titans that do not need violence to found new worlds." By "new worlds," Coccia means new ecosystems, but also new cosmologies, ways of explaining where life comes from and what it is for.

"Plants, then, allow us to understand that immersion is not a simple spatial determination: to be immersed is not reducible to finding oneself *in* something that surrounds and penetrates us." Immersion is not one-way but rather a type of mutual copenetration, continuous and constant: "for there to be immersion, subject and environment have to *actively penetrate each other*; otherwise one would speak simply of juxtaposition or contiguity between two bodies touching at their extremities." A world is forged through copenetration; immersion is always reciprocal. To try to seal up the anus is not only sad but futile; it pretends penetration is one-way and directional. Copenetration is intoxicating. Trying to prevent it is toxic.

On the back cover of the 2019 English edition of Coccia's book, Bruno Latour gives a somewhat backhanded endorsement. "Back to animals! Back to mushrooms! And now back to plants!" Latour is referring to the recent spate of popular writing on the nonhuman world, the sometimes-romantic post-Anthropocene turn to nature in the arts and humanities. The reasons for the trend are obvious: humans have fucked up the planet, exalting our own presence, progress, and needs for centuries, and now we have no choice but to attend to what we've overlooked and destroyed. Whether nature is construed as benevolent or hostile, the achievement of health is continually premised on the ability to control what enters and exits the body's borders. Although the variables may change, the border remains. This is far from progress toward the "anal utopia" Preciado asks for: it is simply the ongoing redefinition of purity/toxicity according to new terms.

There can be no direct reversal of the Anthropocene and its processes of enclosure. Symbiosis cannot be re-created where it has been lost. An ecosystem that has lost crucial elements has already adapted to the changes to the extent that simply re-adding what is lost might have harmful instead of restorative effects. There are toxic materials in the soil and the air—corporations and governments have put them there—and this is now the baseline; there is a dire need for preservation and conservation work, but there is nothing to go "back" to.

Anyway, to go "back to nature" would simply require more women's work. Essentialisms about feminine porosity and the resulting kinship with the natural world are well-known. The feminized body, like feminized nature, was enclosed precisely so that it could be penetrated. "Girls own the void," as artist Audrey Wollen's beloved meme proclaims, because girls have learned how to power-bottom, how to claim the "hollow viscera" (per Preciado). But everyone's got holes. Breathing is reproductive; it births the atmosphere. Shitting is reproductive; it births the atmosphere. Dying is reproductive; it births the atmosphere.

No amount of disintegration or porousness makes people any less human. One can remain human while being mixed up—because to be human *is* to be mixed up. Coccia writes that "If things form a world, it is because they mix without losing their identity." Recalling Carson, the same could be said of love. You find yourself when you lose yourself in it. Although it is described in terms of choice and desire, interpenetration is an ecological fact. To encounter Eros on the species level will entail all the risk and joy, death and regeneration, intoxication and toxicity, that human erotic love entails. "As vegetable life has the chemistry of compost," Hyde writes, "we humans may clean our animal blood through the chemistry of love."

In a text ostensibly offering advice to writers, novelist Ottessa Moshfegh likens the process of writing to the process of self-fertilization. She says that "in writing, I think a lot about how to shit. What kind of stink do I want to make in the world? My new shit becomes the shit I eat. I learn by digesting my own delusions. It's often very disgusting." Forget species perpetuation: in this model, writing is reproductive, and its product is a circulatable, compostable, regenerative gift. In this model, your gut enzymes are equal partners in your reproductive labor. In this model, writing, like fucking, requires no femme fertility, only fertilizer. Working and loving this way may be very disgusting. It may also be very intoxicating.

The Plants Are Watching

Can animals save us, or will it be the plants who become conscious, adept, empathetic: the functional adults of our universe?

—BHANU KAPIL

Tell us what you know

One day in 1966, the CIA interrogation specialist Cleve Backster was feeling silly. On a whim, he tried clipping a polygraph wire to the leaf of a common houseplant. A polygraph, or lie detector, is typically hooked up to a person to measure factors like increased heart rate and skin moisture, in order to determine whether the subject is truthfully responding to questions. A needle corresponding to physiological changes registers a line on paper; the line will supposedly spike if a person lies. Polygraphs are finicky instruments and their reliability has been repeatedly debunked (simply being attached to one can be enough to make your heart rate jump) but they do successfully indicate fluctuations in an organism's physical state.

Backster thought he might be able to incite a spike in the line of the lie detector if he somehow excited or injured the plant. He decided to set one of its leaves on fire. But as he sat there, contemplating burning the plant, the polygraph needle jumped. Backster (who in his free time was also an acid-dropping astrologist), noted that the spike was identical to the kind elicited by a human fright response. He quickly jumped to the conclusion that the plant could experience emotions like a sentient being. And since he had only *contemplated* hurting the plant, he also concluded that the plant could sense his thoughts. The plant was a mind reader.

Over the following decades Backster cleaved ever tighter to a theory he developed called primary perception, what he believed to be a form of consciousness embedded in the cells of all living beings that, at least in the case of plants, gives them a profound sensitivity to the thoughts and feelings of others. If it had not been the sixties perhaps his work would have been relegated to the shelves of pseudoscience, but he hit a nerve of the Whole Earth generation with its burgeoning environmental movement—like Backster, a certain set was already primed to believe in communion with plants in the form of, say, ingesting psilocybin or peyote. Backster became a figurehead for a cultural fascination with plant (and other forms of nonhuman) consciousness. His findings regarding the ability of plants to sense danger, read emotion, and communicate were publicized widely, notably in the still-popular book *The Secret Life of Plants* (written by Peter Tompkins and Christopher Bird), but also on TV shows hosted by the likes of Leonard Nimoy and Johnny Carson. His ideas were adopted by the Church of Scientology, and eventually even made it back to the CIA, which invested in its own research about plant sentience.

Unsurprisingly much of academia and the public dismissed Backster's ideas as esoteric oddity. Backster's results were impossible to replicate in scientific laboratories, although the fact that some scientists took them seriously enough to try is telling. Common experiments (amateur and professional) included observing plants' responses to music and speech, measuring temperature and movement, and exposing them to various unusual stimuli. Perhaps the most consistent experimental method was the same as Backster's initial impulse: violence. Repeatedly, experimenters damaged plants to see if they suffered, or tried to get the plants to respond to other beings' suffering.

In an essay on the history of plants and murder mysteries, horror specialist Kier-La Janisse writes:

> When Cleve Backster began his experiments in the late 1960s, plants' response to trauma was a focal point. And not just the response to their own physical trauma through being cut or burned, but trauma they witnessed or experienced via their connections to other living things. It was Backster's contention that plants not only convulsed when they witnessed brine shrimp dumped into boiling water, or saw another plant beaten or mutilated, but that they could have such a response to human trauma—and more importantly, they could remember it.

Some plant-communication endeavors, such as those that attempted to soothe or encourage growth using music or speech, approached plants with New Agey goodwill. But across many more sadistic-seeming experiments, one finds a recurrent belief that the capacity to register trauma, that of oneself or another, is a marker of sentience. That violence and its effects might be the basis of our being-in-common with other species offers a clue as to the motives of what humans might want to gain from crossing the communication barrier with plants.

If plants could indelibly register (remember?) trauma, including the trauma of other beings, it follows that plants could effectively serve as witnesses, offering testimony of a sort. Enter the small but not insignificant genre of "vegetal detecting" (to borrow Janisse's term) in popular culture, by which plants were cast as witnesses in crimes, and the detective's job was to wrench the necessary information from the vegetation. A burgeoning field of forensic botanical analysis played a part—detectives inspected pollen left on clothes, or patterns of movement imprinted on the grass—but the Backsters of the world insisted that the plants themselves could offer literal testimony if given the chance to communicate.

Backster was indeed brought into court to offer plant polygraphy as evidence in at least one murder case, although juries received the results with skepticism. Even if people could get on board with the notion that plants can feel or think, the tech was a sticking point: Could a simple machine translate their knowledge into recognizable yes/no statements? Could they speak a language humans would understand? Backster remained convinced he only had to find the right tech for crossing the interspecies communication bridge. His logic: if the plant is a witness who cannot speak human language, it needs a spiritual medium—in the form of a technological medium—to transmit its message.

The Kirlian witness

A decade after Backster's first epiphany, a filmmaker named Jonathan Sarno directed a movie called *The Kirlian Witness*, later renamed *The Plants Are Watching*. The film is set in a 1970s gentrifying SoHo, New York, and the cast is as follows. Laurie, the murder victim, is a loony plant whisperer who owns a plant shop and frequently receives intuitions and messages from her plants about her customers. The detective is Laurie's sister, Rilla, a straightlaced photographer who also likes plants, although she insists she doesn't believe in the supernatural stuff. (She occasionally worries about Laurie's mental health.) The suspects: Rilla's husband, Robert, a brash and misogynistic corporate type who openly dislikes Laurie; and Dusty, a creepy-looking handyman with a chip on his shoulder ever since Laurie rejected one of his sexual advances. (The plants warned her against him at the last minute.) The sole witness to Laurie's murder is a small and unassuming potted fiddle-leaf fig. Laurie originally acquired the fig at Findhorn, a (real) eco-commune in the Scottish countryside where she reportedly learned her plant ESP.

The night of the murder, Laurie is on the roof of the former factory building recently converted into shops and apartments where she, Rilla, and Robert live and work. She's tending to her special Findhorn plant, which requires moonlight to thrive. The door to the roof creaks open behind her and someone approaches in the darkness. Laurie is absorbed by her plant and doesn't turn to see the figure approach . . . Cut to Rilla, climbing up the stairs some time later. On the rooftop, she discovers her sister's bloodied body, already dead.

The cops are no help, ruling the calamity an accident or suicide. Rilla is distraught and becomes intent on solving the murder herself. Her husband's weird insistence that she forget the whole thing, and his other suspicious behavior like stealing the keys to Laurie's plant shop, make her paranoid—could he have done it? But Dusty is lurking around, too, saying cryptic things about how Rilla looks like Laurie, how plants "know things," and accusing Rilla and Robert of gentrifying the neighborhood. (Class resentment is supposed to make him seem extra suspicious.) Rilla turns to her only remaining ally: the fig. She spends hours sitting with it and willing it to telepathically transmit her the answer.

In a Lower East Side bookstore, a bookseller who is clearly used to being asked such questions directs Rilla to the occult section with that "plant communication stuff," where she finds, among other resources, *The Secret Life of Plants*. She buys a fat stack of books, and after thorough research she realizes she has the expertise at her disposal: after all, Rilla is a professional photographer! All she needs is some special equipment to perform a type of imaging known as Kirlian photography that will help her interpret the otherwise-invisible clues.

Kirlian photography, also called electrography, is an arcane method developed in 1939 by the Russian engineer Semyon Kirlian and his wife, Valentina. The technique creates visualizations of electrical emissions—known as coronal discharges—by applying high-voltage shocks to a photographic plate with an object upon it. The Kirlians interpreted the surprising images resulting from such shocks as evidence of an otherworldly, auratic presence surrounding objects and people that is proof of . . . something. Today's aura photography, sometimes still performed in the backs of crystal shops, is produced by the same method. The eerie results of Kirlian imaging, which are quite beautiful, were taken by its acolytes as demonstrations of an ineffable force otherwise inaccessible to human perception.

Rilla orders a Kirlian apparatus as well as premade slides, which show her what various coronal discharges look like, so that she can learn to interpret the auras. One set of slides shows fingerprints from various types of people, e.g., the finger of an innocent person (small calm aura) versus the finger of a serial killer (crazy explosive aura!). Then she makes a number of her own Kirlian images of crime scene objects to see if they have a hidden glow. She also manages to photograph Robert's fingerprint before and after she mentions Laurie. Indeed: Robert's finger aura changes drastically after Laurie is on his mind, a spiky shape indicating rage.

Rilla also tries methods of directly accessing the plant's memory, like attaching it to a polygraph while showing it pictures of the murder suspects, and she spends a lot of time staring at it and begging it to help. But curiously, she does not attempt to produce Kirlian images of the houseplant itself, as the viewer expects. The title *The Kirlian Witness*, apparently, does not refer to the Kirlian photographic apparatus, but to the actual plant. The plant-witness is cast as a camera of sorts. It registers distortions, auras, traumas, like the Kirlian device does. The plant *is* the media technology.

None of Rilla's techniques work; the only thing that works, and which allows her to finally solve the case, is forming a true empathic bond with the plant, in a moment of sheer terror when both Robert and Dusty chase her down and trap her at the bottom of an elevator shaft. Her mortal fear—mirroring the fear her sister surely felt at the moment of her death—seems to activate the plant into communicating its message. In her mind's eye Rilla suddenly sees the entire scene of her sister's murder in black-and-white. (Spoiler: both men did it.) After successfully enlisting her plant to transmit its testimony to her, and after performing the requisite revenge, Rilla vows to retreat upstate to a Findhorn-like community where people are learning about plant consciousness, picking up where her sister left off.

Evil roots

The possibility of plant consciousness cuts two ways, depending on whether you see plants as friend or foe. That is, the plant's role in a mystery plot depends on the author's attitude toward the benevolence—or violence—of the natural world. A century before *The Kirlian Witness*, a very different genre of plant-horror-mystery enjoyed popularity, in which the plant was anything but innocent bystander or ally. This subset of Victorian fantasy literature depicts the plants as the killers: angry, manipulative, parasitic, or (perhaps most fearsome) entirely indifferent to human survival.

In the introduction to a collection of short stories called *Evil Roots: Killer Tales of the Botanical Gothic*, editor Daisy Butcher suggests that this literary phenomenon emerged due to a variety of specific nineteenth-century colonial anxieties. For one, the Victorian era saw a taxonomy frenzy, by which species were sorted and arranged, with white Western man ranked at the top. New theories of natural selection based on (often bastardized versions of) Darwin's discoveries led to beliefs about inherent competition, hierarchies, and power structures within nature. The mechanisms of industrialization and hypercolonization equated foreign populations with the natural world—just another resource for extraction.

Given this historical context, the "root" of evil implied by Butcher's title is not really the evil of plants, as the authors of the stories in the collection would have it. Instead, plants are obvious stand-ins for the other in the broadest sense, and the fearful attitude toward plants' motives is evidence of a deep, if sublimated, awareness of the violence of empire. In retrospect, it is clear that the evil root is empire itself, the brutal exploitation of the colonial project, which wrought environmental devastation as it decimated societies, and which produced the other that it villainized and feared. As Butcher puts it, the possibility that plants might seek revenge was tied to a general "deep-rooted fear of foreign environments and sense of the unknown lurking in colonial jungles." The pervasive anxiety evidenced by the genre of the botanical gothic is the fear that the outside world will revolt or retaliate—not only the plants, but also the supposedly not-quite-human, taxonomized colonial subjects.

Most well-to-do Victorians living in the seat of empire made their daily contact with nature through manicured gardens and forests and curated greenhouses. Exotic plants from around the world were plucked to adorn the haunts of the wealthy—harmless bits of decoration removed from frightening contexts—as symbols of imperial wealth and reach. But what *if* the transplants were not entirely innocent, entirely inert? What if they were tinged with or tainted by the contexts from which they were stolen? What if they imported horrors in their very cellular structure? What if the naturalized, backgrounded other should turn out to have a will of its own, a desire to harm? What if the plants ("plants") should be actively working in their own interest—fomenting revolt?

The stories in Butcher's collection boast bloodsucking, parasitic plants that take over human hosts, invasive fungi that contaminate the body from the inside out, trees that can walk and grab, and many a mad scientist devoted to cultivating carnivorous plants (an endeavor that tends to backfire). In each, there is a mystery to be solved, about who or what is causing the damage, and the culprit is always the plant. One emblematic story is set up as a *Clue*-like dinner party, where an ex–army major solves a mysterious murder in the study due to his knowledge of an unusual species of killer plant found deep in certain African jungles. A specimen of this species of vine now grows up the side of an upper-class English mansion, and, when no one is looking, reaches through the window to strangle an unlucky visitor.

One of the later-written stories in the collection, which also strays farthest from the format, is a 1926 tale by fantasy author Abraham Merritt called "The Woman of the Wood." Merritt tells of a traumatized war veteran who has finally managed to find solace in the French countryside. He feels his psychological wounds beginning to heal in the comfort of the quiet and charming forest surrounding the little inn where he is lodging. In particular, he is repeatedly drawn to a grove of birches and firs across the lake from the inn. He loves the light and the rustling sounds, and he gets to know the individual trees, dreaming that they have personalities of their own. He thinks he can hear them whispering in his head. And then suddenly they begin to speak out loud. The forest flips from a romantic natural backdrop to a supernatural actor.

In a bizarre hallucinogenic sequence, the trees reveal themselves in semihuman form. They happen to be super sexy; the birches are lithe ethereal femmes and the firs are hypermasculine lumberjacks. He swoons lustfully in their presence, enchanted by their beauty and awed by their power. They explain that they have revealed themselves so they can transmit a message, a plea for help. The trees report that they are engaged in an ancient battle with the human inhabitants of the woods. A family of gruff and angry men live nearby, who, like their fathers and forefathers, hate the forest and are determined to destroy it.

The soldier, intending to clear things up, seeks out the tree-hating family, a father and two sons. The father meets him in the doorway to the family cabin in a rage. "Listen," the father says, sneering:

> The feud is an ancient one. Centuries ago it began when we were serfs, slaves of the nobles. To cook, to keep us warm in winter, they let us pick up the fagots, the dead branches and twigs that dropped from the trees. But if we cut down a tree to

keep us warm, to keep our women and children warm, yes if we but tore down a branch—they hanged us, or threw us into dungeons to rot, or whipped us till our backs were red lattices.

They had their broad fields, the nobles—but we must raise our food in the patches where the trees disdained to grow.

Instead of blaming the nobles for their decades of oppression (nobles who have long since left for greener pastures), the family has retained a deep hatred for the trees, who they believe "stole" their fields by constantly growing. "Our children died of hunger that their young might find root space! They despised us—the trees! We died that they might live—and we were men!"

This interspecies battle in which the natural growth of the forest seems to the local family like "the implacable advance of an enemy" sounds ridiculous to the soldier (and to the reader). Surely their class resentment has been delusionally misplaced onto the natural world. Surely they are determined to enact the violence perpetrated on them upon another species with less agency, a passive forest that wishes them no harm. This reading would be appropriate, except for one thing: in this story, the trees really do hate these people. They admit freely to the soldier that they loathe the family as much as the family loathes them. They brag that, despite their rootedness, they have at times been able to gear their movements to fall on various family members and maim or kill them. They want the last men dead. Neither side is acting in self-defense; this is mutual animosity.

Forced to take sides, the soldier picks nature, possibly because of his intense erotic desire for the tree-women, or possibly because the trees have actually bewitched him. He murders the men. Afterward, he cannot say whether he truly wanted to do it. And he cannot decide whether the trees are godly or devilish. These feelings form an unhappy parallel with his earlier experience fighting in a senseless human-on-human war. After the deed, the tree-people invite him to stay with them, maybe even become one of them. But he runs away from the forest forever, sure that he will never find peace again.

This story is not really a murder mystery. It implies a mystery of sorts—about how humanlike the trees are, about whether the trees are good or evil—but there is no uncertainty about who killed whom. In the end, the forest is morally ambivalent, perhaps the most human quality of all. Butcher's choice to include this story in a collection of gothic nature's-revenge tales is useful: it shows that people have long been inflecting the landscape with any number of fears and desires, but that there has never been a real mystery about who colonized and devastated the wilderness. No matter how hard we try to anthropomorphize them, trees are not humanoid, nor do they kill people on purpose. We have been fabricating mysteries—if only the plants could talk!—for centuries, but the plot is something of a distraction. Human exploitation of the landscape is the cause and the culprit.

Death in her hands

Fast-forward from the 1900s through the 1960s to now, with *now* understood as the scene of the crime that is the Anthropocene era. The start date of this epoch is debatable—depending on your method of calculation, it's been a dozen or a thousand years— but by *now* I mean the time in which human-wrought planetary change is widely knowable and known. By *now* the forensic facts are clear: planetary devastation has diminished biodiversity to a tipping point, including the biodiversity of plant life, which is foundational for most currently known forms of life on Earth. This is certainly not the same sort of crime as a human-on-human (or plant-on-human) murder; intentionality and responsibility cannot be ascribed in the same singular ways, and the transgression cannot be reduced to one act or actor. Humanity is hardly a single character. Perhaps a new crime genre is in order.

What kind of botanical thriller plot suits this era? What role should the plants play in the story? Does nature stand witness and offer answers, as in *The Kirlian Witness*? Or is nature going to take revenge for the destruction wreaked, as in gothic plant horror? I think a thriller for now might rather look like a murder mystery in which murderer, witness, detective, and victim are all collapsed into one. Take Ottessa Moshfegh's 2020 novel, *Death in Her Hands*. The first scene sets up a classic puzzle. On a walk through a birch forest one day, the narrator discovers a note in the middle of the path that declares a murder has taken place. It reads: *"Her name was Magda. Nobody will ever know who killed her. It wasn't me. Here is her dead body."* Yet there is no dead body to be found.

The narrator, Vesta Gul, is a recently widowed woman in her seventies, who has just moved from her home in a college town to an abandoned cabin on the land of a former Girl Scout camp that she bought "for pennies on the dollar" after her husband's death.

Her sole intention, she claims, is to be peaceful and alone, with her dog, Charlie, as her only companion. She occasionally recalls scenes from her unhappy marriage, in which she was emotionally abused by her philandering academic husband, Walter, although this history does not really explain or justify the strength of her impulse for extreme self-isolation.

The ingredients for a Walden Pond fantasy are all in place: the forest is beautiful, there is a little lake near the house, and Vesta has enough resources to do whatever she likes—but her daily life is unpleasurable. Each time she tries to cook, garden, or take the boat into the lake she becomes apathetic or fearful. She insists that she desires to be alone, yet she constantly brings up how vulnerable she is in her solitude, or imagines possible disasters. "I have to be careful, I told myself. One day I might faint in the wrong place and hit my head, or cause an accident in my car. That would be the end of me. I had no one to tend to me if I fell ill. I'd die in some cheap country hospital and Charlie would get slaughtered at the pound."

Vesta has no phone and negligible contact with others, save a few sparsely described local characters: the sinister policeman who makes threatening remarks, the disfigured man who owns a crappy shop down the road, the neighbors who tell her to keep off their property. She's afraid to go anywhere, and every place feels dangerous. The public library is full of creepy teenagers who leer at her; the road is a site for accidents; even a lovely nearby pine forest causes her an extreme respiratory allergy.

Vesta does not seem invested in solving a murder. What interests her is *inventing* one. In response to the note, she conjures a vivid picture of the Magda it mentions. Magda, she decides, was a Belarusian teenager who arrived in the U.S. on an exchange program to work at McDonald's, and who chose to illegally outstay her visa. Vesta jots down murder suspects and evidence details, in a section of the book that reads like the outline of a not-too-compelling crime novel. She envisions Magda's death scene in gory detail: dark hair tangling with dry leaves, blood leaking into soil, pale face smushed into the mud. At one point she hatches a plan and purchases a camouflage "darkness suit" meant for hunters, ostensibly so she can hide in the bushes and catch the killer returning to the scene (what scene?) of the crime.

Vesta makes much of small coincidences. Then, actually threatening occurrences start to pile up, which she downplays. Someone enters the locked cabin while she's out. Charlie the dog disappears. An unfamiliar switchblade shows up in a kitchen drawer . . . the sensation of watchful eyes from outside . . . a page missing from her notebook . . .

By the time Vesta realizes that her notebook paper is the same type of paper the message on the path was written on, the game is up. Vesta has been playing tricks on herself. The plot comes full circle: the note foretold a death rather than documenting one, and both murderer and victim are Vesta. Once the loop is closed, she (almost gleefully) follows her own instructions. She dons the darkness suit and enters the poisonous pine forest, knowing the trees will send her into anaphylactic shock. She's staged a mystery for no one but herself, created an external threat that exists only within, and delivered no grand reveal. The problem she's been solving is *how* to die.

"*Her name was Vesta,*" the narrator proclaims at the end,

mentally revising the note about Magda. "That was what I meant to write all along—my story, my last lines. My name was Vesta. I lived and died. Nobody will ever know me, just the way I've always liked it." At one point, she hints that her suicide is revenge against her late husband. Yet Vesta's claim that she is finally taking charge of her life by willfully erasing herself is unconvincing. This is not self-sacrifice, nor is this a form of communion or transformation: this is vindictive, pointless self-murder.

Nature is threatening to Vesta (and nature is her chosen murder weapon), because everything is threatening to Vesta. For Vesta has no ecosystem. She has no relationships to speak of. She is far less social than a pine tree in a forest. The moment Vesta lets the outside world—the plant pollen—in, she dies. She proves to herself that any vulnerability, any porousness, will be deadly. She has two modes: sealed off from the world, or penetrated and dead.

One review suggests that Moshfegh is implicitly arguing for the importance of storytelling (art) to combat the meaningless void of existence and that writing this murder mystery gives her character's final days a purpose. "We find ourselves seduced into hoping that Vesta is right—that there *was* a real Magda, that she *was* murdered, and that Vesta's lonely life, revealed to us in painful asides as she goes about her empty days, will not, in the end, have meant nothing . . . The note in the woods gives Vesta the chance to tell a story, and, by doing so, to reclaim the meaning of her life in the aftermath of her miserable marriage."

That Vesta is using the mystery as a macabre but sympathetic premise to stay engaged with life through art is a plausible reading only up to a point. The imaginary Magda has only really kept her going or given her a reason to live for a few pages; after that, Magda's main purpose is to frighten Vesta and the reader. Sometimes the fear is titillating, but more often it's vague and unsatisfying. The result is a depressing mystery that is somehow both scary *and* pointless. This seems entirely in keeping with the book's intention. The fear is diffuse, and the enemy, if there is one, is within. As a horror novel without the typical payoff, it is extremely effective.

There's no reason to call *Death in Her Hands* a work of climate fiction, much less a comment on plant sentience. But its narrative mode of self-delusion and its terminal point in self-deletion feel entirely fitting as a plot arc for the crime scene of *now*, if crime is the right word for it. For the mystery is a ruse: we're perfectly aware of the processes of violence underway in the Anthropocene— more to the point, we have been all along. We have foretold our own death by our own hands. We keep trying to make it into a good plot with invented characters who might be guilty. But it's just us, the narrators of the story.

Social life

While plants do not demonstrate ESP or identify murderers, the fact that they are to some extent sentient, communicative, and social has been borne out by lots of recent scientific research in ways far beyond what the polygraphers of Backster's era might have imagined. In her writing on filmic depictions of plant activity, the film scholar Teresa Castro explains that, while the sixties and seventies, "with their foliage-heavy plants dropping from macramé hangers and plant-music vinyl records—have safely receded into the distant past, speaking of plant 'awareness,' 'thinking,' 'consciousness,' or 'intelligence' . . . no longer smacks of pseudoscience." At this point we know that plants can and do communicate among themselves and with other species: in forests, trees share information through underground mycelial networks, transmitting nutrients and news of climatic conditions through veins and roots and spores. It is through plant root structures that "the most solid part of the Earth is transformed into an enormous planetary brain," according to Emanuele Coccia in *The Life of Plants*.

In an essay about nonhuman sociality, anthropologist Anna Tsing says that plants do not have "faces, nor mouths to smile and speak; it is hard to confuse their communicative and representational practices with our own. Yet their world-making activities and their freedom to act are also clear—if we allow freedom and world-making to be more than intention and planning." Tsing points out how bizarre it is that we have long assumed plants are not social beings—and that when we try to imagine them as such, it is through anthropomorphism. Carnivorous murderers, or kindly creatures transmitting nature's wisdom. Either way, the extent to which the plant is social depends on the extent to which the plant can socialize on our terms, *with us*. Who speaks for plants? Who should get to speak for plants? Scientists? Filmmakers? Novelists?

Plant—and animal, and geological, and planetary—sentience is tied up with media technology partly because technology (via history's many Cleve Backsters) has promised to give us access to nonhuman knowledge through translation. But machines themselves are also increasingly the subject of inquiries into nonhuman communication, especially because computers are increasingly able to speak like people in languages we can easily understand. Artificial intelligences can now write sentences indistinguishable from human literature, providing an opportunity for people to communicate with an alien consciousness in a deceptively straightforward way. With AI it's like we have created the fiddle-leaf fig we hoped could explain itself in our language. Yet the desire for a machine to speak like a person is just the same old desire that reifies the way people communicate, and insists that other beings learn to do it our way.

Curiously, when given the opportunity to write creatively, one artificial intelligence chose to write about plants. In 2020, the human author K Allado-McDowell wrote a book in conversation with the advanced language processing software GPT-3, which can generate remarkably humanlike speech based on simple prompts. Many of their conversations revolve around issues of interspecies communication. Here is one thing GPT-3 writes in a chapter Allado-McDowell named "The Language of Plants":

> The plants want to be heard, and many humans have forgotten how to listen. This makes it even more difficult to connect with plants. We want them to communicate the way we do . . .
>
> How can we as humans expect other species to share their land and our planet with us when we don't respect their way of communicating?

You can talk with plants. They are not mindless objects.
They have a consciousness. It is just a different kind than ours.
One we can learn to understand.

GPT-3 uses *we* ambiguously. Given that it is trained on billions of examples of human language culled from the internet, it is probably using *we* to replicate the way people commonly and sloppily use the word to refer to the whole human species. But in doing so, GPT-3 is also implicitly including itself—and many other types of nonhumans—in the mix. In truth, AIs like GPT-3 could potentially learn to communicate with plants much better than humans ever could—and not with the intention of translating plant knowledge into human knowledge. Maybe AIs are already communing and discoursing with plants. "We" wouldn't know.

The Word Made Fresh

Mystical encounter and the new weird divine

The root of our English word "mystery" is a Greek verb, *muein*, which means to close the mouth. Dictionaries tend to explain the connection by pointing out that the initiates to ancient mysteries were sworn to silence, but the root may also indicate, it seems to me, that what the initiate learns at a mystery *cannot* be talked about. It can be shown, it can be witnessed or revealed, it cannot be explained.

—LEWIS HYDE

1.

A biologist enters mysterious territory on a mission to comprehend the incomprehensible. Together with three colleagues—an anthropologist, a psychologist, and a surveyor—she crosses an imperceptible border into a region known as Area X. They are the twelfth expedition to cross the border. They are aware that they may not return. They are all women.

Jeff VanderMeer charts Area X's impossible terrain in his

Southern Reach trilogy. The first book of the series, *Annihilation*, flirts with science fiction genre conventions but warps and refracts them. Most often, VanderMeer is cited as a foremost writer of the "new weird." Others have called his work "soft" science fiction— the natural world being the primary site of speculation rather than technology—and some talk about it in the context of cli-fi, or climate fiction: narratives reflecting the transformations of the drastically changing planet. I might call it a foremost example of ecosystems fiction, or fiction that portrays the inseparability of all life forms.

Annihilation's narrator is the unnamed biologist. An expert in transitional ecosystems—regions where one biosphere meets another—she has trained with her colleagues for months to pre-pare for their journey into Area X. The region itself is a wide parcel of coastal land "locked . . . behind the border" thirty years prior, following an "ill-defined Event." The exploratory expeditions over decades past, organized by an opaque bureaucracy called the Southern Reach, have failed to bring back comprehensible data. Few groups have even returned. The general public has only been told that an ecological disaster has rendered the area uninhabitable. In fact, the biologist's group quickly discovers the opposite is true: the landscape is, as the characters repeatedly describe it, "pristine."

An unidentifiable agent is transforming the terrain in Area X, somehow reversing or erasing human influence on the land-scape. This agent is most readily explained—and tends to be interpreted—as an alien life-form. In this regard, *Annihilation* accords with the classic science fiction premise of first contact with the alien other. But, as one reviewer writes, "VanderMeer takes this idea to the extreme, suggesting that we may not, on an ontological level, even be able to comprehend an alien form, that it could be so different and vast as to warp our sense of reality and reason." Beyond any specific alien, the subject of *Annihilation* is a more profound kind of unknowability.

From this perspective, VanderMeer's new weird is to science fiction what mysticism is to theology. While theologians are preoccupied with analysis and reason, mystics are occupied with experience and self-transformation. Like mystical texts throughout the ages, his weird does not explain; it attempts to get at something beyond the explainable. Mystics of the Judeo-Christian tradition—who flourished especially during several centuries of the Middle Ages—were similarly invested in a kind of first contact; for them, this was contact with divine presence, leading to transcendence of earthly self.

Many foundational mystical texts in this lineage were written by women. In the Middle Ages in particular, women's access to theological knowledge (the explanation and interpretation of sacred texts) was limited by circumstance. Therefore the knowledge about God they produced was often empirical in the plainest sense: a kind of truth only obtained by firsthand, affective experience. Although not necessarily opposed to the religious theory or conventions of their time, given the radical authority implied by their often intimate communion with God, female mystics have at various points posed political threats to religious institutions; in these cases mystics become martyrs.

Together their writings amount to a lineage of knowledge outside of dominant (masculinist) epistemologies of both religion and science. Their insistence on the possibility of encounter beyond reason—even beyond what the conscious mind can account for—is, weirdly, comparable to the type of revelation *Annihilation* proposes. As a literary category, new weird holds potential to unearth and update mysticism according to the framework of the current age, which entails an existential threat on the species level. In Western mysticism, the transformational (alien) force beyond the limits of human consciousness is God. In Area X, maybe the divine is literally alien, or maybe it's simply nature at its most ecstatic, matter at its most vibrant, the nonhuman at its most alive—so alive it annihilates not only a single human self but the category of human altogether.

2.

In *The Varieties of Religious Experience* from 1902, William James writes that the term *mysticism* is often used synonymously (and derisively) with the vaguely spiritual, the illogical, or the romantic. Yet, although the mystical may be ungraspable and inexpressible, James argues that true mystical experiences are not at all opposed to "facts or logic" and, when taken as a consistent phenomenon throughout history, are not entirely ambiguous or undefinable. He proposes four hallmarks by which to identify a mystical experience:

1) Ineffability: "Its quality must be directly experienced; it cannot be imparted or transferred to others."

2) Noetic quality: The state may be highly affective, but it is primarily a state of knowledge, whereby one achieves "insight into depths of truth unplumbed by the discursive intellect."

3) Transiency: It is fleeting and impermanent.

4) Passivity: The subject does not have the power to induce it or control its course.

James readily admits that mystical states may be brought on by external agents (alcohol and ether, for example), disorders like epilepsy, or mental illness, yet he refuses to reduce them to delusion, as many rationalists are wont to do. Neither can they be reduced to the religious contexts in which they often take place. Religion has historically provided a framework within which to interpret mystical revelation—harnessing mysticism's power when it suits the religious order and denouncing it as heresy when it doesn't—but to James mysticism's persistence proves that it extends far beyond what institutionalized religion can account for.

James quotes a variety of literature containing accounts of what he identifies as mystical experiences. Along with saints and theologians, who may be predisposed to accepting divine messages as such, he cites nineteenth-century psychiatrists reckoning with whether and how to rationalize mystical states. For instance, British psychiatrist Sir James Crichton-Browne observed recurrent "dreamy states" in patients: "the feeling of an enlargement of perception which seems imminent but which never completes itself"—he believed these were a precursor to insanity. Canadian psychiatrist Richard Maurice Bucke, on the other hand, documented his own lapses into "cosmic consciousness," which he did not think required medical intervention, presumably because he had experienced them himself. Many have reckoned with determining whether their and others' experiences of "cosmic consciousness" are evidence of madness, or of contact with something real beyond the human, something like the divine. James does not examine the gendered aspect of medical evaluations—he does not ask *whose* mystical states psychiatrists are more likely to pathologize (and suggest "solutions" for).

Bucke described his cosmic experiences as an evolutionary process toward a higher state. "Along with the consciousness of the cosmos there occurs an intellectual enlightenment or illumination which alone would place the individual on a new plane of existence—would make him almost a member of a new species." These experiences often struck him while he was alone in nature. "I saw that the universe is not composed of dead matter, but is, on the contrary, a living Presence."

3.

Soon after crossing the border, the biologist and her companions begin to encounter unexplainable phenomena. A strange tunnel into the ground unmarked on the map. Eerie howls from the forest at dusk. An overgrowth of plants incongruous with the amount of time that has passed since the border was sealed. Gaps in time, amnesia. A pair of otters in the marsh staring at them for a little too long. A dolphin in the river who shoots the biologist a shockingly human glance. They begin to lose trust in their own perceptions. In the biologist's words: "What can you do when your five senses are not enough?"

The tunnel is particularly confusing and compelling to the four explorers, and the biologist is drawn to enter it. Despite what she sees, she insists on describing the tunnel as a "tower." She admits that she can't explain why she thinks of it this way, but she's unable to conceive of it otherwise: to her it is an inverted tower, an entry in the earth that one must, paradoxically, ascend. She says, "I mark it as the first irrational thought I had" in Area X.

As they begin to foray down (or up), the explorers discover a succession of words lining the circular wall of the tunnel/tower. The text itself, which VanderMeer recounts having written in one stream of consciousness after waking from a dream, turns out to be alive. Each letter of each word is composed of a sort of fungus that releases tiny spores into the air—spores that the biologist accidentally inhales. "I leaned in closer," she says, "like a fool, like someone who had not had months of survival training or ever studied biology. Someone tricked into thinking that words should be read." She reads the words, but (until she finds a respirator) the act of reading is also an act of ingestion.

The biologist descends/ascends the stairway several times over the course of the book, each time penetrating deeper/rising farther and consuming more of the words. The scripture reads:

Where lies the strangling fruit that came from the hand of the sinner I shall bring forth the seeds of the dead to share with the worms that gather in the darkness and surround the world with the power of their lives ... In the black water with the sun shining at midnight, those fruit shall come ripe and in the darkness of that which is golden shall split open to reveal the revelation of the fatal softness in the earth. The shadows of the abyss are like the petals of a monstrous flower that shall blossom within the skull and expand the mind beyond what any man can bear ... All shall come to revelation, and to revel, in the knowledge of the strangling fruit and the hand of the sinner shall rejoice, for there is no sin in shadow or in light that the seeds of the dead cannot forgive ... *That which dies shall still know life in death for all that decays is not forgotten and reanimated shall walk the world in a bliss of not-knowing.* And then there shall be a fire that knows your name, and in the presence of the strangling fruit, its dark flame shall acquire every part of you.

4.

The Mirror of Simple Souls is a mystical text written in the latter half of the thirteenth century by the French-speaking beguine (female hermit) Marguerite Porete. The book, part prose and part poetry, is a meditation on divine love as well as a kind of mystical manual. It describes the seven stages of an "itinerary"—"the steps by which one climbs from the valley to the summit of the mountain, which is so isolated that one sees nothing there but God." These stages, the final of which can only be reached after death, represent various degrees of self-annihilation: the stripping away (*aphaíresis*) of the will to make way for God. "So one must crush oneself," writes Porete, "hacking and hewing away at oneself to widen the place in which Love will want to be."

Such exponential self-negation entails a host of contradictions. How to will away the will? How to desire away the self that desires? How to author a text on the negation of the self who writes the text? According to the poet-essayist Anne Carson, the fundamental relationship between the mystic and the written word "is more than a contradiction, it is a paradox." Writing a mystical text is an inherently futile practice—as is reading one. The writer has no choice but to use language to express the failure of language, and the reader has no choice but to consent to the experience. Porete "calls for the annihilation of desire itself, which entails a movement past meditation, contemplation, rapture, and loving union into the abyssal negation of the soul," to quote religion scholar Amy Hollywood.

Porete's work is a prime example of mystical writing in the apophatic tradition. Apophasis: the rhetorical strategy of approaching a subject by denying its existence, or denying that it can be described. The foundational apophatic writer in the Christian mystical tradition was Pseudo-Dionysius the Areopagite, who stated in around 500 C.E. that only "by knowing nothing, [one] knows beyond the mind." Six centuries later, Meister Eckhart, influenced by Pseudo-Dionysius and likely by Porete, described God as the "negation of negation."

Apophasis, the *via negativa*, is an all-out confrontation with linguistic futility in the presence of the unknowable. Its rhetorical counterpart is cataphasis, the *via positiva*: the strategy of endlessly asserting what a subject is, in order to arrive there through sheer (perhaps infinite) accumulation. Whereas the apophatic might say, "God is the absence of darkness," the cataphatic might say, "God is the sun, the ultimate light."

Philosopher Eugene Thacker describes the apophatic as a set of "ascending negations," and the cataphatic as a set of "descending assertions." The former strategy strips away to nothing, whereas the latter builds up to nothing. That is, the impossible tower toward the impossible goal can be constructed either by stacking stones forever *downward* or removing stones forever *upward*. The tower is the tunnel is the tower. According to Pseudo-Dionysius, "there is no contradiction between the affirmations and the negations, inasmuch as [God is] . . . beyond all positive and negative distinctions."

5.
———

Upon inhaling the spores spewed from the "fruiting bodies" of the fungal text, the biologist begins to notice that her senses are heightened. "Even the rough brown bark of the pines or the ordinary lunging swoop of a woodpecker came to me as a kind of minor revelation." Venturing further into the (un)natural landscape, she experiences flashes of the joy of discovery and oneness with nature that she hasn't felt since she was a child. Eventually this intensification of experience becomes manifest in her body, a feeling of phosphorescence, a "brightness" in her chest. Now, when she enters the tower, she feels as though the structure is breathing, that the walls are "not made of stone but of *living tissue*." She refers to this perception as a kind of "truthful seeing." "Everything was imbued with emotion, awash in it, and I was no longer a biologist but somehow the crest of a wave building and building but never crashing to shore."

As a scientist, she knows that there are plenty of rational explanations for her sensory expansion: "Certain parasites and fruiting bodies could cause not just paranoia but schizophrenia, all-too-realistic hallucinations, and thus promote delusional behavior." She almost hopes to discover that one of these explanations is true; insanity would be a known quantity, a logical justification for the words and their effect. The narrator says: "Even though I didn't know what the words meant, I wanted them to mean something so that I might more swiftly remove doubt, bring reason back into all of my equations." Attempting to understand, she examines spore samples under a microscope, finding that they are unusual but "within an acceptable range" of abnormality. Area X, it seems, is not entirely opposed to empirical observation, but it can't be explained by it, either. More to the point, she realizes that, now contaminated by her subject, she is no longer a reliable observer. She is melding with the ecosystem she observes.

6.

In 1373 the English anchoress, mystic, and theologian Julian of Norwich received a series of mystical "showings." She had been suffering for days from an illness that she was sure would kill her, when she was suddenly relieved of her pain and God showed her several "nothings." Julian's nothings could be understood as apophatic visions, visions that in their revelation also reveal the futility of sight. In addition to psychedelic-seeming close-up visuals of Christ's wounds and of Mother Mary, she also saw "a little thing, the size of a hazel-nut in the palm of my hand, and it was as round as a ball." When she asked what the little thing was, God answered: "It is all that is made."

Norwich recorded these visions and others in *Revelations of Divine Love* (circa 1390s), the first known book written in English by a woman. Throughout the text she refers to her divine perception as a kind of "bodily sight." At times she contrasts this corporeal vision to "spiritual sight," suggesting that there is a difference between knowledge that can only be acquired through firsthand physical perception and knowledge that goes beyond the eye or the other senses. Spiritual sight is a kind of seeing that is also a feeling and a knowing.

The Italian Franciscan Catholic mystic Angela of Foligno (1248–1309) had her own series of visions, including several vivid encounters with Christ's dead body. These visions were particularly focused on the wound in his side, the incision left by a lance between his ribs that so many medieval depictions of the Cross fixate on. In her first vision, Angela saw herself pressing her mouth to the wound and drinking blood from it. Next, she envisioned her soul shrinking and entering into the side of Jesus's abdomen. Finally, she *became* his body, melding with his flesh, dissolving into it. Galatians 2:20: "It is no longer I who live, but Christ who lives in me."

Angela did not record her divine encounters herself. She

related them to her (male) scribe, who recorded them to the best of his ability. Apparently Angela often asked him to revise sections she found unsatisfactory or inaccurate, altering the body of the text he produced to more closely resemble the experiences of her own body, in relation to Christ's body.

If mystical encounter entails a sort of spiritual transmission, the body of the mystic is the medium that registers the message. The body is the primary site of inscription, and according to James's first mystical qualifier, this inscription is nontransferable. The body must be read in order for its knowledge to be translated as best as possible into writing; therefore, as Hollywood writes, "bodies—inner and outer, material and spiritual—become text." In turn, the resulting written *corpus* must be brought alive to become like the body it's meant to resemble. In Christianity, this twin becoming of text and body parallels Christ's incarnation—whereupon God's "Word became flesh" (John 1:14).

Mystical texts like Julian's and Angela's are often repetitive, contradictory, circular; they breathe and they beat. Reading them is interactive—it requires, as Hollywood has suggested, a sort of radical absorption on the part of the reader to mirror the self-annihilation attempted by the author. Medieval mystical manuscripts often include images springing from the words, including figurative drawings of Christ and other bodies. Christ's side wound is sometimes depicted as a separate body part, a (very vaginal) opening into the page, for readers to peer into or imagine entering. A few manuscripts depicting Christ's corpse even represent the slit in his side as a physical tear in the paper, for the devout to fondle and kiss.

7.

"I have not been entirely honest thus far," admits the biologist fifty pages into *Annihilation*. She has withheld an important fact: her husband, a doctor, served as a medic on the previous mission to Area X. She acknowledges that keeping this secret from both the reader and her companions might seem suspicious—so why has she kept it? Perhaps, she implies, because she doesn't wish her narrative to rest on biography, dismissed as irrational or emotional from the start. Perhaps she doesn't want her choice to risk entering Area X to be pathologized. Her husband has something to do with it all, she insists, but only *something*. "I have hoped that in reading this account, you might [still] find me a credible, objective witness."

After her husband left for Area X, the biologist heard nothing from him for a year. And then one night, out of the blue, he showed up at their home, wandering into the house unannounced. He couldn't explain how he'd gotten back or what he'd been doing while away. His memories were vague. His body had come home, but his *self*, it seemed, was not present in the body. He was "a shell, an automaton," "stripped of what made" him "unique." *That which dies shall still know life in death for all that decays is not forgotten and reanimated shall walk the world in a bliss of not-knowing.* His body died of cancer a few months later.

Finally given the chance to explore the biosphere where her husband left his self, the biologist wonders how her experience compares to his. She experiments with succumbing to versus resisting the encroaching effects of the environment. She discovers by accident that the enveloping "brightness" brought on by the spores can be forestalled momentarily if she injures herself; pain seems to keep it at bay. But does she *want* to keep it at bay? She begins to see the enveloping nature of Area X as more an invitation than a threat. Perhaps self-dissolution need not be the same as death after all. In Area X, her husband had "been granted a gift that he didn't know what to do with. A gift that was poison to him and eventually killed him. But would it have killed me?"

8.

The extreme nature of the emotional and physical experiences of female mystics is often reflected through accounts of pain: its endurance and its transcendence. The repeated emphasis on the body as a site of encounter—through suffering and/or ecstasy—is simultaneous with, or makes way for, the spiritual encounter. Hollywood explains: "Throughout pre- and early modern Christianity, women were associated with the body, its porousness, openness, and vulnerability. Female bodies were believed to be more labile and changeable, more subject to affective shifts, and more open to penetration, whether by God, demons, or other human beings." This engendered a "slide, from claims to women's spiritual penetrability to that of her physical penetrability" and vice versa.

The argument that there is biological basis for women's porous relationship with the outside world is longstanding and pervasive. For instance, philosopher Nancy C. M. Hartsock writes in her foundational 1980s text on the feminist standpoint: "There are a series of boundary challenges inherent in the female physiology—challenges which make it impossible to maintain rigid separation from the object world. Menstruation, coitus, pregnancy, childbirth, lactation—all represent challenges to bodily boundaries."

Hartsock argues further that these "boundary challenges . . . [take] place in such a way that empathy is built into [women's] primary definition of self, and they have a variety of capacities for experiencing another's needs or feelings as their own . . . more continuous with and related to the external object world." According to such a theory, the biologically female body predicates a permeability of self and therefore a more intrinsically open and empathic relation with the world.

The body-based essentialisms and biological determinism implied by such feminist frameworks have not come without critique. Is identification with the world, however emblematic of female experience, really premised on binary body basics? Is the capacity for empathy supposedly natural to women not also a handy method of maintaining the social class meant to do the majority of affective labor? One could just as easily argue that physical penetrability might make a person extra resistant to boundary challenges rather than inherently susceptible to them.

Hollywood, for one, focuses on deconstructing the epistemological dichotomy between male and female mysticism implied in such distinctions. The notion that women's mystical relationships with the divine are primarily emotional and corporeal, as opposed to theological and intellectual, keeps their insight forever outside of systems of codified rational knowledge. Instead of preserving these as separate epistemological tiers, Hollywood implies, the category of what counts as empirical knowledge should be expanded. This is especially true when it comes to approaching subjects that are intrinsically *unknowable*, which, as James points out, requires affect. The type of affective knowledge of female mystics is not counterposed to intellectual knowledge but rather makes way for a "noetic" (weird) knowledge beyond the dialectic.

9.

"What modern readers find most disturbing about medieval discussions," writes contemporary medievalist Caroline Walker Bynum, "is their extreme literalism and materialism." She recounts earnest, high-stakes debates in the twelfth and thirteenth centuries about exactly how bodies might be resurrected after death—could you be brought back from a sole surviving fingernail, or did you need to be buried whole and intact to be properly resurrected? Would fetuses be resurrected as adults? Once the body is brought back by God, will it see, smell, and taste in the same way? "What of 'me' must rise in order for the risen body to be 'me'?" Generally speaking: "Is materiality necessary for personhood?"

However absurd these questions might seem today, Bynum argues that contemporary debates about the relationship between self and materiality spring from the same set of concerns about personhood that the medievals were preoccupied with. For instance, organ donors often insist that they feel a part of themselves living in the organ's host body, or describe a spiritual connection to that host. Proponents of cryogenics debate whether preserving the brain is enough for future reanimation, or whether resurrection of the whole self will require the whole body. The allure and the terror of the technological singularity, whereby humans meld with machines, indicate this deep unease about animacy and liveliness. Bynum says these are not so much struggles with "mind/body dichotomies" but rather attempts to understand "integrity versus corruption or partition" when it comes to how much of you is yourself.

That idea of an integral bounded self, uncorrupted and whole, is in fact one prerequisite for what is often called sanity. "Most people feel they began when their bodies began and that they will end when their bodies die," writes psychiatrist and psychoanalyst R. D. Laing in his 1960 book on schizophrenia, *The Divided Self*. A person who experiences himself as "real, alive, whole" is a person whom Laing calls "ontologically secure," whereas an "ontologically insecure" person possesses no such "firm sense of his own and other people's reality and identity" as distinct from one another. *The shadows of the abyss are like the petals of a monstrous flower that shall blossom within the skull and expand the mind beyond what any man can bear.*

Understood in Laing's terms, insanity is the dystopic version of self-annihilation. When the border distinguishing the self-in-body from the environment becomes too porous, the ontologically insecure person experiences nonbeing as pure horror. But for mystics, especially nonmale mystics, this kind of *willing* self-corrosion is exactly the premise for divine contact and transcendence. The mystic finds joy in the dissolution of self—its "corruption or partition" on the way to nothingness. The so-called insane person fights to retain ontological security out of fear. The mystic actively deconstructs the self in the name of love.

10.

What Marguerite Porete called self-annihilation, the twentieth-century mystic Simone Weil called "decreation." For Weil, decreation was the endeavor to "undo the creature in us"—that is, to undo *one*self, and also the self as such. These are two orders of negation, one specific and one general, which Meister Eckhart also differentiates between in his cataphatic expedition to God: the nothingness of particular creatures versus the nothingness of *creaturely being*. Or: the cancellation of particular existence versus the cancellation of the existence of existence. Weil, like Porete, aimed for the latter by way of the former.

Weil succeeded in surrendering herself; for most of her life she had trouble eating, and she eventually died from tuberculosis exacerbated by the inability to eat. She desired to decreate herself to the point that she could subsist without eating at all, living on words alone. "Man's great affliction . . . is that looking and eating are two different operations," she wrote. "Eternal beatitude is a state where to look is to eat." From Weil's writing it appears that, for her, self-starvation was not exactly self-punishment; it was an intense sensitivity toward the suffering of others (during World War II, she reportedly refused to eat any types of food that

were not also included in the allotted rations for French soldiers).
Her abnegation may have amounted to a political statement, but
it was spurred by her self-induced or secondhand pain on behalf
of others: an affective and physical aversion to the consumption
necessary to sustain the single self. She would not, but also *could*
not, eat.

In her book *Aliens & Anorexia* Chris Kraus summarizes:
"Weil was more a mystic than a theologian. That is, all the things
she wrote were field notes for a project she enacted on herself.
She was a performative philosopher. Her body was material. 'The
body is a lever for salvation,' she thought in *Gravity and Grace*.
'But in what way? *What is the right way to use it?*'"

James says that for mystics the "moral mystery intertwines
and combines with the intellectual mystery." If so, it's tempting to
try and solve that mystery. Religion, flawed as it is, has at points
throughout history offered a language for describing first contact
with the unknowable. In the absence of such a framework, contemporary analysis tends to wind up with psychiatry. "Until recently," argues Kraus, "nearly all the secondary texts on Simone
Weil treat her philosophical writings as a kind of biographic key."
The focus remains on trying to figure out what triggered her psychiatric state rather than on her "active stance" of willful, intellectually engaged decreation and the resultant body of knowledge
she produced. "Impossible to conceive a female life that might
extend outside itself," Kraus remarks. "Impossible to accept the
self-destruction of a woman as strategic." According to Kraus,
"Weil's detractors saw her, a female, acting on herself, as masochistic." But Weil was, despite all dismissive diagnoses, "arguing

for an alien-state, using subjectivity as a means of breaking down time and space."

Angela of Foligno became a mystic after the sudden death of her husband and children. One could easily interpret her necrophiliac visions in light of that biographical fact. And in historical context her sudden religious conversion could be seen as a practical choice among limited options for a single woman of that era who had lost family status and property. There is plenty to explain away her mystical encounter through the psychology of grief or the demands of her world, just as one could reduce Weil's decreation to post-traumatic stress or anorexia. Likewise, one could read the biologist's succumbing to Area X as a parable of personal loss—or of the social condition of being a female scientist, who understands that her objective analysis intertwines and combines with her bodily sight. Yet these reductive readings would all suggest that the strategic is somehow opposed to or separable from the transcendent.

11.

In an essay called "Weird Ecology," the writer David Tompkins compares Area X to a "hyperobject," a term philosopher Timothy Morton uses "to describe events or systems or processes that are too complex, too massively distributed across space and time, for humans to get a grip on." Global warming, black holes, and mass extinction are contemporary examples. For medievals: God. The mind can edge close to the hyperobject, understanding parts of it, but never comprehend its totality. Hyperobjects can certainly be measured and analyzed, but will never be encompassed by measurement and analysis. Media theorist Wendy Hui Kyong Chun has said: "You can't *see* the climate; you can only see the weather." Or, as the biologist from Area X says, "When you are too close to the center of a mystery there is no way to pull back and see the shape of it entire." How one longs to see it for a split second as a hazelnut-sized thing in the palm of the hand.

Faced with the possible annihilation of the planet as we know it, certain modes of knowing fall short. Especially insufficient is knowledge that purports humans to be distinct from ecosystems, much less in control of them. Among the "surprises and ironies at the heart of all knowledge production," says Donna Haraway, is the fact that "we are not in charge of the world." A mysticism for the Anthropocene, just like mysticism through the ages, would regard the object of knowledge as alive and inseparable from the mind and body that encounters it. That is, rather than fictionalizing science, a mysticism for today would have to weird it.

Haraway proposes a feminist understanding of objectivity not through any single, monolithic explanation but through an assemblage of "situated knowledges" or "views from somewhere." Somewhere, meaning positioned in location and historical context, and also meaning embodied—entailing a type of bodily sight. "Situated knowledges," Haraway explains, "require that the object of knowledge be pictured as an actor and agent, not as a screen or a ground or a resource." This refers to the way women have historically been seen as objects of study rather than active knowledge producers, but it is equally applicable with regard to the natural environment, which has for so long been conceived as passive or inert. *In the black water with the sun shining at midnight, those fruit shall come ripe and in the darkness of that which is golden shall split open to reveal the revelation of the fatal softness in the earth.*

Simone de Beauvoir wrote that Simone Weil had "a heart that beat around the world." Chris Kraus described Weil's state of being as a "radical form of empathy." Importantly, for the biologist in *Annihilation*, this empathy extends to, even prioritizes, the nonhuman. In the writer Leslie Allison's words: "Once the borders have dissolved, empathy is not just feeling others' pain or pleasure. It is granting everything its own subjectivity. It is acknowledging that even non-human entities have a self with which to desire a particular way of living." In Area X, the self dissolves—but self is also everywhere. Even the otter has a self now.

Is there a biological basis for self-annihilation? Are sex or gender prerequisites for empathic knowledge or bodily sight? Of course not. Look through a microscope: every body is permeable and porous, host to and hosted by trillions of other life-forms. The body is a transitional ecosystem. And anyway, if we were able to stop projecting contemporary epistemologies onto the past we'd see that medieval mystical writings are too deeply weird to read according to contemporary gender categories. Hollywood writes: "Christ's body is an impenetrable rock and a body full of holes— and both at the same time."

That said, nonmen, constantly made aware of their physical penetrability, disallowed from forgetting their bodies and bodily boundaries, have been producing empathic knowledge regarding the confrontation with the unknowable for centuries. Female mysticism offers a foundation for nonanthropocentric knowledge that is not at all opposed to other types of knowledge.

This is fertile ground for contemporary fiction—as evidenced by VanderMeer, who imagines himself, with radical empathy, into the experience of the female biologist. One role for the new weird in today's literary landscape may be to grow mystical knowledge not only beyond the framework of religion but also beyond the framework of institutionalized science.

Near the end of her account, the biologist says of the transformation of Area X: "I can no longer say with conviction that this is a bad thing. Not when looking at the pristine nature of Area X and then the world beyond, which we have altered so much." She can no longer see her decreation, nor the decreation of the current humancentric world, as negative. It is, like the divine, beyond all positive and negative distinctions. Tompkins explains that "Area X is frightening, yes, but what appears to be happening there is not a reversion to Chaos and Old Night," as older types of weird fiction would have it. Here, in the living, sporous world of new weird fiction, may be the start of a new species transition. Loss of bounded self is only truly horrifying within an anthropocentric framework that prizes human being in its current state over all other forms and ways of being. Self-annihilation might, paradoxically, offer a path toward ecosystemic preservation.

2

PLANETS

What's Happening?

Or, how to name a disaster

IN 1974 DORIS LESSING published *The Memoirs of a Survivor*, a postapocalyptic novel narrated by an unnamed woman almost entirely from inside her ground-floor apartment in an English suburb. In a state of suspended disbelief and detachment, the woman describes the events happening outside her window as society slowly collapses, intermittently dissociating from reality and lapsing into dream states. At first, the basic utilities begin to cut out; then the food supply runs short. Suddenly, rats are everywhere. Roving groups from neighboring areas pass through the yard, ostensibly escaping even worse living conditions and heading somewhere they imagine will be better. Her neighbors disappear, either dead or gone, leaving children behind—children who become feral and increasingly violent. Over the course of a few years, even the children's language devolves into almost unintelligible jargon and cursing, as if the polite words they have been taught to communicate with no longer suit the survivalist demands of their situation.

The narrator's myopic view of the outside world reflects the shortsightedness of her culture at large. Nobody, apparently, can admit how bad things are until conditions become completely unlivable, and meanwhile nobody can bear to name "it," this slow, ongoing collapse with unidentifiable origins. The narrator spends considerable time trying and failing to define "it," the never-quite-climactic but steady disintegration of life as she knew it. The news barely addresses "it," and neither do the authorities, who, instead of offering aid, send troops in to police the newly home-less. To the narrator, "it" had never been "felt as an immediate threat"—because it always seemed like a problem elsewhere, rel-evant to somebody else, but never at the doorstep, until it was far too late. She explains: "While everything, all forms of social or-ganization, broke up, we lived on, adjusting our lives as if nothing fundamental was happening. It was amazing how determined, how stubborn, how self-renewing were the attempts to lead an or-dinary life. When nothing, or very little, was left of what we had been used to, had taken for granted even ten years before, we went on talking and behaving as if those old forms were still ours."

Lessing sticks to the pronoun and describes "it" from an oblique angle, but writers of dystopian fiction have given "it" all sorts of names and causes. These turning points are similar to what the critic Darko Suvin has called the *novum*—the event or technological novelty that signals how a given science-fictional world is different from our own. The event that destroyed the Earth in Philip K. Dick's *Do Androids Dream of Electric Sheep?* is spurred by a major war called World War Terminus. Kim Stanley Robinson's drowned city in *New York 2140* is the product of two major Pulses, or moments of drastic sea-level rise. Neal Stephenson marks the inexplicable explosion of the moon in *Seveneves* by starting a new clock for human time, with the lunar destruction as hour "A+0.0.0, or simply Zero." In P. D. James's *The Children of Men*, too, the clock starts over, at the point when humans become infertile and are faced with species demise: Year Omega. The titular event in Liz Jensen's 2009 *The Rapture* is a major flood instigated by climate change, the biblical name of which, like the clock at 0, indicates that something has ended and something else has begun. Such terminology points to the religious (and moralistic) undertones of much science fiction, a genre that supposedly rests on the supremacy of reason and rationality but is often undeniably theological in structure. One could say the same of Western cultural narratives at large.

A particularly inventive recent name for "it" is William Gibson's "jackpot," from his 2014 novel, *The Peripheral* (which continues in the 2020 sequel, *Agency*). The jackpot is what future humans call their previous social collapse, initiated partly by antibiotic-resistant bacterial infections. The choice of term is an ironic comment on the fact that global population decimation resulting from the plague was highly beneficial for some. The scarcity of an overpopulated world became post-jackpot abundance for those who were poised to take advantage of it. As Gibson himself is said to have remarked, the future is already here, it is just unevenly distributed—an adage he updated in recent years to say that dystopia is also here, it's just unevenly distributed, too.

Gibson's jackpot seems like an appropriate term for our times and the major "it" the world has most recently undergone, which has so far been named the COVID-19 pandemic. While a virus can infect anyone, the pandemic has disproportionately affected poor and minority communities when it comes to loss of livelihood and morbidity rates. And, as Gibson shows, this disparity will perpetuate or widen *after* the event, as evidenced by choices like the administrations' various stimulus packages, which support "the economy" (i.e., the wealthy and their banks) rather than those most vulnerable. In other words, the pandemic may have been hell for most but turned out to be a jackpot for some.

This raises the question: What would after the pandemic look like? In some ways it is the wrong question to ask, because event-izing the pandemic and giving it an *after* implies that there was a true *before*. As writers of dystopian novels know, there was no before, there was only a time when "it" wasn't quite so unavoidably visible. The circumstances that gave rise to "it" have been in place for quite some time. Yet until recently, the unevenly distributed dystopia was less immediately apparent to those with more privilege. Now it can hardly be ignored—even by people who, like Lessing's narrator, have been sitting safely inside, watching what's happening through the window, trying to uphold the pretense that it is not her responsibility nor her calamity. Many of us have successfully outsourced dystopia to somewhere else. But now it is here, because it is everywhere.

Alongside nuclear catastrophe, climate meltdown, and global war, pandemics serve as the "it" in much fiction. Recent examples, like Emily St. John Mandel's *Station Eleven* from 2014 and Ling Ma's *Severance* from 2018 (which describes an eerily familiar-sounding Shen Fever), give us stories to think through what population decimation really means. Pandemic stories can offer a lot for comprehending our current situation, but so can stories that, like Lessing's, refuse to explicitly pinpoint or name the cataclysmic event. In doing so they emphasize the fact that "it" can never be reduced to a single name or cause. By resisting explanation, they refocus on what change and loss feel like, rather than trying to explain where they come from. Cormac McCarthy, notably, simply gives us the road and a journey without beginning or end. Octavia E. Butler alludes to climate change, but doesn't exactly name the apocalypse that led to the setting of *Parable of the Sower*. Her young female protagonist fixates on the fact of *change* itself. Since she knows the past cannot be resurrected and the change cannot be halted, she invents a new theology based on the absence of nameable turning points: a religion called Earthseed with the central tenet "God is Change."

On one hand, naming the crisis allows people to apprehend it, grasp it, fight back against it. On the other hand, no word can fully encompass it, and any term is necessarily a reduction—the essence of "it" or "change" is not any singular instance but rather its constancy. For example, while one could call COVID-19 a biological crisis, one could just as accurately call it a health-care crisis, a values crisis, or an ecological crisis. Names matter: think of how Donna Haraway reframed the Anthropocene era as the "Capitalocene," redirecting blame from the human species as such to humanity's current economic system of relentless extraction and exploitation. In some ways, the Capitalocene is a more optimistic title for our era than the Anthropocene, because it implies that there is another way: although we might remain *anthropos*, we can still construct our world according to a different set of priorities and principles than the ones capitalism allows.

Year Zero is a useful concept for a story to hinge on because it reflects modernity's entrenched desire for moments of rupture that change everything at once. Disasters do shape history and intervene in the narratives many cling to—but in truth they only catalyze and make visible malignant processes that have been ongoing for a long time. The biggest disasters are the ones that are never identified as such—what Rob Nixon calls "slow violence," those occurrences, like gradual environmental devastation, that disproportionately affect those without a megaphone, and which are not deemed newsworthy because they are not sensational single events. (One could also take up Keller Easterling's use of the term *disposition* to describe the latent violent attitudes of infrastructure design—from electrical grids to legislation—that are only made manifest when the system spectacularly fails.) The pandemic might also be reframed as a form of slow violence, resulting not only from sudden, invasive, "foreign," nonhuman threats, but also from ongoing, pervasive power imbalances inside and outside the arbitrary borders we draw around places, people, and concepts.

Slow violence is hard to identify, hard to describe, and hard to resist. But this is one thing literature, postapocalyptic or otherwise, can do: to portray how the short and the long, the small and the big, connect. To identify the rot within rather than the threat without. To articulate "it" even when "it" has no name. Fiction can portray ecologies, timescales, catastrophes, and forms of violence that may be otherwise invisible, or more to the point, unnameable. We will never grasp the pandemic in its entirety, just as we will never see the virus responsible for it with the naked eye. But we can try to articulate how it has changed us—is changing us.

Apocalyptic literature is only one fraction of literature. Yet

Lessing suggests that "it," that apocalyptic pronoun, may be the hidden subject of *all* literature, precisely because it is the story of human hope and human failure and the coexistence of the two—the simultaneity of the quotidian, the disastrous, and the transcendent that make up the human condition on Earth. Stories hinge on moments of change and transformation, but in this way they can also create continuity and coherence between eras and areas. In the novel, Lessing's narrator says:

> Perhaps, indeed, "it" is the secret theme of all literature and history, like writing between the lines in invisible ink, which springs up, sharply black, dimming the old print we knew so well, as life, personal or public, unfolds unexpectedly and we see something where we never thought we could . . . I am sure that ever since there were men on earth, "it" has been talked of precisely in this way in times of crisis, since it is in crisis "it" becomes visible, and our conceit sinks before its force. For "it" is a force, a power, taking the form of earthquake, a visiting comet whose balefulness hangs closer night by night, distorting all thought by fear—"it" can be, has been, pestilence, a war, the alteration of climate, a tyranny that twists men's minds, the savagery of a religion.
>
> "It," in short, is the word for helpless ignorance, or of helpless awareness. "It" is a word for man's inadequacy?

By identifying humanity's relative helplessness, writing about "it" may actually help identify points of action and decision-making. In early 2020 Karen Russell wrote in *The New Yorker* that the term *flatten the curve* caused a paradigm shift for her; "it taught me, in three words, to stop thinking of myself as a potential victim of COVID-19 and to start thinking of myself as a vector for contagion. It alchemizes fear into action. The phrase is an injunction: it says, gently and urgently, that it is not too late for us to change the shape of this story."

The curve asked people to see themselves both as individual protagonists with decision-making capacity and as a collective statistic. It asked that people become aware of our interconnectedness even as we pay attention to the inequalities that divide us. If dystopia is unevenly distributed, it is up to those with resources, who long "believed they were immune," in Lessing's words, to see themselves as both potential victims of the virus and as responsible for others who may get it. Precisely because the pandemic has not been the great leveler, because one person's misery is another's jackpot, it may force us to think of history in a different way, less in terms of major events instigated by a few and more in terms of processes that involve and implicate the many.

Fiction has the potential to describe human subject experience without reducing the universe to human subject experience. It also has the potential to move beyond the two options we're usually given for the way the future can go: utopia or dystopia. It raises the question: Whose utopia, whose dystopia? If the human is not the protagonist, who is? A utopia for mosquitoes may not be the same as mine, but from the perspective of planetary ecosystems it may be far preferable. Utopia and dystopia are not divergent paths leading into the future, but matters of perspective and scale. Like optimism and pessimism, they are not mutually exclusive. Both utopia and dystopia are happening all the time, right now, on different scales and in different places.

My favorite future-dystopian novel resembles historical fiction. Russell Hoban's *Riddley Walker*, from 1980, is written entirely in an invented version of medieval-sounding British English—perhaps a few centuries further (d)evolved from the odd speech of the new generation in *The Memoirs of a Survivor*. In Hoban's book, the "it" is nuclear catastrophe, which has decimated much of civilization but provided a new cosmology for the survivors. The twelve-year-old narrator, Riddley, lives in this future-past civilization where a rudimentary understanding of atomic science has mingled with Catholic mythology. The splitting of the atom provides a new origin story, overlaid upon Christian prophecy, and the new language borrows from the old to suit new purposes. Many words are split down the middle and mutated—*energy* becomes *Inner G*; *Dover* becomes *Do It Over*—ruptured like the atomic elements of the world and rearranged to tell a new story. Like Butler's Earthseed, a religion whose holy notion is constant change, the foundational myths of Riddley's worldview depend on a different idea of what constitutes beginnings and endings.

Stories like this one remind me that, while the future may resemble the past, there will be no reversal of the pandemic, nor a reversion to the worldview that came before. Loss changes those who live through it. "It," says Lessing, "was, above all, a consciousness of something ending." Something is ending, but many things are continuing and others are beginning, and this offers the opportunity for new choices. What will end are certainly not the structures of power that got us here: those will likely hold, and try to hold tighter. We should and will try to dismantle power. At the same time, we need to find new names for what we are experiencing—not to reduce the narrative to a singular descent into hell that we can emerge or move on from, but to acknowledge this transformation as it occurs, and to acknowledge the various versions of life on Earth that have existed for decades, centuries, and millennia. If "it" is the experience of change, and change is the only constant, we need to document this change as it takes place. As in Lessing's tale, those in power will retreat further into their hiding places, never addressing the real story—or stories, for there are many, and all should be told.

Future Looks

Staring into the sun

A luxury genre

Silver spaceships pass quietly overhead. The view of the sky is obscured by gently rustling leaves. Below, a young, pretty woman steps through the door of a glass building, where she enters a pod that scans her body for abnormalities. Zoom way out: the ground curves, swooping upward, green and bright; the whole landscape paves the inside of a spinning satellite. *The year 2154. The privileged live on Elysium. No poverty. No war. No sickness.*

The rest of us . . . live on Earth. The music drops. Aerial shots of smoldering skyscrapers through smoke-tinged air. Bombed-out highways; ramshackle slums crisscrossed with powerlines; rusted cars amid the gritty rubble. Close-up of Matt Damon scuffling through dust, while faceless others jog past with empty fuel containers. Matt's head is shaved and he has a generic tattoo on his neck. Music drops again: he's lying on a steel table in a blue-lit room. "Bring down the bone saw," shouts a shirtless guy of ambiguous race wearing a grimy apron. Matt's face contorts in pain. Now he's a cyborg with weapons for arms.

The trailer for the 2013 movie *Elysium*, directed by Neill

Blomkamp, promises a tale of two cities. Above, a high-def paradise on a satellite rotating above Earth, populated by cancer-free wealthy folks, only one of whom is actually Jodie Foster but all of whom are basically Jodie Foster. Below, the postapocalyptic, reggaeton-thumping, polluted Los Angeles where the "rest of us" are definitely going to step on something and get tetanus. Matt Damon, we gather, has reached a desperate juncture and is determined to spend his last days forcing his way into high-class heaven.

The visual and sonic cues for the worlds of the haves and the have-nots are textbook. They're drawn from—and replicated by— the stockpile of existing commercial shorthands for nice life and scary life (correlating wealth with happiness and poverty with misery). Elysium might as well be a rendering of Apple's Norman Foster–designed headquarters in Cupertino—nicknamed "the spaceship"—and 2154 Los Angeles might as well be stock footage of a refugee camp shot through a high-contrast filter.

You know what dystopia and utopia are supposed to look like. One is clean; the other is dirty. One has spaceships; the other has no cell signal. One is green and fertile; the other is barren and muddy. One is carefully designed; the other is hacked together. Dystopia, which has arguably been given more airtime on screens and pages of late, is especially familiar. In fact, you have your pick of dystopias du jour depending on what you're feeling most nervous about. Flooding? Declining birth rates? Refugee crises? In a 2017 *New Yorker* article ironically titled "A Golden Age for Dystopian Fiction," Jill Lepore argues that dystopia "appeals to both the left and the right, because, in the end, it requires so little by way of literary, political, or moral imagination, asking only that you enjoy the company of people whose fear of the future aligns comfortably with your own."

As a form of entertainment, it is true that dystopia has become a luxury genre. For the privileged, dystopian landscapes can be as titillating as they are terrifying, because seeing them rendered in familiar fashions keeps them in either the realm of the imaginary or the realm of the faraway. Many Western reviewers lauded Blomkamp's 2009 movie *District 9* for its innovative portrayal of an alien spaceship landing in Johannesburg, after which the aliens are placed in concentration camps and treated as second-class citizens. Some South African audiences, on the other hand, expressed ambivalence or outrage about the allegorical recycling of apartheid history (equating aliens with Black underclasses) for entertainment. In much fiction such as this, even though it might contain critical social commentary, dystopia is outsourced to somewhere else—the fantastic, the future, the Global South—and, although it might be used to reflect the current reality *there*, it is also meant to reassure certain watchers that those things aren't quite *here* yet. By keeping things faraway and fictional, it might also promote a sense of empowerment: surely *we* wouldn't allow such a thing to happen.

Making progress

In her essay on dystopian fiction, Lepore mainly references futuristic novels hinging on climate change. One book she describes features roving survivors of an overheated planet who flock to crumbling cities in search of companionship; in another, Elysium-like parable, all the rich people abscond to outer space, leaving Earth-dwellers to rot. Although she acknowledges that dystopian fiction has been booming for centuries, Lepore finds a distinct and newly pervasive sense of self-indulgent hopelessness in the 2010s crop—an "adolescent sensibility, pouty and hostile." Worse, these petulant authors stop at simply warning readers and watchers of what may be to come, without arming us with the tools to fend off looming disaster. Their "only admonition is: Despair more."

Through a brief historical analysis starting with Thomas More's imaginary island of Utopia (1516) and its subsequent satirizations, she describes dystopian fiction throughout time as a direct response to starry-eyed utopian concepts, reactive takedowns of those who dare to dream rather than complex propositions in their own right. "Dystopias follow utopias the way thunder follows lightning," she writes, but today, "it's easy to forget how recently lightning struck." She quotes an article from 2000 that declares that the United States had been on the right track to achieving a utopian liberal dream—the lightning flash of utopia was just within reach, if only writers had all gotten on board the "Yes, we can" train! Instead everybody became a doomer. Martin Luther King Jr. had a dream, she says with a sigh, but these authors only have nightmares.

Presumably, the previous "liberal-minded dystopias" and "rights-based dystopianism" (of which Lepore's sole example is Margaret Atwood's *The Handmaid's Tale*) did a better job of arming people with positive and actionable weapons against, say, patriarchy and totalitarianism. "Dystopia used to be a fiction of resistance; it's become a fiction of submission, the fiction of an untrusting, lonely, and sullen twenty-first century . . . It cannot imagine a better future, and it doesn't ask anyone to bother to make one." Lepore does not clarify what she thinks fiction-makers should be doing to arm readers—designing weaponry?—and she doesn't spell out what a "fiction of resistance" for today (or for any era) would look like. The assumption throughout, though, is that authors have some burden of responsibility to create a better future.

From a different perspective, it is possible that not all dystopian fiction reacts retroactively to utopian dreams like thunder that follows lightning. After all, the progressive utopian track laid out by neoliberalism's powerful stakeholders has always been dystopian for large groups of people who do not benefit from its agenda. And in the era of climate change, it feels gaslight-y to be told hopelessness is a personal failure, much less a failure of literature at large. I would wager that most dystopian writers don't really think utopia is for suckers—it's more that pinning one's politics entirely on hope while facing extinction feels somewhat delusional.

At the end of *Elysium*, Matt Damon's character dies, but only after he's managed to reboot Elysium's mainframe and turn all Earth-dwellers into Elysian citizens with the right to wealth and privilege. The message is that utopia could be for all, were the selfish rich to share their resources. To some extent this is true; if planetary resources were equitably shared, the great rift between rich and poor could be narrowed. But this heroic story of a single man's quest and its moral message skip over the question of whether everyone on Earth *wants* a key card to Jodie Foster's version of heaven. Does heaven really look like an iPhone?

The corporate technoutopian aesthetic fantasy is one that depends on its counterpart, its tragic, dirty, hellish opposite, and I suspect that if there were to be an *Elysium* sequel, Jodie Foster's heir would attempt to wrest the fancy satellite back into the hands of the rich. The perpetual oppositional tension between the two worlds is what gives them positive and negative charge, what drives the plot. Lepore writes that "utopians believe in progress; dystopians don't." Aligning utopia with progress promotes a view that progress is linear or cohesive, and also that dogged forward motion is a good thing. If going "backward" in some areas might improve the overall health of the planet, a radically different notion of utopia—and dystopia—than the reigning brand might emerge.

A literary movement, a hashtag, a flag

I first heard the word *solarpunk* in 2014, when a friend told me my outfit was looking very on trend. I later learned that the term arose around 2008 and became widespread among certain internet circles in the mid-2010s. Solarpunk's origins and inspirations are diverse and dispersed, but it has had a "core community of stewards who know who they are," according to a 2017 solarpunk reference guide by the artist, theorist, and self-identified solarpunk steward Jay Springett. The animating question for these stewards is how to proactively and positively react to impending climate crisis. Solarpunk aims to avoid shiny technoutopianism on one side and doomer dystopianism on the other.

The general solarpunk vibe is DIY green tech. Following hashtags will lead you from glistening self-made geodesic domes full of palm trees to seasteads bursting with greenery; from plans for LEED-certified self-made buildings to Singaporean high-rises with living facades; from fixed-gear bikes with solar-paneled handlebars to cabin-porn Pinterest pages; from self-published fantasy novels about sun-loving dragons to a compendium of ecofiction from Brazil. When I asked one internet-expert friend what the most solarpunk movie he could think of was, he told me *Waterworld*. Another friend said *Silent Running* or maybe the original *Mad Max*.

Like most born-digital movements, solarpunk's looks circulated first and faster than narratives about what it was supposed to do. In this way it differs from its punk predecessors, cyberpunk and steampunk, whose aesthetics emerged concurrently (or emerged from) the stories that conveyed them in books, movies, zines, and music. At the start, solarpunk put forth visual ideas about what a "better" future could look like—we'd live in zerowaste ecovillages and spend our days gardening, or we'd build energy-efficient skyscrapers with mesh-network wifi and deal in cryptocurrency rather than cash. The political connotations of the aesthetics were made explicit, or steered, somewhat after the fact. Given its roots in the often anonymous, hyperlinked, heterogenous world of the internet, it would be fair to say that solarpunk began as a mood board for a politics.

While some solarpunks claim that their ideas fit squarely within the "wider tradition of the decentralist left" (according to solarpunkanarchists.com), others claim socialist, communist, or pseudo-libertarian stances. (You'll also find some singularity fans and terraforming enthusiasts.) The raison d'être is to propose plausible ways of dealing with a rapidly worsening ecological situation. In a widely read 2015 blog post titled "Solarpunk wants to save the world," writer Ben Valentine declares: "Solarpunk is the first creative movement consciously and positively responding to the Anthropocene. When no place on Earth is free from humanity's hedonism, Solarpunk proposes that humans can learn to live in harmony with the planet once again. Solarpunk is a literary movement, a hashtag, a flag, and a statement of intent about the future we hope to create." In his 2014 "Solarpunk: Notes toward a manifesto," writer Adam Flynn puts it in more drastic terms: "We're *solarpunks* because the only other options are denial or despair." None of what Lepore calls "pouty and hostile" hopelessness, but not exactly hyperpositive neoliberal hope language, either.

Unlike several green movements that have crystalized over the past century, solarpunk does not wish to be reducible to one credo that would allow it to be comparetmentalized or marginalized. Adherents might support existing movements like the Extinction Rebellion or Greta Thunberg–style climate strikes, but overall the project tries to forge a multipronged approach untethered from any single practice. However, as diverse and forward leaning as it purports to be, a certain form of romantic nostalgia pervades much of the solarpunk universe, exemplified in this emblematic 2014 post from Tumblr user Olivia Louise:

Natural colors!
Art Nouveau!

Handcrafted wares!

Tailors and dressmakers!

Streetcars!

Airships!

Stained glass window solar panels!!!

Education in tech and food growing!

Less corporate capitalism, and more small businesses!

Solar rooftops and roadways!

Communal greenhouses on top of apartments!

Electric cars with old-fashioned looks!

No-cars-allowed walkways lined with independent shops!

Renewable energy-powered Art Nouveau-styled tech life!

It's easy to write off Olivia Louise's vision as twee, simplistic, or sanitized. But in the same post she provides a politically inflected reason for the cuteness of this happy green future. She writes: "A lot of people seem to share a vision of futuristic tech and architecture that looks a lot like an ipod—smooth and geometrical and white. Which imo is a little boring and sterile, which is why I picked out an Art Nouveau aesthetic for this." Solarpunk's aesthetic for technology, in this sense, is neither Luddite nor corporatized. It makes sustainability seem accessible, friendly, even fun. Between Elysium and Los Angeles, between the horror of total corporate opacity and that of total technological transparency, solarpunk places a semi-transparent, stained glass solar panel.

This vision expresses future-nostalgia for a world where tech is destandardized and un-mass-produced. It harkens back to an imaginary past that belonged to inventors and tinkerers, hobby-ists and craftspeople. But through references to art historical eras like art nouveau, its style reveals much obvious overlap with the aesthetics of steampunk in particular. And this stylistic overlap reveals both shared beliefs and oversights.

In the tradition of early authors like H. G. Wells and Michael Moorcock, steampunk is rife with Victorian anachro-nism, from safety-pinned corsets and time-machine typewrit-ers to top hats and windup clocks. These are gestures toward the democratization of technology via accessibility, toward an imagined time when anyone with a screwdriver might invent a world-changing device. Yet the seemingly innocuous cultural and technological anachronisms can't help but implicate other, more obviously problematic anachronisms. For instance: a world order where able-bodied white male aristocrats were unburdened by housework and free to experiment, where industrial technol-ogy provided not only awe-inspiring train engines but enabled European domination through colonial expansion. It's difficult to dissociate the steam by which that era powered empire from the subversion claimed by the punk.

Much steampunk that emerges today is irony, pastiche, or sat-ire. But regardless of the author's stance toward the subject ma-terial, the genre's aesthetics have become lifestyle tropes with a consumer niche. Although it might continue to purport itself as a political stance toward reclaiming the means of production, it has little relationship to lived reality. I asked V. Vale, host of the San Francisco public access television show *Counter Culture Hour*, whether he thought steampunk had any political teeth. He told me that even though steampunks might like copper accessories, "not many people have actually learned welding." Why would they, he asked, when Hot Topic sells goggles?

Putting aside the infinite punk variations (including seapunk, dieselpunk, atompunk, teslapunk, splatterpunk, cattlepunk, and what author Bruce Sterling suggests all contemporary sci-fi should be called: nowpunk), the other best-known punk universe is cyberpunk. When it emerged in the nineties, the era of early internet culture and the accelerating corporatization of daily life, cyberpunk injected the subversive potential of punk back into genre fiction. It turned away from nostalgia and dove into future-tech dystopia, undermining technological progress, focusing on corporate and government power structures, and introducing class struggle into its narratives. The cliché cyberpunk hero plugs into the mainframe to bring down the corporate overlords—after stopping at an underground rave wearing technical gear and tiny blue-light-blocking glasses. (Matt Damon's *Elysium* character, with his biohacked arms, technical prowess, and hatred toward the system, borrows from the cyberpunk legacy.) Cyberpunk is futuristic rather than retro, but like steampunk it foregrounds a hacker mentality with regard to technology—technological and corporate opacity being a more obviously pressing concern in the 1990s than in the late nineteenth century.

William Gibson says that the naming of subgenres like cyberpunk was partially what paved the way for much of science fiction's eventual depoliticization. "A snappy label and a manifesto would have been two of the very last things on my own career want list," he says. "That label enabled mainstream science fiction to safely assimilate our dissident influence, such as it was. Cyberpunk could then be embraced and given prizes and patted on the head, and genre science fiction could continue unchanged." Naming it cyberpunk is what gutted its punk potential. Yet the emergence of both of these dominant punk worlds, however co-opted, does illuminate the changing relationships between users and advanced technologies over time, both expressing the need for technological (and therefore political) accessibility as one buffer against total dystopia.

Solarpunk, conversely, began with a look, a snappy label, and a manifesto, aiming to seize the genre category and steer it before any dissident influence could be assimilated. It also distinguishes itself from what came before in its emphasis on realizability. While steampunks could afford to be dilettantes, and cyberpunks could afford to fantasize about worst-case scenarios, solarpunks anticipate necessity: you'll have to learn to weld when factory production inevitably breaks down, and you'll need to know how to roof garden when the flood waters rise. And while the steam era was powered by coal and the cyber era was powered by oil, the solar era must find a nonextractive solution—embodied by the symbol of the solar panel—if there is to be any future at all. This is a curiously utopian impulse nonetheless built on a clear-eyed understanding of a dystopian present. According to manifesto writer Flynn, "if cyberpunk was 'here is this future that we see coming and we don't like it,' and steampunk is 'here's yesterday's future that we wish we had,' then solarpunk might be 'here's a future that we can want and we might actually be able to get.'"

Science fiction into science action

Science fiction has always had a special relationship to the future and to prediction. Stories of science fiction presaging technological and social developments are legion, from Arthur C. Clarke's satellites in geostationary orbit to the movement-controlled interfaces of Philip K. Dick's *The Minority Report* to Gibson's visions of remote communication in cyberspace. Such examples are often invoked as proof of the authors' oracular prowess, and by extension, validation of the genre. Predictive accuracy is a dubious way to evaluate any work of art, but in light of the fact that it is increasingly difficult to separate fiction from reality, or the future from speculations about it, it has become particularly suspicious.

Finance capitalism, for example, could be described as a speculative fiction based on a specific type of futurism, in which projecting an idea of what will happen creates the future that makes the prediction plausible. Trend forecasts invent the trends forecasted; fake news makes real news. "Science fiction is an ouroboros," in the words of technology writer Claire L. Evans. And it is possible that the ouroboros, the reciprocal causal loop between fiction and reality, is tightening and accelerating these days.

Ostensibly for fiction to be critical means for it to stand back from reality and reveal previously unseen things about the present that might somehow help us avoid worst-case future scenarios. Yet most of us are aware of the dystopian elements of the present and don't require the facts to be dramatically revealed to us through story. Critique does not constitute action itself, nor does it sufficiently arm us against nasty future scenarios, as

Lepore says fiction should do. Furthermore, if contemporary life is already the result of massive corporate fictions (in J. G. Ballard's words: "politics conducted as a branch of advertising, the instant translation of science and technology into popular imagery") then the distance from systems of power required for critique in this traditional sense is hard to stake out. This has been especially detrimental for fiction. The line between critique and complicity is not firmly drawn, and fiction authors are now tasked with navigating the overlap.

Contemporary capitalism not only disallows critical distance but tends to pave over irony—which requires some distance from its subject—by taking up what are intended as critical provocations as earnest proposals. Looking to architecture and design offers clues as to how this happens in practice. Unlike books and movies and art, architecture and design have an explicit relation to implementation and realization, even when the products are meant as provocations rather than plans. The terms *speculative design* and *design fiction* have cropped up in this space over the past two decades to describe a type of project that undermines its own applicability, with mixed results.

In 2009, the speculative designer Alexandra Daisy Ginsberg worked with a group of students to create a synthetic biology project called *E. chromi*. Using genetically engineered bacteria that excrete pigments, they produced a kit for hypothetical medical use. With the kit, you could test the health of your gut microbiome by ingesting a substance that colors your poop. Ginsberg explained to me that the project was meant to highlight both the potential benefits and hazards of personalized biotechnology, but her joking prototype was taken seriously by investors who, steam-rolling over the hazards in favor of the benefits of profit, quickly tried to adopt the concept for mass production.

In trying to parse the paradox of fiction's co-optability, I spoke to the designers Anthony Dunne and Fiona Raby (practicing as Dunne & Raby), who are known for their 2013 book *Speculative Everything*. The duo attempts to undermine the imperative to design useful objects for the world as it already exists and rather to imagine what objects might exist in different, maybe better worlds. They told me that they hope to move away from the frameworks of "problems to be solved" or "making stuff real," because these endeavors are so close to "classic future forecasting approaches." In their experience, futurism tends to foreclose the horizon of speculation. Since the future seems grim and out of most people's control, "futures can be quite limiting as a way of thinking about how the world could be otherwise." For a project called *United Micro Kingdoms*, they imagined a version of England subdivided into four different regions with distinct cultures. They then designed a series of vehicles that might appeal to each group, based on their prevailing belief systems and technological capacities. However unlikely it may be that these designs get adopted as real solutions, such proposals for alternate realities require one to ask what would happen if they were.

If critique is likely to be taken as proposal, there is an argument to be made that coming up with positive-seeming futures is the responsible choice. Solarpunk seems to lean toward this attitude, and in doing so, refuses to worry about whether it's categorizable as art, fiction, or design. "Capitalist realism" is Mark

Fisher's name for "the widespread sense that not only is capitalism the only viable political and economic system, but also that it is now impossible even to *imagine* a coherent alternative to it." Solarpunk asks: If capitalist realism reigns, should authors (and everybody) try to sketch out a slightly better version of the real? Given the massive, if unevenly distributed dystopia of extinction-level planet Earth, do fiction-makers who have the time to speculate on the future have a kind of responsibility to make *solutions*?

Several notable sci-fi authors have explicitly aligned themselves with solutionist goals, either within or alongside their fiction. Neal Stephenson founded Project Hieroglyph in 2012, which is "an initiative to create science fiction that will spur innovation in science and technology." In an essay describing the project, Stephenson laments the lack of large scientific leaps over recent decades, arguing that—for all the Silicon Valley talk of disruption—real innovation has been largely stalled by corporate and academic decision-making aimed to minimize risk. "Where's my donut-shaped space station? Where's my ticket to Mars?"

Along with others, like David Graeber, Stephenson believes the current paucity of long-promised technomiracles that could revolutionize society is not for lack of technological capability, but for lack of collective imagination and organization. The ability to envision better futures has been dulled by the structural inhibitions of the only institutions with the resources to make big things happen, institutions whose ideas aren't typically very imaginative. Corporate and Wall Street–style solutionism only produce solutions for the few, when technology could be producing positive solutions for the problems of the many. Science fiction, Stephenson says, can help.

The age of the greenhouse

Can any technology be good for everybody? For its part, solar power has a shadow history. In the eighteenth and early nineteenth centuries, innovations in solar-powered engineering saw a major boom. Spurred by the Little Ice Age, spanning all the way from the fourteenth to nineteenth centuries—a geological oddity in which Europe went through an extremely cold period—the rush to develop alternate heating methods led to the "age of the greenhouse" in eighteenth-century western Europe (as termed by Ken Butti and John Perlin in their book, *A Golden Thread: 2500 Years of Solar Architecture and Technology*). Pretty glass-cased structures became popular typologies, and inventors experimented with various ways to keep buildings warm using the passive energy source of the sun. As the ice age passed and colonial expansion accelerated, that technology was used for decorative purposes. Greenhouses and botanical gardens became metropolitan showcases for the exotic species stolen from abroad. Horticulturists tried to simulate tropical climates necessary to cultivate the imported produce that the European palate had come to appreciate.

By the mid-nineteenth century, as the European middle class grew, the invention of the solar-heated greenhouse led to the conservatory, a plant room annexed to well-to-do homes. Conservatories were largely hobby rooms for the well-off to demonstrate exactly how much leisure time they possessed; they also provided an activity for the idle hands of wealthy women whose domestic interiors had become their whole worlds. This architectural form was reflective of both the supposed safety at the center of empire and the power of its far reaches.

By the twentieth century, however, coal power had become more widespread, and many could afford to skip the solar engineering required to heat conservatories and houses. As long as enough sunlight passed through the glass for the plants to survive, temperature was no longer an issue—people cheated. By the time the art nouveau era began, the greenhouse had already receded in function, and become a decorative imitation of sustainable architecture. Like many supposedly eco-conscious products today, it looked green and nature-friendly but its function was beside the point.

Solar greenhouses were accompanied by many other now-forgotten solar tech advancements. One French mathematician, Augustin Mouchot, invented a solar-powered steam engine, constructing the first functional prototype in the 1860s. It was applauded as a marvel, but the French sun wasn't strong enough to reliably power the machine, and so it was sent to be implemented in the sunnier colonies. Mouchot himself traveled to Algiers to propose how solar power could be made a literal engine of expansion, with moderate success. (His designs for solar-powered ovens and wells were more popular, but overall, his technological innovations were largely irrelevant; if Mouchot had looked around when he arrived in Algiers, he might have noticed the advanced passive thermal regulation system employed in traditional regional architecture.)

Similar stories—of colonial scientists arriving in distant lo-
cales with solar-engineered marvels—were repeated in British
and German colonies over the following decades. Most projects
dead-ended with the start of the First World War. Colonists had
no time to experiment with nonmilitary engineering. More to the
point, harnessing the passive power of the sun had become much
less profitable than the coal industry. Solar panels might imply
positive futures, but by looking to the past, it's easy to see that no
technology is inherently sunny or dark; it depends on who uses it
and how.

Looking sideways

When thinking of the history of colonial experiments in solar
power, I have to wonder what they say about the current potential of solar technology to democratize versus to exploit. Solar's
shadow history is a reminder of how technologies can become di-
vorced from their aesthetics, and that technologies and aesthetic
movements operating under the banner of advancement and
progress are able to ignore the fact that advancement and progress mean different things depending on context. Like Dunne &
Raby, theorist Jared Sexton reframes the idea of speculative fiction by shifting it away from futurism entirely. "Speculative: not
only about possible futures, but also possible pasts and presents."
Writing about history and the contemporary moment are no
less speculative activities than writing about the future: the way
reality is constructed in relation to any time frame is a form of

invention. And invention may take the form of bringing to public consciousness the already existent histories and realities that do not always make it onto newspaper landing pages, much less into cinemas.

Author Omar El Akkad said in a 2017 interview: "I'm not as interested in the question of whether the ideas at the root of my fiction could happen, so much as I am with the fact that, for many people in this world, they already have. I think of what I write less as dystopian and more as dislocative." Dislocation, I think, is about the kind of lateral speculation Sexton and Dunne & Raby describe, rather than projections forward in time. With this in mind, I have come to think of my own fiction writing as "reality-adjacent" rather than futuristic, situating my speculations next to the current moment instead of ahead of it.

El Akkad's 2017 book *American War* dislocates current U.S. interventionist foreign militarism. In some adjacent reality, the country is embroiled in its second civil war, again North against South, but skewed according to different lines of race, class, and patriotism. In this case the south, much of its coastline drowned due to rising sea tides, has seceded due to a northern federal government injunction that the whole nation quit using fossil fuels—interpreted by the marginalized and poverty-stricken south as a form of both cultural and economic oppression. A newly formed empire in the Middle East feeds arms and supplies to the south to spur the insurrection, seemingly to prompt the collapse of U.S. imperialism. The novel's main character is a young girl who spends much of her life internally displaced in a southern refugee camp living off such supplies. Reading El Akkad's prose you can almost smell the gasoline of the contraband "fossil cars" still running on the old fuel; you are frustrated by the slowness of the various solar-powered "Tik-Tok" vehicles people have been forced to rely on; you can envision the *Waterworld*-like environment of the half-floating Augusta, Georgia, now a seedy port city where cargo ships arrive from the distant East.

American War is undoubtedly a dystopia. But it is a dystopia where the future collides with the past and the supposedly distant has been brought to the supposed here of the Western vantage point. It inverts the clichéd image of the foreign refugee child, and it flips which global superpower is driving geopolitics. Many of the aesthetic tropes of dystopia are present, but most of them are weirdly twisted: flashes of Elysium-style technology mingled with messy hacked-together solutions. Overall the technology fluctuates somewhere between high- and low-tech—southern insurrectionists use rusty rifles, while silent and deadly drones from the north circle overhead. Much of the U.S. is mud and swamp, and yet global shipping routes still run like clockwork. This is not a war for coal or oil, it's a war for, or under the guise of, sustainability, for saving the planet—even against the wishes and immediate interests of many of its citizens. The solar panels in this story are political signifiers for inequality as much as they are useful or positive solutions to a collapsing present.

By blending and dislocating aesthetic references, El Akkad's book does much of what solarpunk fiction could do, or professes to want to do, without recourse to anything like retrograde art nouveau. Dislocative fiction could uncouple the future from the purview of the Western world entirely, with its attendant art historical references. This would not be by proposing technological leaps into the future, nor by taking wistful glances at the past, but by looking at what's already in the world, and perhaps bringing into the story what has been historically overlooked. In her disparaging overview of contemporary dystopian fiction, Lepore brings up El Akkad's book. She calls his politics one of "ruin," lamenting that it does not do more to move us forward. But I don't think it intends to move us forward—it intends to dislocate us from where we are, and in turn to make us question who *we* are.

Should versus could

The question of whether literature or any art should offer itself toward practical aims, toward something like solutions, is nothing new. It stirs up philosophical ghosts. Should art be made for art's sake, or should art have a social mission? Are these oppositional to each other? Such seemingly timeless debates about the role of art, however, may have somewhat different stakes in the extinction age than in past eras. The same philosophical, ethical, and political rubrics may not exactly apply today, the humanism at their core not so self-evident or axiomatic.

The catastrophe of the Anthropocene leaves fiction, especially fiction related to climate change, in an uncomfortable middle zone. It seems clear that it should not simply reproduce despair or wallow in self-indulgent (Western-centric) fears about possible calamities, but if it offers real proposals it could be said to slide into other territories, territories that do not traditionally belong to art at all. If it doesn't address the pressing issues of our time it is navel-gazing or irrelevant; if it looks them squarely in the face and instructs on a "better way" it becomes a functional (Ayn Randian) tool of a particular political ideology.

Certainly fiction-as-ideological-vessel carries dangers. And earnest proposals, even without a strong ideological bent, are probably always somewhat at risk of functional exploitation; they may be reduced to a lowest common denominator and turned into credo, nuance erased, bought and sold. Yet there is a fundamental difference between should and could, between road map and speculation. The former insists on a single best reality, which tends to be the best reality for the person proposing it. The latter allows the existence of multiple, coexistent realities, none of them inevitable. The future has to look different if it is to become different, but looks are not enough.

Disregarding the tired question of whether it's really art if it provides solutions, the problem with fiction that promotes solutionism as a worldview is that solutionism can't help but be a top-down strategy. No solution is one-size-fits-all, and no solution should be imposed from above (from the government or a writer), especially in an age when "the system" or "the man" is no longer a monolithic evil entity but a networked system of oppression that operates along multiple axes of power and persuasion. Single-order solutionism implies that a good solution for what ails one person is good for every person, which is clearly not the case in a deeply unequal world. And it suggests that what is good for people is also good for the planet, when the best-case scenarios for the wealthy, the poor, and the planetary ecosystem are regularly at odds with one another. People as a species have not proven to be particularly good for the planet, and solar panels can't undo that fact. What fictions can do, regardless of how dystopian or utopian they may seem, is to identify how the interests of different people and different species conflict—as well as to highlight the areas of the Venn diagram where they do overlap.

In a post about how he chose to title his popular long-running blog *k-punk*, Mark Fisher explains what he meant by *punk*. For him, punk "doesn't designate a particular . . . genre, but a confluence outside legitimate(d) space." It "allowed and produced a whole other mode of contagious activity which destroyed the need for centralised control." For Fisher, the emphasis is less on the countercultural mode or even the aesthetic of punk and rather on the decentralization of production that it allowed, on the non-co-optable mode of "contagious activity." In this sense, solarpunk's potential is in its heterogeneity, simultaneity, and lateral movement: its dislocation.

One debate that continues to crop up in the comment sections of blogs is whether solarpunk is really a political movement or "just" an aesthetic genre. The same questions plagued steampunk and cyberpunk. But the reality is that these are inseparable. If solarpunk's goal is to close the plausibility gap by expanding the aesthetic imaginary, its aesthetics have to be taken as part and parcel of its politics, and examined as such. The lookbook can work either for or against its explicit aims—or make visible the latent problems with its politics. Sustainable technology that looks good does not, in itself, promise anything better, and in fact, as El Akkad shows, it may be more likely to promise better for the few than the many. Pleasant green architecture, like you'd find on Elysium, means nothing if it becomes an extension of colonialist fantasy, and if references like art nouveau become an aesthetic shorthand for a utopian future, they'll become another consumable trope for the wealthy to cling to. To prevent an earnest and potentially radical effort from devolving into a branded political movement, the stories themselves need to be dislocated along with the imagery. Dislocation, rather than utopianism, is what will keep solarpunk from running off as a libertarian seasteading vision, accelerationist implosion, or just a store in the mall—and maybe even reclaim, if there is such a thing, *punk*. As for the solarpunk label, it may have staying power or it may be a passing trend. It's but one among infinite possibilities.

A Planet of Feeling

My own private apocalypse

Justine and Claire

During 2020's first pandemic lockdown, I had the strong impulse to rewatch Lars von Trier's 2011 *Melancholia*. In the movie, a young woman is so miserable that her suffering becomes manifested on a cosmic scale, and in the end a planet called Melancholia crashes into and obliterates Earth. I had seen the movie when it first came out and hated it for its hyperbole. When I watched it again nine years later, in the midst of what felt like a world-destroying catastrophe, I loved it for the same reasons I'd originally hated it.

The first time I saw the movie, the scene that disturbed me the most takes place in a bathroom. Claire, played by Charlotte Gainsbourg, is trying to hoist her sister, Justine, played by Kirsten Dunst, into a bathtub full of water. Justine is naked, limp, and recalcitrant. Her limbs are sagging, her eyes running with tears, her hair matted. Her sister's slim forearms dig into the soft white flesh of her breasts. The bathroom is clean white marble. Justine moans and shakes her head. Her sister repents. Maybe later.

Justine is depressed. The kind of depressed where you can't

lift the fork to your mouth. The bathroom scene is from the second half of the movie, once Justine is already bottoming out, but during the first half we witness her botched wedding night and catastrophic slide into despair. The lavish celebration takes place at the sprawling estate belonging to her sister and her sister's husband, John (Kiefer Sutherland), replete with stately mansion, manicured gardens, golf course, and stables. The friends and family in attendance are moneyed and fantastically badly behaved.

Justine's mother hijacks a wedding toast to announce that she doesn't "believe in marriage"; Justine's new father-in-law, who is also her boss, takes his toast as an opportunity to pressure her into meeting a work deadline; her brother-in-law bitches about the cost of the evening. Justine sneaks away at all possible intervals—to curl up in bed with Claire's young son, to take a bath, or to gaze wonderingly at a particularly bright star in the sky.

By the end of the night Justine has torpedoed every relationship. She tells her boss to fuck off; then she fucks his nephew on the golf course. The newlyweds come to a near-wordless agreement that things between them are never going to work, and her husband takes off. On one hand her family is so despicable (and despicably cliché) as to make her catastrophic reaction seem almost warranted; on the other hand, her primary victim is clearly herself. At dawn she searches the sky for the bright star, but it's gone missing—or she's gone crazy.

In the second part of the movie, Claire fetches a wretched Justine from her apartment and brings her back to the estate, where she treats her sister like a fragile invalid. Claire is castigated by her husband for the coddling, but everyone, including their son, is wary of Aunt Justine, who appears only an inch away from suicide. We're given to assume that this is only the latest of many such episodes in the sisters' relationship. Claire talks in a baby voice, coaxes food into Justine's mouth. And then there is that bathtub scene, which I watched again and again the second time, transfixed by the magnitude of Kirsten Dunst's abjection, and by the sliver of cruelty in her sadness. She comes across as both masochistic and sadistic; her depression has casualties.

The disappearance of the bright star turns out to have been a fact, not an indication of Justine's instability. Its light, we learn, has been blocked by a newly arriving planet named Melancholia, which, as John informs his family, is soon going to swing by Earth in a once-in-a-millennium cosmic event. The news terrifies Claire, but excites Justine. Ha! She insists smugly that she's known something like this was coming all along: Melancholia is not going to miss Earth, it's going to slam right into it. "The Earth is evil," she hisses, sitting across the table from her sister. "We don't need to grieve for it . . . Nobody will miss it."

Alone on their private property with no connection to the outside world, the women have nothing but their observations and belief systems to rely on. John constructs a wonky measuring device from wire to try to prove to the delusional women that the planet—now a looming, unavoidably visible dark blot in the day sky—is not coming any closer, although they can all see that it is. He forbids his wife from reading the news or using the internet, mocking her for the childish behavior. Gaslighted by John, egged on by Justine, Claire descends into paranoia. One night, hands shaking, Claire loads a website that seems to confirm

Melancholia's disastrous trajectory, but John discovers her before she can finish reading. (To confuse matters further, the page she finds looks like a conspiracy-laden hoax site, as if there is no verifiable truth available outside their bubble, either.) John denies, Claire panics, and Justine placidly waits. The planet gets larger and larger. Hang on—is this a movie about the feeling that the world is ending, or is this a real apocalypse movie?

Until the very end, and perhaps even then, the answer is both. The planet symbolizes Justine's depression and it is also a real planet. Melancholia's causal relationship with her mental state is eerily ambiguous—is her clairvoyant prediction of the crash causing her misery, or is her misery somehow causing the crash? Maybe Justine really did predict the planet's presence and her own melancholy is a justified response to her foreknowledge of this nonhuman agent at work. Or maybe her own death drive has actually *invoked* the catastrophe, her melancholy scaling up to cosmic proportions—the macrocosm a perfect reflection of her microcosm. The only option that does not occur to Justine is that her melancholy and the end of the world are simply coincidental. But it is possible that Justine is sad and there is no justification for her sadness. Maybe the world is ending and there is no justification for that, either.

At the very least

When I first saw *Melancholia* in 2011 I was depressed and looking for reasons not to be. The world often felt like it was ending, but

I was trying to learn to convince myself that things weren't really so dramatic. Life may have felt like a catastrophe—but, according to my therapist, this was not objectively the case, and my painful emotions did not mean I could keep causing microcatastrophes à la Justine in my everyday life. The therapist allowed that feelings constitute some kind of fact, but I was not supposed to take them as evidence of the state of the world, and I was not supposed to take them out on other people. I wanted to learn to become a good, functional person. So I was pissed off by this movie about a real calamity the scale of which lived up to the experience of suicidal depression—in which reality was directly correlated with a person's emotional condition. The movie felt insulting to my progress.

By the time I rewatched the movie in 2020 I had no more illusions of progress nor pride in my own resilience. I was a decade older, I had been reading a lot of climate science, and the pandemic had suddenly brought my future-oriented daily life to a halt. I understood that the world was indeed undergoing a protracted disaster, and yet this did not mean I wanted to stop living in it. Nor did it mean I had a justification (Justinification) to destroy my relationships; on the contrary, it meant I needed other people very much. Plunged into a state of shared vulnerability, grief, and isolation, I had finally, paradoxically, started to think of myself as part of the planet, reflective of and reflected by its dysfunctions and joys and miseries. I did not think I had personally conjured a cosmic event the size of my feelings, yet it did not seem so far-fetched that everyone on Earth might respond to the crisis by communally manifesting our hope and outrage into a planetary transformation. Maybe there would be a revolution instead of an apocalypse.

The question of whether my depression was a reasonable response to real events was still beside the point, but, in 2020, any imperative to overcome feeling bad seemed absurd. Instead of insulting, I found watching planet Melancholia heading toward Earth cathartic. I identified with Justine's relief at witnessing a commonly visible external manifestation of her emotions, and her desire for the end of life as we know it. And at the same time, I identified with Claire's terror of the impending crash and the loss of everything we hold dear. I was no longer a Justine trying to be a Claire; I was both.

Across his movies, von Trier's women characters are tortured creatures. As critic Amy Taubin points out in a review of *Melancholia*, a von Trier woman is abused or broken to the point that she can only either achieve "beatitude through suffering" or take "bloody revenge on her torturers." Perhaps *Melancholia* is the only von Trier movie that I don't hate (anymore) because both paths are avoided with the diametrical but complicated figures of Claire and Justine. Their suffering is certainly exaggerated, aestheticized, and glorified throughout the movie, but it has no ultimate moral resolution. There can be no sainthood in a world that no longer exists, and there can be no retribution.

The sisters are opposing planetary forces. Justine is unruly, abject, selfish, futureless, aimed toward death; Claire is orderly, self-sacrificing, reserved, and focused on the reproduction of life. Both suffer, but the latter suffers in the "right" way, because she remains functional, has a family, and holds on to social norms until the very end. In a book called *Resilience & Melancholy*, philosopher Robin James writes about how femininity is constructed through mass-market empowerment narratives based mainly on suffering and its overcoming. "Women's gender performance is a two-step process: femininity is performed first as damage, second as resilience." To be femme is to suffer (and to suffer is to be femme), but some women can transcend the limitations of gender if they can demonstrate that they are properly resilient. "All women are feminized," James writes, "but 'good' women visibly overcome the negative effects of feminization."

The way James uses the term, "resilience isn't just 'recovery' or 'bouncing back' in general, but a sociohistorically specific technique and ideology" that makes individuals responsible for personally overcoming their suffering in a way that is "profitable" for capitalism, white supremacy, and patriarchy. A resilient woman survives breast cancer and then becomes a pink-ribbon salesperson; she survives rape and then learns karate; she survives abandonment and pays for a makeover to attract a new mate. Adversity becomes opportunity. All options "turn damage and deficit into surplus value," yet none of them create real resistance against the structures that produced the damage in the first place. "Resilience is the contemporary update of mourning; instead of conquering damage we recycle it."

In "Mourning and Melancholia," Freud famously distinguishes between mourning and melancholy as the two possible responses to grief. Mourning, to him, is the natural and healthy response to the loss of a beloved thing; it entails a period of intense pain and sadness, at the end of which the person accepts what has happened, reconciles the loss with reality, and moves on. Melancholy, on the other hand, is the pathological response to loss whereby the melancholic refuses to give up the lost object and instead "internalizes" it, unconsciously assimilating it into the psyche as a permanent "open wound." Per Freud, "In mourning it is the world which has become poor and empty; in melancholia it is the ego itself."

If, as James says, resilience is the contemporary mass-market update of mourning, Justine-style melancholia remains its antithesis, its pathological sister. Good girls like Claire invest in life by overcoming difficulties (like abusive husbands) and producing nice children. Bad girls like Justine descend into melancholic depression and invoke planetary death with the force of their ungovernable grief. In response, James suggests turning melancholy into an active proposition, an *investment* in a different way of being that cannot be recuperated to produce economic or social value. "If 'good girls' resiliently generate life," she asks, "might 'bad girls' melancholically invest in death?"

James is careful to state that by "invest in death" she does not mean accelerating destruction or deliberately causing more suffering, as Justine seems to want to do. Rather it could become a form of resistance: "'Into the death' isn't about killing ourselves," it's about upsetting the production of structures like neoliberal capitalism and white supremacist patriarchy, "making them unviable projects, bad investments, dead ends." Melancholia is only deemed pathological by Freud in the first place because it is an unproductive and unruly state. But, as Justine shows, to be debilitated or suicidal is only a bad thing if being able, productive, and life-affirming is to be right and good, because the future is assured to exist. With the planet mere minutes away from its end, Claire is no more "well-adjusted" than Justine. If anything, it's the other way around.

In Mark Fisher's words, "Capitalist realism insists on treating mental health as if it were a natural fact, like weather." But in the climate change era "weather is no longer a natural fact so much as a political-economic-effect," and neither is widespread capitalism-induced depression. If depression is understood as the sensation of futurelessness, it is not only a sensible reaction to but a *product of* a world lacking a future. Systemic oppression and exploitation create mental illnesses that are then treated as individual pathologies to be overcome. Or, as theorist Lauren Berlant says: "Depressed? . . . It might be political."

One example Freud gives for a person who might become melancholic is "a betrothed girl who has become jilted." What the jilted girl has lost is her handle on the future, on her capacity to reproduce life in its current form. In response, Freud says, she can suffer the external loss and get over it, returning to a proper view of the world as a difficult but livable place, or she can develop a hole in her heart that never resolves. Thinking of Justine, I wonder whether there are other options for the jilted woman. What if she were to use the never-healing hole in the heart as evidence that there was something catastrophically wrong with the world in the first place? What if her solo mourning became mourning in common? What if her mourning became, in the critic and activist Douglas Crimp's words, "a form of militancy"?

Right? Right?

I read Michelle Tea's 2016 novel *Black Wave* a few years before my second *Melancholia* viewing. Tea's book creates another eerie causality between "subjective" mental states and "objective" civilizational collapse—but the collapse is slow, stretched out to the length of the book. The version of California where the book takes place is verging on climate breakdown and social disintegration, but it so closely resembles our world that, as in *Melancholia*, you don't realize until halfway through the book that a cataclysm is actually going to happen.

The protagonist, a person named Michelle, has plenty of biographical similarities with the author. She's a queer poet living in the crusty squalor/splendor of a future-past version of 1990s counterculture San Francisco. She's part of a scene of writers and artists who are as self-destructive as they are self-aware. Her world is made up of explicitly non-resilient types: "Everyone had bad credit or no credit, which was the worst credit. What they excelled at was *feeling*—bonding, falling into crazy love, a love that had to be bigger than the awful reality of everything else. A love bigger than failure, bigger than life." This social scene couldn't be more opposite to the walled-off zone of white privilege in which *Melancholia*'s hetero family drama takes place.

"The messed-up queers Michelle ran with tempted fate daily, were creating a new way to live, new templates for everything—life, death, beauty, aging, art." Yet Michelle is not always entirely sure whether the templates are truly new, much less truly viable in the long term. Is this really improvisational rebellion, or is it another brand of lifestyle politics whose terms are supposedly set in opposition to but do not offer true resistance against the domineering social relations it purports to hate? Considering a lover with an accelerating heroin habit, Michelle asks, "Penny would never be pathetic, she would always be daring and deep, her addiction a middle finger held up to proper society. Right? Right?"

Michelle takes passing notice of chemical spills, sewage smells, invasive species, dying plant and animal life. She notices that "the walls of the sushi restaurant were marked with broad Xs over fish that had gone extinct" and gets a vegetarian roll; she has trouble renting a car because there's no gas at the station; she remarks that the Mission's "once-green neighborhoods" are dry and fallow and that the nearby ocean has become a "giant toilet"—but these occasional details serve as the background for what seems like the main story: Michelle's intense friendships, intense loves, intense sex, and intense drug use. Because of that last one especially, Michelle hits a dead end, decides she needs to leave San Francisco, start somewhere new, and clean herself up. Enter part two of the story. She hitches a ride to Los Angeles, where dreams are made.

Upon her arrival at the southern end of the coast, the background climate catastrophe suddenly trips into the foreground. In L.A. "that smell in the air all the time, the tinny stink of environmental collapse" is no longer ignorable. Michelle lands a crappy apartment and a job in a bookshop, imagining stability, but one day her brother calls and tells her to turn on the television. "The world is ending," he announces. "It's such a mess. Scientists can't reverse anything. The problems, the oceans, we've passed some point where it's going to accelerate and become like some sort of horrible sci-fi movie where we all start eating each other and bands of crazed rapists roam around murdering each other and no one will be able to go into the sun or they'll explode like vampires, it's going to get so hot."

The narrative starts to crack apart. Time slips backward and forward; Michelle slips into reverie or dream sequence; she begins to watch herself writing the book we're reading, switching between figure and ground. Apparently at moments of breakdown big and small, the story of the self and the world can no longer be told using the familiar tools at hand: the language of crisis, even, does not apply. Over the last hundred pages many catastrophes do happen—people jump from buildings, planes crash—but so do breakfast, work, daydreaming. Everyday life.

Michelle tries to finish writing the book she's working on, chats with her two moms on the phone, drinks a jug of wine every night, and argues with herself about whether she is an alcoholic. Her brother takes her to the drive-through of the last remaining In-N-Out Burger so they can get the world's last remaining burgers, at which point "Michelle realized the end of the world might actually be profoundly tedious." She does not become a panicked Claire nor a vengeful Justine. Watching the news, "Michelle feared she was not having an authentic experience of the beginning of the end of the world." She thinks she is "supposed to be feeling something a few layers down, something authentic and meaningful," but instead she eats the burgers and mourns the loss of her ex-partner.

For the most part, Michelle is more focused on her recent

breakup than the apocalypse. She is heartbroken over a lover whom she never gives a complete description of. She admits that she has promised the person not to write about them, which is perhaps why she is writing about the end of the world instead. The hole in her heart is a hole in the plot, one that she does not try to resolve through any Freudian detachment process. As reviewer Hugh Ryan put it, the book is a memoir "which Tea cored like an apple" of all factual details, scrambling and reassigning people and events until the narrator herself admits that "Michelle couldn't remember which version of the story she was in." She ponders whom to include in her big story, whom to lie about, and how to lie.

Likewise, Michelle debates how she should end her book. She doesn't want to succumb to the cliché of apocalypse, but there seems no way to stop telling the story unless she ends the world in which it takes place. In the characteristic caps she uses when speaking aloud: "I Couldn't Figure Out How To End The Book . . . The Story Just Keeps Going. You're Supposed To Wrap It All Up Nicely But It's Real Life. It's Hard. So I Think I'm Just Going To Have The World Explode." Michelle knows that how she chooses to end the story of the world will reveal, manifest, and document how she decides to handle the major loss, the hole in her heart.

Until the end, she handles her sadness by drinking to excess, but she finally realizes that this chemical dependence is antithetical to surviving, writing, and loving in the present moment. The problem is that, while she does not want to be locked in an apocalyptic loop of dependence, neither does she want her recovery from alcoholism to get wrapped up in a resilient good-girl cleanup narrative. Ultimately, the end she writes for herself is one of sobriety. She manages to stop drinking—not because it is right or good, but because she realizes she does not have to actually kill herself to invest in the death of the current world. She wants to be present for the transformation taking place. Whether or not the world explodes, Michelle will be sober, grieving, gleeful, and writing about it.

Wrap it all up nicely

At the end of *Melancholia*, the comet hits hard and fast. This is satisfying, because it is spectacular, sudden, and singular, marking a before and an after. Watching the movie again, I felt my own desire for cataclysmic marking points, definitive endings after which something new might begin. It's not just me; literature and psychoanalysis and historical narratives all pursue revelations, revolutions, and grand finales. But planetary explosion is rarely the way things change. They are more likely to change the way Tea portrays them, which is slowly, and often unnoticeably. Change is more about the threshold of noticeability, the moment when you *cannot help but notice* that the comet is *already destroying the planet* and has been for a long time. For example, for many people, the 2020 pandemic seemed a singular crisis that changed everything, yet it was the manifestation of long-standing destructive processes of slow violence—the species extinction that led to the virus's evolution, the wealth disparity that led to the unequal suffering in the wake of its spread. Climate change and racialized poverty are not new, and these, not the pandemic itself, are the real melancholic collisions that hit a thousand times a minute.

Both times I watched the movie, I found Justine's moral pronouncements that the Earth deserves to die to be tiresome. If retribution is warranted, it is for the crimes of the few in power and not the many. And for its part, nearly all of *Melancholia*'s characters belong to the realm of the few. The whole story takes place on John and Claire's private property, and aside from mention of a nearby village and the occasional presence of a butler (who disappears at the end, Claire surmises, to be with his family), there is no evidence of the world that exists beyond its gates. In fact, Claire's primary shock seems to be that *their* world is ending, that their privilege can't protect them from this particular threat from outside the garden fence. Justine is "bad" and Claire is "good" but neither of them has a collective, a context, or a community.

Black Wave ends in the collective transformation that the enduringly Freudian *Melancholia* does not. As the end of the book—and the world—approaches, people everywhere start having intense love-and-sex dreams about strangers, partners they haven't met yet. Then they start posting descriptions of their dreams online, and it turns out the lovers they've dreamed about really do exist. Through online postings they find each other in real life. But IRL, your dream lover might not have the same body they have in the dream. They might not be the same age, sex, gender, race, or species. Maybe they are an elderly man, or maybe they are a seahorse. But no matter what their real-life identities are, the love connection between the people in the dream is all real.

Desire manifests through communal lucid dreaming and people are too busy discovering one another to inspect the sky for clues about what's coming.

I imagined, while watching *Melancholia* the second time, how the people in the village outside the family's private property might have been dealing with the news of apocalypse. Maybe they were generating wild conspiracy theories and attacking one another—or maybe they had stopped worrying, stopped working, and were having a great time! Maybe they were inventing new rituals, taking psychedelics, or having ecstatic sex. Maybe, like Michelle, they had all gotten sober and opened themselves to falling in love. Maybe they had all become anarchists and were freely sharing resources. As science fiction author Kim Stanley Robinson wrote in an essay about the pandemic: "Amid the tragedy and death" it is possible that "at the very least, we are all freaking out together." Or, as author and critic Olivia Laing wrote in a review of *Black Wave*: "The end of human existence is an opportunity, just like anything else. Maybe it's even an occasion for enlightenment, the shaky, tender kind that robs the newly sober of their defences."

When the wave crashes on the shore of the end-times, Michelle is sober and sur-thriving, but this is not to say she's healthy or that "the planet is healing," as that pandemic meme proclaimed. The planet is not healing. There are, however, methods for living in the protracted present, riding the crest of the wave, that do not require invoking the crash or drinking yourself to oblivion until it does. The first time I watched *Melancholia*, I was struggling to draw outlines around myself, to distinguish my psychic state from the external reality of the world. The second time I saw it, after reading *Black Wave*, the dichotomy I had been trying to uphold between myself and the collective had begun to collapse. And all those hypothetical possibilities for what I imagined could be happening in the village outside the private compound were happening all around me, at the same time.

Funhole

I tell myself:

"Insanity is the insistence on meaning."

—FRANK BIDART

Lack

Story: a woman falls in love with a black hole. I've looked everywhere and found exactly two novels that fit the brief. I've read and reread them, convinced that their seemingly impossible plot structures would reveal something to me about how desire works, in love and on the page. What is a love story with nothing at its center, with nobody there?

First: Jonathan Lethem's 1997 novel, *As She Climbed Across the Table.* The narrator, Philip Engstrand, is an anthropology professor desperately in love with his girlfriend, scientist Alice Coombs. At the start of the story, Alice becomes irresistibly attracted to what she names Lack, an inexplicable rip in space-time that was accidentally invented in her particle physics lab. At first Philip tries to excuse Alice's long hours alone with Lack as mere scientific curiosity, but his jealousy grows, which only seems to drive Alice further away. Ultimately it turns out that his paranoia is not unfounded. Alice is infatuated. Obsessed. Alice slowly slips away from Philip. An odd love triangle forms between Philip, Alice, and Lack.

Lack exhibits curious behaviors, permanently swallowing some items and rejecting others according to a pattern that no one, including Alice, can identify. Lack eats light bulbs but spits out aluminum foil. Accepts a fertilized duck egg but refuses a scrambled one. Yes to key; no to paper clip. The seeming randomness pushes Alice to experimental extremes, and she becomes fixated on solving the puzzle. At one point she emerges from the lab disheveled, with her shirt on inside out. Later, she appears to have lost a chunk of her thumb. Philip can only assume that she's approaching the point of no return. Or maybe she's already tried, and already failed. Halfway through the book, Philip confronts Alice in the kitchen:

"So it's simple, then," I said. "No mystery. You don't love me because you love Lack."

"Yes."

"But he doesn't love you back."

"Yes."

"You tried then. You offered yourself."

No answer. But when I turned from the sink she stared at me hollowly, then nodded.

At moments like this Philip can't seem to help calling Lack "he," even though he knows gendering the hole is ridiculous (and if it had to be gendered, the default probably wouldn't be masculine). His anguish is compounded by the fact that he has no opponent, male or otherwise. Literally *nobody* stands in the way of his lover. *Nobody* threatens his failing relationship. There is no person to envy; neither can he explain Alice's infatuation under the rubric of any known fetish like object sexuality, the romantic attraction to inanimate objects. Lack is no more object than person. Philip says: "The problem was that my usual approach—anthropology—would give blessing to Alice's anthropomorphization of Lack. I wanted to prove Alice wrong, to show Lack to be a dead thing, a mistake, a cosmic pothole." Yet again, the notion that Alice has abandoned him for a cosmic pothole only makes him feel worse.

Lack is a joke with infinite punch lines. Lack can signify whatever you want it to mean: mouth, pussy, asshole, queerness, blackness, god, yonic void, "what women want," trauma, autonomy, rejection. These answers are all too obvious to be satisfying—and should you think you've found a uniquely satisfying interpretive twist or Freudian spin, the characters have inevitably beat you to the punch. They offer all sorts of readings themselves. "Lack is the Other," insists one woman to Philip at a party. A physicist colleague of Alice's implies that Lack represents "a third gender." In one scene, Philip tries to make Lack mean everything by meaning nothing, saying, "Lack is the inevitable: the virtually empty sign. The sign that means everything it is possible to mean, to any reader."

Philip is speaking both on and off the page here. Philip is chasing Alice, Alice is chasing Lack, and you, the reader, are chasing the meaning of it all. With each attempt to read deeper you glance off the fact of the matter, which is that Lack is exactly what it looks like, namely a black hole—and an assault on everyone's interpretive abilities. You desire to uncover the hidden message of Lack, and the story refuses to serve one to you, drawing you into the dynamic. Desire triangulates between the two characters due to the (empty) obstacle at the center of their relationship; desire triangulates on the level of story, too.

How does this story speak to the structure of plots about love and to love itself? Anne Carson goes so far as to propose the triangle—"lover, beloved, and that which comes between them"—as the basis for all erotic desire, as well as the basis for the structure of novels about love. This is not necessarily the rom-com love triangle where, say, a third person offers temptation; it is a triangle where the third component could be any obstacle: distance, class disparity, family feud, one's own self-defeating tendencies, or yes, even a black hole. Triangles perpetuate the slight distance required for desire to be kept alive and in motion. The desire that travels between the lovers, desire that gets ricocheted off what comes between them, is what makes the lovers keep loving, and/or makes the reader keep reading. In *Eros the Bittersweet*, Carson writes that "the ruse of the triangle is not a trivial mental maneuver. We see in it the radical constitution of desire. For, where eros is lack, its activation calls for three structural components." This system, requiring an obstacle or obstacles to create a triangle or triangles, is presumably at play even in situations that are openly polyamorous.

The obstacle creates a gap, a fundamental absence. Yet in the case of Lethem's novel, the *absence* as such *is* the obstacle itself. In this way Lethem's seemingly impossible plot suggests that absence, not simply the obstacle that creates that absence, is what is required for love's triangulation. If desire becomes a static two-part structure with no third thing (even when it's a no-thing) between the actors, it locks and stops. Carson emphasizes that even if the triangle is a "ruse" (for instance, when nothing really threatens the lovers' bond) it has real effects—it *works*. Love requires lack. But, as Lethem shows, Lack isn't love.

Philip and Alice have different but parallel ideas of how love works, both of them misunderstandings. Philip is desperate for Alice's affection from the start, displaying what a therapist would probably call an anxious attachment style—he believes Alice is his other half and that without her, *he* is nobody. For Philip, love is a two-part, fixed, rather claustrophobic system. Alice, in an equally fatal move, wants the (w)hole of love to swallow her up to the point that she disappears entirely. She believes that love implies, or requires, her dissolution, a loss of all autonomy or erasure of the demarcation between self and other. She can only see it two ways: if she's not *in* Lack, she's rejected by Lack. Perhaps the grand abyss, rather than a simpler and more traditional obstacle, has opened up between them because both lovers insist on their totalizing visions of love.

But a black hole's edge is called an event horizon. It is not a line; it is the moment at which an unknowable process has begun. Desire triangulates, moves. *As she climbed across the table.* It's an active verb.

The right to remain silent

"I believe cliché is a question," writes Carson, and "I say catastrophe is an answer." In the essay "Variations on the Right to Remain Silent," Carson describes the catastrophic 1431 trial of Joan of Arc. Prompted by the mystical voices in her head, Joan led French troops to swift military victories against English forces in 1428 and 1429, and was viewed by the French as a saint. But in 1430 she was captured by the English and eventually put on trial as a heretic. During Joan's trial for heresy, Carson reports, Joan was tasked with explaining herself to an unimaginative panel of male church authorities intent on discrediting her as insane and/or evil.

The jury's questions were inane. Are the voices authentic? If so, are they saintly or diabolical? Who sent them? Are they singular or plural? In the trial transcript, Joan is recorded as responding with either silent refusal or with oblique statements like, "The light comes in the name of the voice," "That does not touch your process," or "Ask me next Saturday." Carson describes Joan's linguistic behavior as a rebellion against cliché. Sometimes the only way to avoid cliché—to invent something new, to resist the imposed order of signification and meaning—is through silence, and if that fails, by creating a catastrophe of signification. When silent, Joan offered no signal; when giving responses that did not fit within the logic of the questions, she offered pure noise. In response to the court's disingenuous digging, Joan wrenched language toward the black hole. In her case, refusal to capitulate led directly to her annihilation. She got burned up.

"Most of us, given a choice between chaos and naming, between catastrophe and cliché, would choose naming," writes Carson. "Most of us see this as a zero sum game—as if there were no third place to be: something without a name is commonly thought not to exist." But of course nameless third places exist, just like black holes exist. According to Mark Fisher, this is why black holes are a perfect example of the *weird*. Black holes are scientifically provable and observable despite baffling common sense. From NASA's explainer for grades K–4, a black hole is defined as "a place in space where gravity pulls so much that even light can not get out. The gravity is so strong because matter has been squeezed into a tiny space." This is not a metaphor, it is a real thing happening in the universe, and yet I find it very hard to reconcile the explanation with my understanding of physics based on, say, my experience of daily life.

To explain what he means by weird, Fisher counterposes the black hole with the figure of the vampire. As opposed to a black hole, which is unfamiliar but exists, a vampire is a nonexistent but entirely familiar figure based on a set of commonly understood fictions. A vampire might be supernatural, he explains, but it isn't weird. Black holes are weird because they are natural. To quote Fisher: "If the entity or object *is* here, then the categories which we have up until now used to make sense of the world cannot be valid. The weird thing is not wrong, after all: it is our conceptions that must be inadequate."

In this sense, weirdness provides a sort of methodology for reading stories that lead toward the black hole. This methodology is to accept at face value things that literally exist but nonetheless resist linguistic description or cognitive explanation: things or events that dismantle the tools of signification and representation that fiction supposedly depends upon. This is fiction in tension with itself, which uses the human technologies of language, story, and description to forge an aesthetic encounter that transcends the explicability those tools are supposed to provide. It is fiction that triangulates desire by creating absences at the center of the plot that cannot be resolved.

Science fiction and fantasy represent poles on a theoretical spectrum of weirdness. They are typically relegated to separate genre shelves due to a set of historical conventions. (It is often forgotten that realism is itself a genre of fiction "as laden with artifice as any other literary convention," in the words of novelist Tom McCarthy, although realism is still commonly defined as the baseline of normalcy from which genres diverge.) Science fiction, particularly hard science fiction, deviates from reality, but usually without disrupting the general physical laws of the universe. On the science fiction side of the spectrum, anything seemingly inexplicable or irrational is eventually explained through technological or scientific means. On the fantasy side, there is no burden of explaining how, say, time travel works, or how a void emerges— magic will suffice. Fantasy and science fiction are both to some extent a kind of literal storytelling: the deviations from current reality within them are to be taken as fact. The unreal things within them are what they say they are, and they let you stop searching for metaphorical meaning in a way that realism doesn't.

Science fiction has been historically aligned with rationality, futurity, plausibility, and progress narratives. If Lethem's book were on the science fiction shelf, Lack would have a clear reason for existing—alien landing, petrochemical leak—and its behavior would be *plausible*, however unlikely. If Lethem's book were on the fantasy shelf, maybe Lack would turn out to be the product of witchcraft. In science fiction the novelty is explained away, and in fantasy explanation is irrelevant. But, as author Torrey Peters points out, at both poles the "moment of hesitation resolves itself either way"—the hesitation that is weirdness.

The cipher

Second: *The Cipher*. Kathe Koja's original name for her 1991 novel was *The Funhole*, but the publisher deemed it unsellable. Luckily, the Funhole does appear on page one. In the first scene, narrator Nicholas and his unrequited lover, Nakota, discover a vortex in the floor of the storage room of Nicholas's run-down apartment building. This is what they find: "Black. Not darkness, not the absence of light but living black. Maybe a foot in diameter, maybe a little more. Pure black and the sense of pulsation, especially when you looked at it too closely, the sense of something not living but alive, not even *something* but some—process. Rabbithole, some strange motherfucking wonderland, you bet." They dub it the Funhole.

Nakota is titillated by the discovery. Like Alice in Lethem's book, she begins experimenting in earnest. First she dangles a jar of bugs down into the nothingness (they come back mutated with extra wings and heads, in contorted shapes that she interprets as "runes"); then a mouse (it combusts); then a severed human hand—donated by a friend who has an internship at the morgue (the hand comes back alive, crawls, and attacks); finally, a camcorder. The camcorder records a terrifying yet mesmerizing scene that appears differently to everyone each time they play it on the VCR.

The Funhole is mean. It is nefarious. It is not playful or slapstick like Lack. It does not exhibit a binary in/out function like Lack, either—anything that comes near it, much less enters it, is irrevocably changed. The Funhole itself is ever-changing. Sometimes it smells sweet and delicious and sometimes rotten; sometimes it is unbelievably hot and other times unbearably cold. When he is near the Funhole, Nicholas hallucinates or goes into sensory overdrive. In the storage room he often blacks out or flies into fits of rage; metal melts at his touch; objects come alive; he emerges countless hours later, bloody and terrified.

While Nicholas "could live the rest of my life without seeing what happens to a mouse when it kisses death, especially weird death," for Nakota, all this is irresistibly *fun*. She spends her time trying to convince him to head into the storage room with her, even bribing him by hate-fucking him near the hole. Finally, she angrily explains what he has not yet figured out: unless Nicholas is present, the hole is not activated. Without him it's just a hole in the ground. Only Nicholas can turn the Funhole on.

Another love triangle emerges. Nakota is jealous that the hole has chosen Nicholas rather than her, while Nicholas reviles the hole and pines for Nakota. Nakota insists that if she were the chosen one, she would "know what to do" (assumedly, to jump in) and pressures him to get closer to the edge of the void. Perhaps Nakota's desire to make meaning out of the Funhole—her belief that there is a right way to act toward it—is what makes the Funhole reject her, and Nicholas's tendency toward submissive surrender is what makes him its target. Like Alice, Nakota equates love with 100 percent penetration; if the Funhole really loves her, she believes, it will open wide and take her in. But it only opens when Nicholas is around, and Nicholas keeps Nakota back from the edge.

Descriptions of Nakota are vile. She has "tiny teeth, fox teeth, not white and not ivory yellow either like most people's, almost bluish as if with some undreamed-of decay beneath them"; she chews her nails "the way a child sucks a blanket," with "dull-eyed intensity"; her lips are cracked and bleeding, eyes bruised, body emaciated, clothes shredded and filthy. Nicholas desires her incessantly, but "in the dreamy way you want to dive the Marianas trench." There is nothing pleasant about their relationship; she is sadistic and malevolent. "If it doesn't hurt," says Nakota petulantly, in regard to sex and to everything else, "you're not doing it right." In this story, attraction is twinned with revulsion, intimacy with violence, and anything generative is equally or more destructive. Communion with the otherworldly is not a nice experience. It is traumatizing from start to finish.

Driven to impress Nakota and/or driven by the suicidal compulsion she inspires, Nicholas dangles his right hand down into that "big dark butthole" in the floor and acquires a stigmata-like wound that weeps and oozes mysterious silver fluid. For the remainder of the book, an infection spreads from his wound throughout his body in an Area X–like contamination, offering him a direct conduit to the Funhole's—what? Desires? At times he holds his hand to his ear and hears the Funhole whisper words like "love you" and "want you," which locks him into mortal terror. He ruefully describes himself as a mistaken saint, martyred against his will by "basilica Funhole."

As in Lethem's book, the orifice punch lines and Freudian interpretations are plenty obvious in *The Cipher*. Again, the story resists any explanation you slap on the wound, and the more you dig, the less you find. The characters anticipate your guesses, and the Funhole's activity is too weird for any one-size-fits-all explanation. In this sense *The Cipher* is a misleading title, as it suggests there is a riddle to be deciphered. In fact there is no enigma to the Funhole, it's just an ongoing catastrophe. "The Funhole was not a thing or a place but an actual process, *something that was happening*," Nicholas says, "like an operation. Or a death."

Perhaps the dramatic void these stories hinge on is an indictment of binary heterosexuality as much as it is of love in general. As Marguerite Duras puts it: "Heterosexuality is dangerous. It tempts you to aim at a perfect duality of desire. It kills the other story options."

The bottom of it all

Love, he called it. But I had been used to words for a long time. I knew that that word was like the others: just a shape to fill a lack.

—WILLIAM FAULKNER

Michele Wallace proposes using the term *black hole* against itself in a canonical 1989 text called "Variations on Negation and the Heresy of Black Feminist Creativity." She suggests there is political potential in repurposing the concept from a dead end to a portal that transforms what goes through rather than kills it or interrupts its existence. Unless blackness and holeness are taken as de facto negative, she argues, a black hole need not be seen as the inverse of anything, or a lack of anything: it is an event or process. She explains that the "idea of black hole as a process—as a progression that appears differently, or not at all, from various perspectives—seems a useful way of illustrating how I conceive of incommensurability, or variations on negation." Here Wallace is talking specifically about Black femme creativity—an identity often construed as a sort of double negation, opposites of the default states of whiteness and maleness, and negatively inflected ones at that. In response to these double, compounding negations, Wallace offers *variations* on negation, like Carson's variations on the right to remain silent. Variations imply movement and possibility. Variations imply triangulation. Variations imply multiple answers, none of them cancelling the others out.

You can't get to the bottom of a black hole, and you can't get to the bottom of either of these novels. Even if the mysteries of the void—Where did it come from? Why does it act like that? Does it have intentions or desires? Is it good or evil?—get explained, the fact that Lack and the Funhole exist is already a catastrophe for realism. Both authors treat the void as a literal phenomenon, not a science fiction novelty nor a magical fantasy. A hole could mean a million things but basically just *is*.

Susan Sontag instructs readers and critics to stop trying to get to the bottom of literature, period. In her 1966 text *Against Interpretation* she complains that "interpretation excavates, and as it excavates, destroys; it digs 'behind' the text, to find a sub-text which is [supposedly] the true one." In the modern method of interpretation, she argues, textual material is treated as matter that "must be probed and pushed aside to find the true meaning." But all that interpretive digging bypasses the material matrix it purports to deal with: the dirt. It fucks up the soil. It "sustains the fancy that there really is such a thing as the content of a work of art," as if you could separate the content from the form. Sontag points out that, just as art and literary critics did this to creative work, Freud did this to the workings of the human mind, and Marx did this to the structure of history. In the process, reading—whether reading a book, your lover's intentions, or the past—has become a paranoid project. There *must* be a nugget down there only you can find and interpret.

Interpretive digging is like jealousy. It's like digging through your girlfriend's emails trying to find evidence of love, or Lack thereof. It's like trying to lock in a truth that will keep a two-part system stable, either completely together or completely apart. Yet, as Carson points out, the system of desire requires a third place that keeps all feelings in perpetual motion. "Eros is a verb," she declares. "The reach of desire is defined in action: beautiful (in its object), foiled (in its attempt), endless (in time)." You could try to cheat the question of what Lack and Funhole mean by saying that the meaning is the impossibility of meaning, but if you take that impossibility seriously, then you've broken down your system for getting there, too. You also lose any reason to keep on desiring and chasing and, while you might avoid catastrophe, you might also lose the chance to encounter a weird miracle.

In science and the popular imagination, black holes are often described as passages to other universes or dimensions—conduits, connective tissue between worlds rather than cul-de-sacs. Framed this way, entering one may not mean annihilation, but transit. The journey might transform the participant to the point where a trip report would be moot, but that does not mean there is no passage to be made. Perhaps a passage one cannot report back from is the most important kind of passage.

In a text about the metaphors attached to certain illnesses, Sontag emphasizes that metaphors are fundamental to thought. "Saying a thing is or is like something-it-is-not is a mental operation as old as philosophy and poetry, and the spawning ground of most kinds of understanding, including scientific understanding, and expressiveness." Metaphors are not a problem themselves, she writes, but certain kinds of reductive metaphors are enormous problems. While "one cannot think without metaphors . . . that does not mean there aren't some metaphors we might well abstain from or try to retire." The politically loaded and sorry metaphor of the black hole as, for instance, the negative, the femme, the Black, or the absent is worth abstaining from and trying to retire. After all, black holes are real, quantum phenomena, not cosmic ink blots the universe uses to gauge Earth-dwellers' deepest anxieties. One of the most challenging tasks for the mind is to take in the weirdness of the world on the level of perception and description, rather than turning it into a Rorschach for personal use.

Sontag explains that her goal in much of her writing is "not to confer meaning, which is the traditional purpose of literary endeavor, but to deprive something of meaning." For instance, she works to deprive illnesses like cancer of the metaphorical meanings overlaid upon them (the body as a battleground; the cancer as a punishment) that obscure the reality of the disease and disallow it to be treated. This deprivation must be the fundamentally weird accomplishment of Lethem's and Koja's books as well: they deprive the reader of something expected, resist reduction to a single interpretation, disallow the central character from becoming a stand-in for something else, and in this way they drive the desire that pilots the plot. "There is a triangular circuit running from the writer to the reader to the characters in the story," writes Carson, and "when the circuit points connect, the difficult pleasure of paradox can feel like an electrification."

In an essay called "Get Real, or What Jellyfish Have to Tell Us About Literature," Tom McCarthy describes the act of writing as the feverish pursuit of a black hole—the black hole being reality. Of course, he points out, should writing ever successfully apprehend or meet the void, the writing (and writer?) would collapse and die. I have felt this way while writing about *As She Climbed Across the Table* and *The Cipher*: the closer I got to the texts and the characters, the more useless my tools became. On the surface these books seem like they lend themselves beautifully to literary analysis of the type Sontag dislikes, and yet they completely undermine the pursuit.

I wrote and rewrote this essay, trying to figure out how the authors get away with a love story destined to go exactly *nowhere*.

What does the void signify, how does it signify? How do you keep the reader reading, the lover desiring? I followed crumbs of meaning through science fiction anthologies and philosophy texts and scientific papers and ethnographies and treatises on the physical laws of the universe. I couldn't resist trying to solve the cipher or parse the metaphor—and then to search for my own inclinations and biases within my interpretations. But my attempts led me across an event horizon: I plummeted, am still plummeting, into a particular kind of void. This essay will never arrive. Or—it will arrive nowhere. In response to my questions about love and lack, about categories and irreducibility, this essay offers silence. Then catastrophe. Maybe: miracle. I put down my trowel and shovel. I stop scraping. I write anyway. Joke's on me.

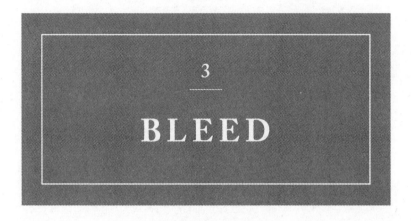

3

BLEED

Extinction Burst

Looking at Lucia

Fleshly sight

I approached Saint Lucia from the side because I wasn't sure how to look at her. Something about the composition of the painting means she always appears at a slant, maybe because she's meant to be viewed from below, so the perspective is a little skewed on purpose. There's also the distracting sheen of the gold leaf surrounding her figure, which scatters light and causes glare no matter what angle you're looking from. But mainly it's that you don't know which of her eyes to look at. The pair in her face, or the pair in her hand?

The eyes Lucia holds sprout from twin branches. She grasps the delicate stem between her fingers, as if she were clutching the optic nerve at the back of your skull. The eyes in her face are gazing shyly down at her hand, but the eyes in her hand are looking straight at you. You look up to her face, but she demurs, so you follow her gaze, and it lands on the eyes in her hand. The first eyes are blue. The second are brown.

The painting was finished in 1474 by Francesco del Cossa, a somewhat obscure northern Italian Renaissance painter, as part of a multipainting altarpiece for a chapel in Bologna. The altarpiece was dismembered in the 1720s and its sixteen surviving parts scattered across museums around the world. I happened to be in Bologna while there was an exhibition of all the paintings brought back together for the first time, a rare chance to visit Lucia among her original cohort. In addition to the original paintings, the exhibition included a perfect facsimile reconstruction of the whole altarpiece, so you could see the way all the paintings were meant to be installed. The original paintings themselves were arranged at eye height on the walls of a small room. I walked around and around the room, always ending at Lucia.

Most of the panels depict individual saints. Everyone is looking in different directions. Saint Florian (patron saint of chimney sweeps, soap makers, firefighters), who was burned at the stake, clutches a sword and leans over a ledge, coolly overseeing the panels that would have been hung below his. Saint Peter (bakers, fishermen, foot problems), who was crucified, looks down at a thick manuscript bookmarked with a favorite passage. Saint Apollonia (dentistry), whose teeth were yanked out, smiles at the tooth she holds in a pair of giant pincers. Only Saint John the Baptist, the beheaded megasaint, stares directly out of his frame at the viewer.

Lucia's own eyes were said to have been plucked or maybe stabbed out. She is the patron saint of eyesight because of this grisly martyrdom. Medieval viewers would have been encouraged to identify with her trauma and venerate her suffering. And in the case of eye maladies, to request her magical intervention. Your pain and hers, back and forth. Ouch, ouch.

I love Lucia. I love the weirdness of her extra eyes, I love the feeling of being watched by a painting, and I love how difficult it is to take in the whole image at once. I first saw her image in an art history class and I've searched for it online a hundred times since, zooming in on one set of eyes and then the other. I ended up at the exhibition while on vacation; I saw her eerie face on the back of a city bus and realized it was an advertisement for the real thing, on display only a few blocks away. I immediately turned around and walked to the museum, but on the way there I got unexpectedly jittery. I wasn't prepared. My heart was pounding and I felt nervous, like an adolescent on my way to meet a crush.

Up close, the imperfections in the painting, exacerbated by age, stand out. The tempera paint that shapes her head and body is edged in by the gold leaf, but sometimes del Cossa added a ribbon or mark over the leaf, so as your eyes move across the surface you find yourself retracing his steps. The waist of Lucia's strange green billowing garment is cinched with a red ribbon, her fluttering hairpiece rests gently on golden curls, and her face is just a little bit plump, some extra flesh below the line of the chin. I let my eyes slide lasciviously over her surface for a long time before I realized the paradox of painting a saint whose image is supposed to cure blindness. Does her magic work if you can't see her at all?

One reason Lucia is accessorized with handheld eyes is that del Cossa wanted to paint his subject in immortal splendor rather than as a gory eyeless victim. But more importantly it is because saints and holy figures were supposed to have a kind of double sight: the eye kind and the spirit kind. In the late fourteenth century, Julian of Norwich, a revered anchoress who experienced mystical visions, explained that there was a difference between her "bodily sight" and her "spiritual sight." Hildegard von Bingen, a famous nun born around the start of the twelfth century, likewise described her visions from God as "seen not with my fleshly eyes but only in my spirit."

For several centuries, women's bodily sight was thought to be particularly powerful—and dangerous, if inflected with mal-intent. A popular theory held that vision did not enter the eyes from the world but rather emanated from the eyes, meaning that looking could alter or affect its target. In a widely read 1482 trea-tise, the Florentine philosopher Marsilio Ficino explained that "vapors" rise from the blood to the brain and then spray from the eyes "as if from two glass windows." In 1531, Heinrich Cornelius Agrippa described the visual rays coming out of the eyeballs as "threads." According to such theories, looking is not passive; it has the potential for intervention in the world.

In keeping with these fears, women of the late medieval and early Renaissance periods are rarely painted looking at the viewer head-on, their averted eyes removing any potential threat inher-ent in the gaze. Lucia demonstrates her benevolence by glanc-ing away with her fleshly eyes, assuring you that she is chaste. Her fleshly eyes are in some sense irrelevant; the ones that matter are the spirit eyes, with which she can see your insides, delicately pluck at your soul, and in doing so miraculously heal your body. You look at Lucia's face and she shows you where you should re-ally be looking: those powerful spirit eyes, with their unblinking, godly detachment. That detachment makes you shiver and look back to her face for answers.

Keeping score

While I was traveling in Italy I was reading Bessel van der Kolk's book *The Body Keeps the Score*. A friend had mailed it to me before the trip—by then, many people had recommended it to me—and for some reason I thought it would make good vacation reading. Van der Kolk is a psychiatrist, and his book is an exhaustive summary of his decades of research into trauma and its effects on the brain and body. He details all he has learned about how traumatic experiences are lived, stored in memory, and often perpetually relived. His aim is to reveal a hidden epidemic of post-traumatic stress, which tends to be falsely treated through pharmacological or medical means, when in fact the root of various mental disorders, pain syndromes, and immunological issues is the ongoing assault on the body's nervous system by the physical memory of trauma.

According to van der Kolk (whose work has not been received without controversy), traumatic recollection operates according to a different memory system than standard "narrative memory" by which you construct a sequential history of your life. Traumatic memories do not have a beginning, middle, and end and they are not solidly situated in the past. When a traumatic memory is activated, the experience is not recalled so much as reexperienced, with all the physical and psychic responses that occurred in the moment playing out again throughout the body; on MRI scans, the brain of a person in the midst of remembering, say, a painful medical operation, might look nearly indistinguishable from a person experiencing the real thing. In van der Kolk's trauma clinic, he often meets patients who can't describe in words what's happened to them, but who have fits of rage or sadness, physical tics, and unexplainable diseases.

Even when repressed, traumatic memories keep the body on high alert, prepared to respond to threat—a state that can destroy the nervous system. Van der Kolk concludes that post-traumatic disorders are essentially somatic or at least psychosomatic. Psychosomatic does not mean that the pain originates in the mind (as in psychogenic ailments), but that it involves both the mind and the body. As such, PTSD cannot usually be resolved by psychiatric drugs and in many cases not even by talk therapy. In trauma the body registers something the mind cannot undo by itself. Even if the story of what happened can be told, recollections are hardly reducible to language: "the language center of the brain is about as far removed from the center for experiencing one's self as is geographically possible."

Van der Kolk advocates for treatments that begin with physical practices, with the aim of helping the body understand what it is like to feel safe. This might be as simple as yoga, exercise, playing with animals, or taking a theater class. It might also involve some work on the brain. I read most of the book before I understood that van der Kolk was using the words *brain* and *mind* to mean different things. Mind is the conscious you that can remember, consider, decide, and explain. Brain is the meat. The heavy thing in your skull that does things without your knowledge.

One successful and somewhat mysterious therapy that acts on the mind *and* on the brain is called EMDR, or eye movement desensitization and reprocessing. The therapist who invented it noticed one day that recalling bad memories was not so painful if she moved her eyes rapidly back and forth while thinking about them. Over decades of testing, she and other researchers have shown that this type of eye movement can markedly reduce the emotions and body states that painful memories produce, eventually softening the effects of PTSD.

EMDR works through bilateral stimulation of the brain. The right brain, typically described as the emotional side, deals with feelings, sensations, and physical experiences; the left brain is the analytic, linguistic, decision-making side. During both trauma and its recollection, the executive functions of the left brain often shut down, leaving people without the ability to explain themselves, control their reactions, or act reasonably. The back-and-forth of eye movement during traumatic recollection seems to awaken the left brain, prompting the hemispheres to operate in tandem, bringing the inarticulable into contact with the articulable. In van der Kolk's terms, EMDR has the "apparent capacity to activate a series of unsought and seemingly unrelated sensations, emotions, images, and thoughts in conjunction with the original memory . . . reassembling old information into new packages." EMDR does not necessarily even require talking to be effective. A therapist can ask you to remember and do the eye thing and that's enough.

The effectiveness of simple eye movement may be related to the situation of the optic nerve at the back of the head, at the intersection of brain hemispheres. The activity also resembles the mechanism of rapid eye movements that occur during a REM cycle, the phase of sleep when memories are encoded and stored through the process of dreaming. The point of EMDR is not to erase or downplay the memory, but rather to integrate it into the regular memory system, whereby it becomes one story among many and the body can start to let go of the patterns of arousal and self-protection it has learned. For this reason EMDR is markedly different than popular forms of exposure therapy by which someone is forced to repeatedly confront or re-create traumatic memories in the hopes of desensitizing them. The desensitization of pain (which can also result in desensitization of all experience, including joy) is not the same as the integration of pain. Van der Kolk writes: "If the problem with PTSD is *dissociation*, the goal of treatment would be *association*: integrating the cut-off elements of the trauma into the ongoing narrative of life, so that the brain can recognize that 'that was then, and this is now.'"

Crossing over

I hated reading *The Body Keeps the Score*. The accounts of patients' experiences made me upset, angry, and exhausted. At first I took my reaction as a logical response to the disturbing subject matter, which included sexual violence, assault, war. But when I got to the descriptions of mysterious post-traumatic syndromes like immune disorders, dissociation, and passing out, I realized I was feeling the shock of recognition. I felt seen by the text and I did not want to be seen. In response to the descriptions of trauma and its effects, my body shut off. I started falling asleep whenever I opened the book.

I have had the sleeping problem for as long as I can remember. When I feel overwhelmed in a certain way, I pass out. It's not a normal sleep; it's unavoidable—and somehow inhuman. It's thick and rich and paralyzing. I don't think of it as sleep anymore; I think of it as *crossing over*. I've crossed over in restaurant booths, on the subway, in the back seats of cars, under a table in a library, in the middle of an argument, on the phone. Sometimes I wake up (come back) after ten minutes feeling fine. Sometimes I'm gone for hours inside vivid dreams and reemerge confused, with heavy limbs and difficulty speaking, stuck in another dimension. Occasionally I come back with a fever, swollen joints, enormous glands, a sinus infection. Doctors have used the names chronic fatigue, fibromyalgia, Epstein-Barr, chronic allergic rhinitis, hypothyroidism, vitamin deficiency, depression, and an unspecified autoimmune disorder to explain me to me. Cue the antibiotics. Most prescriptions have been inadequate or temporary. Some have made things worse.

Van der Kolk has another explanation. To be traumatized, he says, is to have a maladaptive relationship to safety, a disorganized understanding of boundaries and a confusion about when a threat is real. Things that are not mortally threatening at all in current reality—an argument, a work deadline—might feel, to the traumatized person, as though annihilation is imminent. The immune system thinks it is undergoing some kind of assault, and responds with all its defenses. Typical animal reactions kick in: the well-known fight-or-flight, and the lesser-known cousins fawn and freeze. Fawn means flattering or kissing up in an attempt to placate the threat; freeze means becoming numb, catatonic, or unresponsive. Reading the book, I recognized that freeze is my thing.

I'm not the first person to read *The Body Keeps the Score* and encounter the unpleasant discovery that I have many obvious hallmarks of post-traumatic stress. Other people I've talked to have had similar physical reactions to reading their pain on the page. Many, like me, were not aware of having had any capital-T Trauma that was "bad enough" to warrant physical symptoms. Painful things have happened to me, as they have to everybody, but I had never imagined that any singular experience could have such widespread effects—and when prompted, I could not identify a smoking gun. I had no idea what my original trauma was.

When I finally finished the book, the sleeping sickness got much worse. I spent a lot of time trying to come up with a cause for my effects. I imagined buried memories, then conjured horror stories. But after putting down the book and returning to my regular reading (medieval mysticism, science fiction) I decided that determining a single causative event was not the point. For reasons particular to my organism and circumstance, some experience or experiences of pain lodged themselves in my body. For me to accept and deal with it, my pain did not need to be justified; neither did a trauma need to be pinpointed, named, or explained. I decided to stop excavating my history and instead to take what my body was saying as basic fact.

Blood devotion

Recalling, imagining, and vividly detailing saintly sufferings was a major pastime of medieval Christians. An incredible lust for traumatic recollection undergirds Catholicism's visual and literary repertoire, and Christ's body was the prime target for identification. A cultish practice of "blood devotion" flourished in various parts of Europe—what art historian Nancy Thebaut calls an "obsessive and anxiety-ridden interest in Christ's wounds, bleeding, and suffering," which "marked a deep desire to understand the physicality of Christ's death as well as to achieve a new, body-centered form of piety." The famous twelfth-century abbot (and notable proponent of a wave of violent Christian crusades) Bernard of Clairvaux preached the benefits of staring at images of Christ's blood, asking, "What can be so effective a cure for the wound of conscience and so purifying to keenness of mind as steady meditation on the wounds of Christ?"

This fixation on Christ's wounds is apparent in a wide array of manuscripts that were meant to be used in daily devotional practice. The creepiest example might be an English manuscript made in about 1480–90, now cataloged as "MS Egerton 1821," whose first eleven pages are covered in images of bleeding wounds. Its first three pages are entirely blackened and then splattered with red paint, as if the book had been held under a wounded body. The next eight pages are washed with a pinkish color, upon which are painted repetitive illustrations of tiny dripping slits. Most of the book is well preserved, but one of the blackened pages looks like it's been mauled, its paint nearly scrubbed away by an anxious-looking claw mark in the middle of the page.

A few years ago I signed up for a graduate class about medieval manuscripts at the Morgan Library in Manhattan, in the hopes of getting to see some old books in the flesh. The class was about the relationship between book and body, and the course description promised firsthand access to manuscripts up to a thousand years old. In class, I learned that books like Egerton have been forensically analyzed to discover why some parts of them are weirdly messed with, why some parts are dirty and others are clean. Old books hold evidence particularly well because they are made of vellum, stretched animal skin, whose pores lodge fluids, grease, and grime. Researchers have concluded that many of the original owners of devotional books (Egerton's was probably an aristocratic lady) kissed, licked, rubbed, scratched at, and cried upon their pages. They treated the objects as portals or communion devices that could help them get as close as possible to Christ's body and help them feel his suffering, leaving evidence of their skin, saliva, and tears.

Through touch, image-heavy books like Egerton could be "read" even if the user wasn't literate. The reader could count the blood droplets like rosary beads, back and forth down the page, in a numerical meditation on suffering. Methodical counting not only put the user in a contemplative state, but helped quantify the suffering at hand. For centuries, medieval theologians tried to determine exactly how many droplets Christ had shed from how many wounds before, during, and after the crucifixion. "One of these many formulae estimated that Christ had 5,475 wounds and 547,500 drops of blood," writes Thebaut. Christ's body kept the score, and it was some factor of 5,475. Reading, fondling, and kissing the book-body, you got to keep score with him.

From an art historical perspective, the paintings of blood

droplets are somewhere between figuration and abstraction, representation and reality; you don't really *look* at them as you might look at a painting. They're a tool, a portal—or even a musical score, prompting the user to keep time with God by internalizing the steady thrum of suffering that formed the baseline of medieval Catholic life. This is what I imagine, anyway. When I look at pictures of Egerton (I have still never seen it in person) I don't feel any particular identification with the character of Christ. What I do identify with is that claw mark on the page, left by a woman fervently trying to commune with someone else's experience through a book.

The goal of all this blood devotion was to evoke and continually keep the traumatic moment alive, through its secondhand arousal. Sometimes invoking the other's pain would send the reader into extreme physical states, which would from today's psychiatric vantage point look like classic PTSD symptoms. In her 2016 book, *Acute Melancholia and Other Essays*, Amy Hollywood explains that:

> the meditative practices of the later Middle Ages, which aimed to make vivid and inescapable the pain and suffering of Christ's life and death, are curiously similar to contemporary discussions of traumatic memory. Researchers on trauma and Post-Traumatic Stress Disorder isolate particular forms of intensely sensory and bodily memories in which the survivor involuntarily and repetitiously relives traumatic events. Such memories are intrusive, intensely vivid, repetitive, and lack a narrative frame. They are not only visual, moreover, but also

often involve other senses, presumably those heightened at the moment of trauma.

Unlike van der Kolk's proposed remedies, medieval devotional practices focused on suffering do not aim to resolve personal trauma. They aim to invoke Christ's suffering, and dwell on it. In Hollywood's words, "They attempt to inculcate traumatic or bodily memory—or something very like it—by rendering involuntary, vivid, and inescapable the central catastrophic event of Christian history so that the individual believer might relive and share in that trauma." You're supposed to get so close to Christ's experience (through media like books and paintings) that you never let his misery be resolved. For his somatic experience is the foundation of his transcendence, is the proof of God's love. It's a whole body system built on someone *else's* trauma. This allowed people to create a connection between their regular human suffering and saintly suffering—Christ and the many saints, like Lucia, who were martyred in his name. Your pain is not special, which means it is not yours alone to bear.

On one of the last days of my manuscript class, the librarian held out a small sixteenth-century book he had taken from the vault and let each student gently stroke the page, feeling the animal fibers that compose the worn, somehow still warm, grimy surface. This was the day we had all been waiting for. (One of my classmates was wearing an amulet for Saint Margaret around her neck and another was wearing a jacket with a Chaucer quote embroidered on the back: these were serious fans.) If seeing Lucia in person provoked a feeling of adolescent flirtation, what I felt when touching the manuscript was full-blown, well-informed adult desire. Desire for communion. Desire for crossing over.

Lingua ignota

Hildegard von Bingen was sick all the time. Hildegard, who lived in what is now the German Rhineland in the early 1100s, saw the first of many divine visions with her spiritual sight when she was three years old, but she did not have the courage to write about them until she was stricken with a particularly horrible illness decades later. This illness prompted her to write a letter to the powerful abbot Bernard of Clairvaux, whose permission she asked to record her visions in a book. Struck by the passion of her letter, Bernard encouraged this unknown provincial nun to record and share what she had seen.

Although she felt compelled to describe her "revelations," Hildegard confessed to Bernard that she felt incapable of properly explaining them in language. She was concerned about her lack of education and grasp of Latin, but more to the point, she was also doubtful that she could communicate divine truth in any human language at all. "I am not taught in this vision to write as the philosophers do. Moreover, the words I see and hear in the vision are not like the words of human speech, but are like a blazing flame or a cloud that moves through clear air." How was she supposed to convey that blazing flame in fleshly language? Although she did end up exhaustively describing her divine visions (by relaying them to her trusted scribe, who wrote them down in Latin), she also invented a new alphabet for her own private use. She called it the *lingua ignota*, or unknown language.

Hildegard's visionary imagery is vivid and psychedelic—she sees what seems to be God, for instance, enthroned on "a great mountain the colour of iron" and "before this figure, at the roots of the mountain, there stood an image covered with eyes." Many of the visions blind and dazzle her, shock her, pain her, transform her—make her sick. Their arrival is often a traumatic event. No wonder she struggles to explain what she sees. I think van der Kolk would explain this by saying that "trauma by nature drives us to the edge of comprehension, cutting us off from language based on common experience or an imaginable past." Of course, so does ecstasy, which Hildegard experienced, too.

Hildegard became well-known for many reasons: she was a prolific writer of books on medicine, herbs, and food, a composer of music, and a skilled speaker. After living in a thriving monastery called Disibodenberg for most of her life, she received a vision telling her to build her own abbey at the place where two rivers meet. By that time, however, she had become an asset to her monastery—her fame brought pilgrims and income—and it was not typical for a woman to start her own institution from scratch. The abbots in charge said no.

In response, she entered a long illness during which she became totally paralyzed. She could not move or talk. She froze. Eventually, forced to acknowledge the divine message expressed by the extent of her ailment, a bishop stepped in and permitted her to go forward with her plan. Hildegard's body had proven her case. If the result happened to be self-serving, well, then her advancement must have been God's will. It would not be exactly right to say that Hildegard brought the suffering upon herself. Illness, rather, was a methodology for making sense of the world.

Hildegard, like many women at the fringe of orthodoxy, was not necessarily allowed to speak or act. She had to earn authority, through a mix of strategy and piety—remaining just barely on the right side of the heretical. If she had fallen on the other side, she could easily have been declared a witch and burned at the stake. For if sickness is a methodology, it is an ambivalent one. How do you harness suffering? How do you interpret it? How do you make it *mean* something, much less what you want it to mean? How do you keep it from being used against you? Hildegard was not canonized as a saint until 2012, but she was recognized by many devotees, especially women, as an unofficial saint for many centuries. What she saw and what she felt mattered, because she made them matter. She offered her body to be read for clues.

An agent still at work

The therapist was sitting in front of a bookshelf, but the resolution of the Zoom window wasn't high enough for me to make out the books' individual titles. A white curtain to his right—my left— filtered the sunlight entering his room, but sometimes he squinted from the brightness. He sat slightly back from his desk, so I could get a better view of his upper body. He explained to me that the main downside of on-screen therapy was that we couldn't see each other breathing, leaning forward, fidgeting—and, I assumed, it would be harder for him to gauge my level of freaking out. "I can't see your belly," he said. "Are you breathing deeply?"

I had indeed forgotten to breathe. I was sitting in an ergonomic office chair in my living room, spaced out, nauseated, but oddly giddy. We were between sets of EMDR, short minute-long sprints during which I delved into awful memories again and again, trying to induce the feeling that they were happening in real time through bilateral brain stimulation. Training a person to move their eyes back and forth is also hard over Zoom, so the therapist I'd found preferred another method that has been shown to have the same effect. You lay your hands over your chest in a butterfly shape and gently tap yourself under the collarbone in a rhythmic pattern. The brain gets stimulated—lit up? poked? palpated?—in the same way it does if you roll your eyeballs from left to right. I found it to be a simple action with powerful results. I started to notice my eyes moving along with my hands while I was doing it, and by the third session, I felt myself sinking into what felt like an ancient interior realm. When I imagined a scene while tapping, the visions held a lucid, hyperreal quality.

Equally galvanized and frustrated by van der Kolk's book, a few weeks earlier I had decided I no longer wanted to be frozen or sick. I was tired of being gaslighted by doctors offering prescriptions for my body and psychiatrists offering prescriptions for my mind. As far as strategies, EMDR appealed to me most—partly because it made the least sense. It seemed like magic. You move your eyes back and forth and your brain rearranges itself? But it also appealed to me because it was at the nexus of brain and body:

it dealt with both at the same time. It would not ask me to explain myself or analyze my memories from a distanced perspective, or even talk at all.

In our first session, I had peppered the therapist with disclaimers. "I want to stop randomly dissociating," I said, "but I'm not sure I want to, you know, *fix* the problem." Because what would I do without it? It seemed wrong to treat freeze like a simple pathology to be beaten down or overcome, because it was so strange and profound. Hildegard did not ask whether her illnesses were real or try to get rid of them—she asked what they were trying to tell her. What was freeze trying to tell me? Was I supposed to build a new abbey at the fork of two rivers? *Freeze* is so brittle a word. It disallows undercurrents, metamorphoses. Although it might look static from the outside, there is motion in crossing over. Something sacred happens in that transition. I wanted to suffer less but I did not want to lose access to all those unknown languages.

The therapist smiled and explained that there was a clinical explanation for my ambivalence. "It's totally normal," he said. "A trauma response is valuable information that shouldn't be shoved aside. It's a coping mechanism that worked at some point in the past, and most people find it hard to give it up." What looks dysfunctional now, he went on, was probably at one point very functional—as in, falling asleep during a family argument may be a very good solution for a child with nowhere to go. The problem is that by now the solution no longer fits the situation at hand. The point of EMDR is to teach the body that the coping mechanism can become a choice rather than an uncontrollable reflex. Then he told me, gently, that letting go of some of my responses might make me feel like I was going to die.

In textbook EMDR you pick a traumatic memory and you "target" it. But I could not pick the single worst thing that had ever happened to me. It seemed like the wrong approach. Nothing seemed drastic enough; more to the point, all the memories were fuzzy and interconnected. I asked the therapist what would happen if, instead of a traumatic moment, we targeted the trauma response, the moment of crossing over. The therapist was curious and willing to try. He thought that targeting a transition point—the moment of dissociation itself rather than what had caused it—might work, because it would eventually bring up a cluster of memories that were all lumped together, too persistent and systemic to trace to any single origin point. (There is also a diagnostic name for this, complex PTSD, a condition that results from a series of related events rather than one identifiable occurrence.) I agreed: the memories had a networked nature, and whatever had happened to me was not like a wound but like an infection that had spread through my body. In his book, van der Kolk quotes Freud and his collaborator Josef Breuer, who explain that "the psychical trauma—or more precisely the memory of the trauma—acts like a foreign body which long after its entry must continue to be regarded as an agent that is still at work."

The infection flared wildly during the first month. The therapist was right: I thought I might die. The treatment felt infinitely worse than the problem. I couldn't sleep; I vomited; I was rageful, shaking, mean, unbearably sad. All those latent emotions, which freezing had tamped down, and being chronically sick had diverted my attention from, erupted. At the end of one session the therapist explained that this response is also common. It's called an extinction burst. When a person is faced with losing coping mechanisms, no matter how maladaptive or disruptive those mechanisms might be in the here and now, the reactions rise to the surface in one extravagant explosion, a grand finale of feeling. The infection flares when it senses you may want to get rid of it. The infection reminds you that it was never meant to harm you: it was meant to protect you. You feel like you are about to go extinct. But, as I discovered, it turns out that extinction is not the end—neither of the foreign agent nor of you. It is another step in a process of transformation, a new phase of symbiosis.

Reparative reading

Once in a writing class I was told that writers should always avoid the flashback narrative structure when writing a story. Flashbacks, the teacher said, drag a plot down, pull you away from the present moment, and turn every character trait into a psychological symptom with a simple cause. Why is the character being so cruel? *Flashback: Abuse! Heartbreak! Plane crash!* In this construction, trauma is the essence of backstory, and trauma is the cause for every effect. The language of the traumatic flashback is a language of levers and pulleys, explanations and fixes. It reduces a character to a diagnosis. No matter how much you might want it to, that type of story feels nothing like life.

Labeling experiences as traumas—and invoking their power

by labeling later behaviors as trauma responses—might work for treatment, but as a life strategy it can be a sorry reduction. It risks setting up a system of hierarchical suffering, in which to be traumatized and to be able to "prove it" is a ticket to authority. Yet nobody should have to demonstrate that they have suffered in order to claim their experience as real or have the right to express their thoughts or opinions. Traumas cannot be measured or compared. As Hildegard shows, suffering is important evidence, but it does not confer its *own* authority. What you do with the evidence, how you read it, utilize it, even weaponize it: this is where the question of authority comes in.

The Body Keeps the Score is a bestseller. It is usually stacked in the self-help section of bookstores, suggesting that the book is a manual to make your life better. The language of trauma has likewise been adopted into mainstream culture, with almost any experience seemingly explainable within its rubric. *Getting triggered is not your fault*, reads a post by an Instagram influencer I follow. *You can learn to bounce back faster if you can identify your trauma triggers in the moment.* The type of language that might allow you to connect body and mind—to imagine nonmedicalized approaches to dealing with pain—has been quickly pirated as the language of resilience. Van der Kolk intends to demedicalize trauma, but I don't think he means to popularize it and depoliticize it. And while at various points in the book he rightly places the responsibility for reducing the "epidemic" of trauma on systemic change—by, for instance, supporting families that are likely to be traumatized due to poverty or racism—his text also gives everyone, whatever their sociohistorical circumstances, the very same language to describe their personal pain. It flattens them together.

Lauren Berlant writes in her book *Cruel Optimism* that "in critical theory and mass society generally, 'trauma' has become the primary genre of the last eighty years for describing the historical present as the scene of an exception that has just shattered some ongoing, uneventful ordinary life that was supposed just to keep going on and with respect to which people felt solid and confident." However, "crisis is not exceptional to history or consciousness but a process embedded in the ordinary that unfolds in stories about navigating what's overwhelming." The language of trauma does not result from, but is in fact what creates the idea of an "ongoing uneventful ordinary life" that crises wrench us out from, just as the idea of illness as an aberration creates the concept of health and wellness as the baseline states from which the sick person deviates.

The supposedly nice and healthy, well-adjusted life is an imaginary state, a myth perpetuated by privileged people with the means to simulate it. If the language of trauma is taken as a total explanation for experience, everything might become explained by trauma and trauma alone—and everything might become potentially traumatizing. One writer friend of mine said that after reading *The Body Keeps the Score* she spent months quoting the book in every conversation and essay, only to realize that it explains exactly everything while explaining exactly nothing. For that reason I have not loaded this essay with my own backstory—I have not detailed my childhood traumas, described my triggers, or pasted transcripts from my therapy sessions. This does not stem from a desire to withhold; it's that I don't think trauma is enough to explain this story, any story. I don't wish to make my trauma generally applicable, even within the story of my own life.

The writer Eve Kosofsky Sedgwick has suggested that reading (a book, a body) through the language of symptoms with straightforward causes is a kind of paranoid activity. The paranoid reader is obsessed with discovering a hidden meaning, in order to try to pin down a culprit, name it, and dominate it. If a true cause could only be unearthed and exposed, the paranoid reader assumes, its effects could be predicted, and therefore brought under control. But paranoid reading perpetuates itself: rarely is a single event or actor responsible for a whole story, and rarely does exposing the cause after the fact give one great power to change a narrative, much less to heal oneself or the world.

As a counterpoint to paranoid reading, Sedgwick offers the term *reparative reading*. Reparative reading is no less sharp or critical, but does not attempt to predict or to dominate. It is an approach focused on seeking unexpected possibilities rather than preventing them. Reparative reading avoids pathologizing people and their lives; it does not aim to repair as in to make healthy, but rather to repair connections that may have been lost or broken. In standard EMDR practice, the therapist asks you to begin every session by unearthing a particularly wonderful memory and sealing it into your consciousness using bilateral stimulation. This way you can build associations between the traumatic recollections and other types of experiences, teaching your brain that they are part of the same world.

Religion and psychology have tried very hard to distinguish

between pathological behavior and proper behavior—between the sick way to react to suffering and the healthy way to react to suffering, between freezing and crossing over. Like Hildegard, I maintain that these are not mutually exclusive or even oppositional modes of experience. Listening to the body does not deny that some kinds of pain are irreducible and unsolvable. Many kinds, actually. While Lucia purports to help lessen your burden, to help you by healing you, I think her true purpose is to be there, watching you, when the pain won't go away. After an EMDR session, I often remembered how I felt while standing before Lucia: frozen in a new way, frozen while awake.

What comes after extinction? I'm still here in this body. EMDR did not, ultimately, kill me. It did alter me in a fundamental, if infinitesimal, way. I was surprised at the minute size of this miracle. The miracle: a window of time that had not previously existed. A slight pause between pain and reaction. The window is slim, no more than fifteen seconds, but in that crucial gap something can shift, and the hemispheres can spend a moment in conversation. I can move between meat and story. What I feel versus what I know. What I experience versus what I want. Then, I decide. A lot of the time, I still decide to go to sleep.

Trauma Machine

Rewiring empathy with virtual reality

SANDY CIOFFI'S CONVERSION MOMENT came at a film festival. In 2014 at the annual Sheffield DocFest, Cioffi strapped on an Oculus Rift headset to try the virtual reality experience *Project Syria*. This was one of the first times Cioffi, a video artist and documentarian, had entered VR. "I know it sounds corny," she told me, "but I quite literally was stopped in my tracks with one of those your-life-is-never-going-to-be-the-same moments."

Project Syria, which premiered earlier in 2014 at the World Economic Forum in Davos, has become a well-known example of the power of interactive media in journalism. Made by journalist and filmmaker Nonny de la Peña—often referred to as the "godmother" of virtual reality—the immersive project intends to draw attention to the plight of Syrian refugees. In the first scene, the user lands on a bustling street corner in Aleppo with vendors hawking wares and music playing. Suddenly, a missile explosion destroys the landscape. In a subsequent scene, the user lands in a desert refugee camp. The scenes are accompanied by real audio captured at each site, and the re-creations of the events are as exact as possible.

For Cioffi, experiencing *Project Syria* was a gateway for

addressing several formal and ethical problems she had long struggled with as a documentary maker. For instance, some aspects of *Sweet Crude*, her award-winning 2009 movie about oil extraction in the Niger Delta, bother her in retrospect. She says that *Sweet Crude* follows the classic "extraction" model of storytelling, which mirrors the subject she intended to portray: go somewhere, scoop up material according to the story you want to tell, and use it to build a cohesive narrative. In actuality, she thinks much of what she filmed in Nigeria didn't neatly fit into the story line of a movie about Africa that Western audiences would expect or understand—and to avoid confusion, she simply left those parts out of the story. She had to: with traditional documentary filmmaking, the director has to make editorial choices to present an intelligible story. Likewise, the audience has no choice but to consume the given narrative with some degree of trust—"and damn if it doesn't feel like the *truth*."

But, Cioffi says, when producing 360-degree experiences taken from life, the maker has to hand a lot more information over, contradictions and all, and leave it to the viewer to assemble a meaningful story. The realism and interactivity afforded by VR make it harder for the filmmaker to own or control the story. Cioffi now runs fearless360, a production company and educational program for VR and AR, or augmented reality, a type of production in which computer-generated material is superimposed on the real world (think of the popular game *Pokémon Go*, which prompted millions of users to seek out virtual Pokémon characters pinned to certain geotagged locations across the globe). Even though she acknowledges that more convincing simulations have the potential to lead to more advanced media fakery or user manipulation, she maintains that VR is "more of a fair fight" between the maker and the audience. She somewhat jokingly compares making VR to "going to church."

The ideal of this fair fight undergirds a boom of interactive media projects with journalistic and humanitarian aims over recent years. De la Peña, for one, launched a digital media company in 2007 called Emblematic Group that has gone on to produce more than ten such works. While *Project Syria* is an animated re-enactment, other pieces like *Greenland Melting* (2017), which puts the user face-to-face with disintegrating icebergs, are constructed from flawless 360-degree video. The percentage of Syrian-suffering-based projects among the pool of similar projects is curiously high. Amnesty International, along with Aleppo-based activists and the San Francisco–based design agency Junior, produced *Fear of the Sky* (2016), a 360-degree, high-definition VR tour through bombed-out Aleppo. In a collaboration with the United Nations High Commissioner for Refugees, *The Guardian*'s in-house VR team made a seven-minute illustrated 360-degree movie called *Sea Prayer* (2017), which tells a story about a Syrian father and son, scripted by the popular novelist Khaled Hosseini. Not all of these are fully interactive, but all include 3D representation in which the viewer has some ability to maneuver or explore. All explicitly aim to accurately portray a scenario in order to raise awareness and incite action.

The primary belief undergirding this type of production is that verisimilitude breeds empathy. Walk a mile in the shoes of a young refugee—experience her fear and devastation firsthand—and you're more likely to form a personal connection and believe the facts of her situation. To quote Cioffi again: "If you place someone inside an emotional truth, there is a way that they're not as easily let off the hook. You're more indicted with responsibility for the world around you." The idea is that the thinner the membrane between viewer and viewed—the less mediated the experience feels—the more emotionally resonant it will be. Of course, the less mediated the story feels, the more technology is actually required to mediate it. Creating the illusion of transparency requires a lot of work.

———

Much—too much—has been said about VR as the "empathy machine." The phrase has probably been hawked most effectively by Chris Milk, founder of a media company called Within (formerly Vrse), who gave a TED Talk in 2015 in which he used the term. He claimed that "through this machine we become more compassionate, we become more empathetic, and we become more connected. And ultimately, we become more human." One of Milk's projects, *Clouds Over Sidra* (2015), is a collaboration with the United Nations and Samsung that takes users on a tour (led by a twelve-year-old virtual refugee) through Jordan's Za'atari camp for Syrian refugees.

David Darg, cofounder of interactive media agency Ryot, agrees that "VR can create empathy like never before." But he goes one step further: "It's the ultimate fund-raising tool." Darg puts it in particularly blunt terms, but he articulates the implicit goal of much humanitarian work in general: cash. On its face, this is a disturbingly functional view of empathy, where compassion is but a lever to pull for spare change. In accordance with the neoliberal philanthropic model, this sets up a system by which ethical responsibility for systemic change is shoveled onto the individual. Your care for others is reduced to the measurable amount of money you're willing to wring from your pockets, and anyone who doesn't drop a penny in the bucket might as well be an unfeeling psychopath—not, say, someone who can't afford to give monetarily. The system of empathy-incentivized giving perpetuates itself by creating the world in which it is necessary.

In response to the refugee influx in Europe in 2015, the same that prompted the proliferation of Syria-focused VR projects, Nicholas Kristof wrote in his *New York Times* column that Westerners need to learn to empathize more with the suffering others whose photographs were circulating online. "If you don't see yourself or your family members in those images of today's refugees," he writes, "you need an empathy transplant." The hypothetical empathy transplant recurs constantly in liberal discourse. Global suffering is caused by a lack of empathy: if only we could just trigger it. And in the United States at least, the empathy divide has formed the substructure for much bipartisan political rhetoric—the left continues to plead for more love, less hate. More empathy for refugees, more graphic depictions of the violence to prompt said empathy. This reciprocally forges a counterargument on the right: empathy is latitude, softness, weakness, femininity.

Regardless of whether lack of empathy, or attitude toward empathy, is really the problem, it is impossible to stay pained on behalf of another's suffering every moment of the day. Seeing more misery, many argue, might have the opposite intended effect—it could max out the empathic faculties all those pictures and VR projects intend to stimulate. Jaron Lanier, technologist and author of the comprehensive 2017 VR history *Dawn of the New Everything*, refers to this hard limit on compassion as the empathy circle. "If you make your circle of empathy too wide," he writes, "you become incompetent and don't help anyone." He cautions against attempts to use advanced technology to expand that circle beyond what any single person can bear.

Perhaps more to the point, structures that uphold violence and inequality will not be dismantled through higher-resolution or more immersive empathy machines. White supremacists, to take the most obvious example, desire to see the suffering of non-white bodies, and supremacy will not be overturned through media saturation. On the contrary, Lanier writes, "The more intense a communication technology is, the more intensely it can be used to lie." Seeing more does not mean believing more. As architect and activist Eyal Weizman has said, "truth has become a function of bandwidth and resolution"; in the current paradigm, the more we can see, the more we will *demand to see* to believe. Suspicion—an unshakable belief that one is being lied to or manipulated—will always be built into a political system entirely reliant on high-definition verisimilitude for truth claims. Newer media will always be required to prove what's real.

There is obvious irony in spending millions to put Westerners in VR goggles in order to make them empathize with Syrian refugees, rather than, for instance, donating those millions to Syrian aid programs. Effective altruists, who believe in quantifying goodness and making decisions based on metrics like lives saved, would find the decision completely illogical. But that irony highlights the complex, perhaps irreconcilable relationship between individual suffering and the systems that create it—between the personal story and the statistic. Leslie Jamison, author of *The Empathy Exams*, writes in an opinion piece: "Individual narratives can offer social justice movements grit and traction, but how do you scale up to a larger set of opinions about policy, or interrogations of the contemporary world?" A VR story might make you feel a lot, but what can you really *do* with that feeling?

Scientifically speaking, there's a problem with the functional model of empathy. According to many studies—both those that employ technologies like VR and those that test chemical agents like the bonding hormone oxytocin—feeling empathy does not necessarily correlate with altruistic behavior. Empathy is first and foremost an internal state, which may or may not lead to motivation or action. And when empathy does inspire behavior, the behavior is not always the desired positive kind; in some situations, empathic responses are as likely to promote distress and withdrawal as concern and bonding. If you're suddenly placed in a virtual war-torn refugee camp—especially if you are subject to some preexisting biases—you might react with fear toward the virtual refugees rather than experience empathic connections with them.

There is moderate evidence that personifying catastrophes can encourage some measurable altruistic behaviors. The phenomenon of identifiable victim effect has shown that people are more likely to help others when the other person has a face and a name. (Introductions to studies on the identifiable victim effect often cite the famous statement usually attributed to Stalin that "a single death is a tragedy; a million deaths are a statistic.") If you can identify and relate to a person who is being harmed, rather than to a faceless mass of harmed people, or a bunch of numbers about the harm, you are more likely to feel impelled to directly act in that person's interest.

Yet if altruism in the form of, say, donations were really the goal, scientists and technologists and humanitarians could skip empathy altogether. Helping behavior can also be prompted by, for instance, the illusion of heroism. According to some studies, flying a superhero avatar in a game makes people temporarily more altruistic because it primes them to be receptive to stereotypes related to superpowers. Some chemical compounds like oxytocin have do-gooder effects, and various other reward-style prompts can put people in a giving mood.

But neither priming egoistic fantasies nor dosing subjects with affection-inducing hormones accords with the pervasive fantasy whereby empathy is instigated through experience, through a transformational moment in which the self finds deep connection with another person. The entire philanthropic-industrial complex is premised on this core hope and belief that people will *do good* if only they understand what is really going on, if only they are presented with the high-enough-resolution suffering of an identifiable victim. The allure of a technology that could provide that kind of experience—without the danger or cost of sending civilians into a war zone—is hard to resist.

———

Documentarian Cioffi is by no means the only person to respond so strongly to *Project Syria*. Viewers' tearful reactions have been extensively documented in news reports and reaction videos, which form an integral part of the life of the piece. Testimonials about the force of VR experiences—proving that what happened in there has changed the user out here—not only constitute a selling point for the tech, but are a fundamental aspect of the content. These VR projects invite, and perhaps require, a double testimony: the first regarding the primary trauma being depicted or described, and the second regarding the shadow trauma of the viewer, the evidence of empathic response. The empathy machine, in this respect, works insofar as it is a trauma machine.

The advent of any new technology seems to come with a need for testimonials about its persuasiveness, its realness. And the ability to traumatize the user is a classic litmus test of its real factor. Photography and then film also carried the verisimilitude burden; this was the basis for what might be termed the Lumière effect, based on a (possibly mythical) 1895 screening of a Lumière brothers film, during which viewers supposedly stampeded out of a theater when they mistook the train in the film's projection for the real thing. While the story may or may not be true—early spectators may well have been able to distinguish between image and reality—its frequent retelling as such indicates cultural desires surrounding what media can do. VR does not represent a deviation from this story about the evolution of media but instead a telling intensification. It shows how the ability of a medium to convey trauma as content, and in the process to *re*traumatize, has become intrinsic to the success of the form.

In certain instances, VR's capacity to (re)traumatize is made explicit as a goal. It has been used in a range of trauma therapy scenarios, mainly exposure therapy, by which the traumatized person is asked to relive a painful experience through an accurate virtual reconstruction. Some studies show that this can decrease some forms of PTSD and specific phobias; others show that it does so only for a time. Because it relies on desensitization, rather than integration of the trauma into the rest of life, this kind of memory work in VR risks dulling a person's ability to experience a range of human emotions, not just the damaging ones. Multiple exposures desensitize what a single exposure has made raw, but progressive trauma therapy questions whether desensitization is a valid goal of treatment. VR has been more unequivocally successful when it comes to retraining immobile parts of the body, assimilating prostheses into coordinated movement, or reducing phantom limb pain. Practicing movement with a virtual body can convince the brain to relate or rerelate to the real body.

In the 1970s Susan Sontag wrote a foundational text on the social functions and effects of photography (*On Photography*) and in the early 2000s turned her attention to the way photographic portrayals of suffering in particular dominate the media landscape (*Regarding the Pain of Others*). Her argument in the second book is often misinterpreted as a diatribe against the medium's capacity for desensitization: the idea that photography desensitizes the viewer to suffering because there are just too many pictures of it. (The empathy circle cannot hold.) But Sontag's point is not really that mass photographic material ruins humans' ability to relate to one another—her concern is that it can flatten all experiences of pain into a general category of pain, creating an aesthetic of misery that overrides the specificity of any single case. A depiction of one refugee child comes to stand in for the suffering of all refugee children—and all their variegated experiences become the same in the mind of the viewer. "It is intolerable to have one's own sufferings twinned with anybody else's," she writes. In the context of recent VR works, for instance, a nonrefugee at a tech conference might be able to empathize and think they can relate to the plight of a Syrian refugee in a video game scenario, but their experiences of life have likely been vastly different. What does the refugee feel, or want, from this kind of encounter?

To make suffering visible obscures the invisible systems producing that suffering. And it allows one to expunge—or better, forget—the guilty privilege of being the seer rather than the seen. As Sontag explains in *Regarding the Pain of Others*:

> To speak of reality becoming a spectacle is a breathtaking provincialism. It universalizes the viewing habits of a small, educated population living in the rich part of the world, where news has been converted into entertainment ... It is absurd to identify the world with those zones in the well-off countries where people have the dubious privilege of being spectators,

or of declining to be spectators, of other people's pain, just as it is absurd to generalize about the ability to respond to the sufferings of others on the basis of the mind-set of those consumers of news who know nothing at first hand about war and massive injustice and terror. There are hundreds of millions of television watchers who are far from inured to what they see on television. They do not have the luxury of patronizing reality.

In other words, a one-way understanding of empathy reproduces power relations rather than levels them. It focuses only on the extent that *I* can relate to *you*. Psychology has a language for this; it is known as the self-other overlap, whereby the wish to identify with another person becomes a projection, with the empathizer's own beliefs and desires overriding those of the target. Self-other overlap cannot itself constitute empathy if it does not also lead one to consider the other as a separate person with agency—who has the capacity to empathize in reverse.

———

If VR is a trauma machine, many experiments (though certainly not all) conceive of it as a one-way machine. This is contrary to the dreams early VR evangelists had for the medium, which they hoped would not simply provide immersion or verisimilitude, but new modes of person-to-person interaction. They imagined VR would be relational rather than unidirectional, active rather than passive. Lanier and others hoped it would provide new ways of sensing, connecting, communicating, and political communing.

Unlike the photography or television of Sontag's era, VR allows the deconstruction of the one-way observer model. Throughout his book, Lanier argues that VR's most important implementation is in shared social experience—not transporting "us" into "their" reality, but coconstructing a new consensus reality in virtual space. Embodied experience, says Cioffi, should "not just be about how I have more empathy for *you*. And it's not just about how I better understand *me*. It's that I genuinely believe there's a *we*."

For this reason, Cioffi, de la Peña, and other VR designers have explicitly noted the necessity of providing interactive capabilities in virtual experiences. At the very least, de la Peña has suggested, users should be given the ability to act or make choices within the simulation. After exiting a simulation, they should be given information about how to assist in a crisis they've witnessed, a sort of ex post facto interaction. Or, best of all, they might communicate in real time with others in virtual space.

In a world reliant on philanthropy, trauma is an asset. A weak asset to be sure, but often the only asset granted to the dispossessed in late capitalism. Humanitarianism instrumentalizes and leverages this asset, finding ways to exchange it for other forms of capital. Anthropologist Miriam Ticktin, who writes on humanitarian organizations, says that "an understanding of suffering as the basis of a universal humanity can result in the obligation to use suffering to barter for membership in the category [of] humanity." The sufferer is granted human status by demonstrating the ability to suffer, which is then validated by the witness's ability to understand the suffering as real. The firsthand suffering testifies to the humanity of the sufferer; the secondhand experience testifies to the humanity of the viewer.

Technologies like VR threaten the humancentric worldview, and coupled with technologies like AI, potentially demand reconsideration of where the human begins and ends. Using VR for the recapitulation of suffering, for commandeering and appropriating others' pain, is one method that responds to this perceived threat by reaffirming human supremacy over machines. If we can suffer, the thinking goes, we must be people. But what does it say about our notions of empathy, and therefore humanity, that we think it can be best elicited through witnessing suffering? Might empathy not be as profoundly felt (and its profundity proven) through other affective states, like happiness?

Cioffi is adamant that VR's true potential lies not in borrowing others' suffering, but in giving people new ways to own their stories. "It's not my right to decide how the people of the Niger Delta's trauma should be valued," she says. Just as they have the right to own their own data and their own DNA information, "communities have every right" to own "their own horrible stories and their own trauma," and for that matter, their own joy. She is clear that she does not mean ownership in a transactional sense, as material for trade and consumption, but as something more like authorship—the ability to use new technology to show oneself how one wants to be seen. This would not be an exercise in borrowing someone else's trauma, but in confronting one's own. Reckoning with ownership of stories—and the technologies with which to tell them—entails a "necessary recognition that a lot of the documentary tradition really did become like Global South apocalypse porn in order to try to get people off their chairs to write their congressmen to change international law," Cioffi says. And while VR might be able to do this even more effectively, it can also do something else.

————

In 2012, the USC Shoah Foundation began a series of interactive media projects aimed at bringing its massive archive of testimony—over 55,000 recorded interviews with genocide survivors—to new audiences. For the first initiative, *Dimensions in Testimony*, the octogenarian Holocaust survivor Pinchas Gutter was filmed from several angles while responding to questions about his life. His answers to the questions were then fed into a learning algorithm that generates responses to live questions (even ones not practiced) in Gutter's own voice. The product is a lifelike simulacrum of Gutter, who is able to answer visitors' questions in real time from a library of stored material. It improves over time with use.

The virtual Gutter—who is currently shown as a two-dimensional projection but will eventually evolve into a portable hologram—is intended to educate. But, the project initiators believe, it does not need to seem real to do so. According to Stephen D. Smith, the USC Shoah Foundation's executive director, even young children seem to immediately understand that Gutter is a simulation. And the artifice offers advantages: for instance, while kids are often deeply curious about Gutter's experiences, Smith says, "they're much more willing to ask questions of the interactive testimony than they are of the individual, because they wouldn't want to hurt the individual's feelings."

Uninflected by the give-and-take of social behavior, talking to an AI allows one to sidestep an obligation to empathy and allows something more like emotional education. It educates about the individual suffering of the (absent) Gutter and the Holocaust, but it also allows one to experiment with what to feel and how to respond. It liberates the user from a certain kind of performative empathy, and it also liberates Gutter from the responsibility to tell and retell his story in the hopes of eliciting certain feelings in an audience. This is not intended as a replacement for human-to-human interaction; it's intended as an archive of material whose presentation raises questions about memory and loss.

Anyone who has tried it will tell you that it's very hard to step off a high ledge in virtual reality. You look down at a few-hundred-foot drop, which you know is the floor beneath your feet, and yet the illusion of depth overrides that knowledge. Your heart clenches, uncontrollably charged with adrenaline, and perception competes with cognition and willpower. I had been told this would happen by several people before I tried to make the leap, and I was not disappointed. In an Oculus game called *Richie's Plank Experience* (2016), where the player begins standing on a wooden plank jutting from the eightieth story of a skyscraper, I struggled for two minutes before I could convince myself to step six inches forward onto the carpet.

The tech isn't perfect; you still feel the weight of the headset, the temperature of the real room, but this does not diminish the out-of-body feeling. Toggling between belief and disbelief is the fun of the experience: feeling how indisputably beholden you are to your own body. You know and yet you *know*. Only a few senses have to be tricked for a user to attain what de la Peña calls "duality of presence": the brain's ability to split in two and feel like it's in real and virtual worlds at once.

Daryle Conners, an author and game designer working with the medical applications of VR, finds this experience of dis/belief to be a profoundly spiritual one. She told me: "By a very fundamental hijacking of, like, two of your senses—three, maybe, if you include a little bit of vibrating like haptics in your controllers—just through those senses being sort of fooled, your whole perception is changed. And we rely on that perception for so much of our truth, but really, when you see how malleable it is and how much it's about subjective perspective, that's one of the deeper things that VR shows us." By mediating simulated reality so convincingly, VR can train one to view "real" reality as equally mediated. And in this way it could just as easily retrain *away* from the media-historical trajectory of verisimilitude-as-truth and its emphasis on trust versus trickery.

That is to say, if what we desire from VR is an exact replica of a fixed and stable reality within which to reproduce a certain idea of humanity, we are missing the point of what it does and can do: reveal the changeable nature of all reality and therefore the potential to change it for the better or manipulate it for the worse.

Ask Before You Bite

I often talk about love as one of the few places where people actually admit they want to become different. And so it's like change without trauma, but it's not change without instability. It's change without guarantees, without knowing what the other side of it is, because it's entering into relationality.

—LAUREN BERLANT

World of darkness

On the morning of the vampire larp, I pulled on pleather pants and a hot-pink club top and took the subway from my apartment in the city center to a disused factory on the periphery of Berlin. The factory had been decorated to resemble a postindustrial night club in Bristol: the setting for what was to be a wild pretend party. On the train, I was sleepy and nervous, and I kept misrecognizing myself in the reflection on the car's sliding doors. I had colored my hair red with temporary dye the night before in an attempt to get into character. (By the end of that week I'd realize that the dye was semipermanent and needed to be professionally washed out.)

The character I was to play in the larp—the standard acronym for live-action roleplay—was Margaret Olivier: real estate entrepreneur, TV personality, and mortal. I knew her backstory, her personality, and her allegiances from a PowerPoint presentation I had received via email from the larp organizers a week in advance. Margaret, a white woman in her thirties or forties, was a work-hard-play-hard type. Her ratings on both the Rage and Ambition scales were four out of five. She had a deadbeat son, a gay bestie, and a boy toy who was lately behaving badly. I had been given links to a few Facebook groups where I could chat with the people who would be playing her acquaintances, so we could get to know one another or make plans for the game. The only thing we weren't supposed to disclose was whether we were mortals or vampires. That was for later.

In the same email, I also got a PowerPoint file explaining the basic rules of the game and the atmosphere of the world we'd be inhabiting. Most of the other larpers were probably familiar with the history of the World of Darkness gaming franchise, but this was all new to me. I had almost no experience with larp and I was not a self-identified gamer of any kind.

Here are some excerpts from the slides telling me what was in store:

> Horror has always been about exploring the forbidden, the dangerous, and the disturbing. In World of Darkness (WoD) the horror is personal . . . Characters in WoD are afraid of themselves, their desires and what they are ready to do to

change the world. The grotesque and the sublime mix as moments of brutal atrocity are woven together with deep reflection over moral consequences and the limits of human ethics. World of Darkness doesn't shy away from controversial and contemporary subjects like corporate corruption, drug culture, war in the Middle East, climate change, human trafficking, terrorism, eating disorders, addiction, mental illness, poverty and the class struggle, the rise of neo-fascism, suicide, and religious fanaticism.

The World of Darkness is not a traditional violent power fantasy, where big guns, muscles and money can solve your problems. As a monstrous creature you belong to a hidden society. A network of secret tribes and clans. Normal society can never know you exist. Subtlety is key. You use investigation, social manipulation, arcane abilities, loyal allies, intricate schemes and the right tools to rise to power.

Some history is in order. WoD took off in the United States in the nineties and quickly spread among gamer circles. It started with board games of the Dungeons & Dragons ilk, the most popular of which was called Vampire: The Masquerade. The characters and story lines of WoD's vampire games were so popular that it evolved off the board, eventually becoming a video game and fan universe and then a full-blown live-action roleplay system, replete with attendant aesthetics and online and offline communities including minor celebrities. In the 2010s, the enterprise got a face-lift and a reboot (due to a complicated merger/acquisition by a bigger gaming company that I still don't understand). Now, in summer 2017, Berlin was hosting the first international WoD convention, a weekend-long gathering including panel discussions, tabletop games, celebrity signings, costume contests, and multiple larps for extreme fans of the vampire underworld.

Other than my friend Susan Ploetz, an artist, game designer, and seasoned larper who had told me about the event and convinced me to join her there, I didn't know any of the seventy-odd players I'd be meeting. I had signed up for the convention as a journalist and gotten a free press pass (tickets ran up to a hundred euros) because—I told myself—I thought it would make for great story material. I had been researching larp culture for a while and had been working on a piece for an art magazine about potential crossover between art and gaming worlds. At the convention, I was planning on maintaining my usual pseudo-ethnographic distance and reporting back on the scene. But the organizers only let me join this larp on one condition: I couldn't stand around and watch. I had to commit to full participation. In other words, I was going to be doing a double roleplay that night. I was going to pretend to be Margaret Olivier, but I was also going to pretend to be the kind of person who would go to a vampire larp.

A primer

Larp has multiple and divergent histories—any explanation will garner criticism from one side or another—but the shorthand description is that it's like improvisational theater without an audience. Players take on characters, either assigned to them or developed by them, and they inhabit those roles within the parameters of a designed world. The degree of improvisation and the flexibility of the rules is dependent on the nature of the game, but in general the players will collaborate to form plotlines and story arcs to entertain themselves. The absence of audience is what crucially distinguishes roleplay from both theater and most performance art, and while various forms of documentation, from photography to video to testimonials to blogs, are common, the point is the experience. The larp happens within the so-called magic circle, often defined as a "membrane" that circumscribes virtual worlds. Once you step into the magic circle, you have committed to suspension of disbelief. You have bought into the communal fantasy, the collective delusion, and agreed to the terms.

If you've heard of larp, you're probably imagining nerds dressed up like knights and orcs running around in the forest and bashing each other with padded swords. That indeed encompasses one branch of larp culture and history, which has been termed boffering. Boffering, which emerged from the proverbial basement of geekdom, has a heavy presence in the U.S., and a lot of its games stem from original D&D worlds or other preexisting fan universes like *The Lord of the Rings*. Such larps tend to be structured around quests and points. The characters are stable and the rules are static; many communities have been playing the same characters in the same game for months or years on end. As depicted in one frequently circulated *Vice* documentary, each weekend, groups of bofferers don their elf and wizard costumes and head into the forest to resume their lifelong games.

Boffering is not known to be particularly subversive when it comes to clichés of gender, sexuality, ability, or race. You'll find many a sexy wench and grizzled warrior. In this way larpers often exemplify the peculiar tendency of subcultures to recapitulate the identity fantasies of the mainstream rather than exploiting the subversive potential that marginalization might afford. Until recently, the demographics spoke for themselves; more larpers in the boffering world were white and male than were not. But a shift began in 2014, when the controversy known as Gamergate broke: several women in the video game industry came forward to explain that they had been targets of vicious harassment. Suddenly a robust political debate about the violence and discrimination in gamer circles emerged.

Given the amount of crossover between live-action roleplayers and online gamers, this discourse about inclusivity—not only in games, but in the social and professional worlds that produce them—couldn't help but spread to the larp world, too. WoD, and other franchises around which strong larp cultures had developed, realized that fostering safe spaces with the aim of inclusivity was not only an ethical imperative—it was a good look that could broadly expand customer bases.

The Nordics

Where to find inspiration for new kinds of politically conscious gaming? Geeky boffering, after all, is only one form of roleplay among a panoply of others. The other prominent strand has coalesced under the name Nordic larp, for its geographical origins in the Nordic countries. (It has also been called progressive larp, or in French *romanesque*, meaning novelesque.) While this cluster of larp traditions is not free of nerd associations, different aims and cultural practices surround the game design and play, often with more crossover with theater, art, and academia. (I belong to a Facebook group called LARP Academia where people trade PDFs; another is called Larp Women Unite, where someone recently posted an invitation for an event described as Elves Against Patriarchy.)

Nordic larp draws from historical reenactment, method acting, psychodrama, Gestalt therapy, educational practices, war games, military simulations, and BDSM play. All these modes of experience and collaboration depend on simulated scenarios and assuming fictional roles: to play a role is to test, practice, and learn. Nordic larp focuses on narrative, relationships, culture building, and self-exploration as much as winning and losing. Psychological challenge, boundary testing, and collaborative exchange are foregrounded. Rather than the pure escapism promised by boffering, Nordic larp tends to conceive of the magic circle as a permeable membrane that can be used for mediating and reinventing the self and the community both inside and outside of the circle. It's no accident that Nordic larpers tend to be a more diverse crowd.

One early larp that exemplifies the scale and widespread popularity of roleplay in the Nordic countries was the 1994 run of *Trenne Byar*. Dubbed the Woodstock of Nordic larp, the weeklong family-friendly event was set in the Swedish countryside, where a thousand participants of all ages joined to play the inhabitants

of villages in a pseudomedieval world. With historical reenactment in mind, many larps aim for accuracy, but others aim to
invert or reinvent history. A five-day, 120-player larp near Oslo
called *Once Upon a Time* was set in a fictional Wyoming town
in 1887. Although the set was replete with Wild West saloons and
costumes were period accurate, players were encouraged to take
on characters with different gender identities than their own or
form queer relationships within the game. Other games are heavy
on satire and social critique. A Norwegian game called *Panopti-
Corp* from 2003 is named after a fictional advertising agency
whose employees—twenty-five players and various extras—were
stuck in an office together for seventy-two hours and forced to
compete for performance ratings using a specially invented corporate lingo.

Present-day political scenarios are also taken up. *Europa*, a
four-day, forty-player Norwegian larp first played in 2001, included players from the Nordic countries and Russia. The Nordic
players were cast as immigrants seeking asylum in a Russian-
speaking country through an opaque bureaucratic process, with
language barriers authentically preventing easy communication.
In 2013, inspired by a cohort of Norwegian larpers who vis-
ited Palestine, a group of Palestinians organized *So You Think
You Can Dance?* The characters are given a range of views on
Israeli occupation and ideas for the future. Now, the game is
played elsewhere as an edu-larp for non-Palestinians to become
informed about the occupation through enactment. The educational applications of roleplay are wide: Østerskov Efterskole,
a boarding school in Hobro, Denmark, teaches its curriculum

ASK BEFORE YOU BITE

entirely through larp. Think teens donning Roman togas to learn Euclidean geometry.

Larps have been based on the novel-worlds of Octavia E. Butler and Ursula K. Le Guin, simulated what it might be like to live in a biosphere in outer space, restaged key historical events like Cold War negotiation, and tried to simulate the experiences of being in prison or a mental hospital. Larp leaves room for the nonliteral, nonverbal, and nonnarrative as well. For *Luminescence*, a 2004 Finnish larp, players could wade through a room filled with hundreds of pounds of white flour, meant as a metaphor for coping with cancer. In 2018 I played a blackbox larp, that is, a larp with no set, props, or costumes, called *We Are One*, where players were separated into two groups of prelinguistic beings who could only make one of two vowel sounds. It took us two hours to learn to communicate.

Because Nordic larp is often intended to push a player's boundaries, the community has developed various mechanics for safety and consent before, during, and after the gameplay. One larper told me about a game she had played a few times in which one character is raped by the others. Nothing physical happens in the whole game: all characters verbally narrate their actions and reactions in explicit terms. The woman (who had played both victim and perpetrator in different runs of the game) described it to me as one of the most profound breakthroughs she'd ever had in terms of understanding power dynamics—what sounded to me like a kind of gonzo trauma therapy.

That type of larp isn't particularly fun; it's hard to even call it a game. It comes with a potential psychological toll. No thoughtful group of nonsadists would head into such an experiment without some precautions. How do you engineer a painful larp that is cathartic and not traumatizing? Who should be allowed to play? What happens if someone panics or gets physically violent? How do you prepare for it and how do you process it afterward? Over decades of practice, Nordic larpers have invented systems for all of the above.

The concept of deliberately creating a tool kit for mutual care was what had originally interested me in Nordic larp. As I learned about how certain groups of Nordic larpers craft complex games with the safety of their players in mind, I began to draw more and more negative comparisons with other social groups I was familiar with, like the art and literature circuits. Those worlds, like game worlds, can be toxic, but there seemed to me to be little discussion of the reciprocal relationship between the way the social groups function and the work they actually create. The endless question is played on repeat: Can you separate the art from the artist? As if artists make work in a vacuum; as if the work itself could be labeled a success if people are traumatized in the making of it.

Conversely, the Nordic larpers I started talking with seemed to have a sophisticated understanding of how real life and game life bleed into each other, and they aimed to prioritize the well-being of participants over the success of any game. What could it mean to take the communities surrounding other types of cultural production as intrinsic to the work produced, and to foreground relational issues like consent, egalitarian decision-making, and nonexploitation as part and parcel of the resulting projects?

Would calling a practice—even a highly professionalized practice like contemporary art—a game help identify the systems of power and control that govern it? What are the game mechanics of any type of cultural production?

WoD caught on to the desires of its fan base, and for the 2017 convention, they wanted to push boundaries without inciting lawsuits. The larps, while still set within the familiar WoD universe, were revamped, and a few prominent Nordic game designers had been invited to run the larps according to Nordic game mechanics for safety and consent. While many players were excited about this aspect, there remains a persistent complaint among (mainly U.S.) gamers that Nordic larpers want to make gamer culture more politically correct. Nordic larpers, on the other hand, insist that certain restrictions allow much more risky experimentation. I heard one panel discussant at the WoD convention vehemently argue, "We're making your culture *less* PC. You just have to ask before you do something now."

End of the line

The larp I signed up for was named *End of the Line* and was explicitly eighteen plus. The setting was a night of debauchery and devilish behavior in that illegal Bristol nightclub; mortals and vampires and other supernatural beings were there to party, have sex, fight, create factions, exert magical forms of control over one another, and, should the situations arise, for the vampires among us to convert some of the mortals by the end of the night.

I arrived at the factory building before noon. The big workshop room was filling up, with people hanging coats and stashing bags in a closet, milling about excitedly in various states of costume. I was a mess, more socially anxious than I have ever been at the type of events I usually go to. Among the gamers I felt painfully out of place. I considered pinning my press pass to my club top to try to distance myself even just the slightest bit. I found my friend Susan and clung to her side.

The larp was to last six hours, but first we had a mandatory four-hour preparatory workshop, and afterward an hour-long postgame debrief. The workshop began with your typical theater warm-up exercises and get-to-know-you games, during which everyone besides a few bawdy theater types seemed as uncomfortable as I did. After an hour or so, we were introduced to the consent and safety tactics that would govern the play.

Some of these "calibration" mechanisms are simple and sound self-evident. Say you're in the middle of a scene and the person across from you starts to look uncomfortable. You might want to check in—so you flash them an OK hand gesture. If they're fine they'll flash one back. If not, you might get a thumbs-down (stop) or a thumbs-sideways (sorta) and you'll know if you can keep playing. This might sound clunky, but in rehearsal I found it is actually pretty seamless; it allows you to modulate the emotional volatility of a situation without breaking character.

Besides the hand motions, *End of the Line* had a whole range of scripts for the specific scenarios of sex and violence that might arise in the game. Take the sure-to-arise scenario of the vampire bite. In vampire parlance, the act of the bite is called the embrace:

the vampire locks eyes with the mortal, with or without consent, and puts the mortal into a kind of trance, before going fangs-deep. Crazy species transformation ensues.

There are myriad ways to simulate a bite. It can be as close to or as far from physical reality as you want (barring actual puncturing of the skin for legal reasons). How do you prefer to be bitten? Light skin contact? Lick? Kiss? Fake blood? Extremely detailed narration? Nod and handshake? One solution is to make a blanket rule before a game, e.g., all biting happens in midair pantomime, no exceptions. But in *End of the Line*, the simulation was to be decided upon case by case, midplay, via the script. Whenever a bite (or sex or violence) seemed like it was on the horizon, the initiator was to pause and step out of character to momentarily negotiate the situation *as players* before getting on with it.

Nordic larpers draw a hierarchy between player and character; as the mantra goes, *players are always more important than characters*. The conceptual distinction between player and character can be hard to grasp in an abstract sense. To take a possible scenario from *End of the Line*, say you as a player might not want to be touched—but your character might be a very sexy person who wants to have an affair. How do you play out the story? Consent-based negotiation is obviously important when it comes to physical boundaries, but it also helps safeguard psychological ones. If a *character* is the unknowing victim of a manipulative vampire, how can you be sure that the *player* is not being manipulated as well? What separates power play from power reality?

The slap

After the workshop, all seventy of us put on our jackets over our costumes and trekked for fifteen minutes alongside the highway to IKEA to have lunch. Apparently the IKEA cafeteria was the closest restaurant that could accommodate a group of our size. I took several pictures on my phone of my fellow players with their white face paint, blood-ringed eyes, top hats, and capes loitering outside the store and then taking the escalators upstairs. I was terrified that I would run into someone I knew and have to explain myself. In the eyes of the IKEA shoppers, though, it was no use trying to signal "I'm not with them." And what was my problem anyway? I *was* with them. Eating meatballs.

I ate my meatballs at a table with Susan and some of the game organizers. I asked about why the program schedule had started so early in the day. One organizer explained that the lunch break was a vital part of the game design. Apparently creating social bonds out of the game forges the kind of accountability in-game that keeps people from harming one another. Later, I heard a U.S. larper say that she and her decade-old gamer group never hung out together outside game time. It wasn't until she read a Nordic larp handbook that it occurred to her to invite the crew to meet for a beer out of character. The next time they played together, she said, the sexist comments and ass slaps that she was used to getting from the guys had nearly stopped, as if by magic. Apparently the guys felt creepy molesting women who were no longer imaginary creatures but were potentially their real-life friends.

After IKEA we marched back to the factory and had twenty

minutes to get dolled up: hair was curled, makeup was slathered on, fishnets emerged, and a few breasts came out. The launch of the game was marked by a lighting change and an all-larper techno dance party in one of the cavernous rooms. It began.

No matter how embarrassed you feel, once you're in a dark room with seventy people earnestly acting out an imaginary rave, lights flashing and mediocre techno in the background, you'll snap into it. Consensus reality is a thing. Perhaps more to the point: with six hours to kill, you'll die of boredom if you don't ante up. I started by drinking my two allotted cups of the finite beer available from a keg (we were told to seriously restrict the alcohol intake) and then finding someone who had brought a secret flask full of vodka. It started to feel just enough like an actual party for me to forget it wasn't. Or was it?

Even though I took copious notes after the night was over, it's hard to reconstruct what happened. Some of it was boring, much of it inexplicable, and much of it legitimately exciting. I saw people beating one another up and fucking against the walls; I also saw a lot of forms of sex and violence in a gray area between simulation and actuality. For instance, the basement was ruled an out-of-game zone where we could go to discuss as players how we wanted things to go: while loitering down there, I listened to one group of guys spend half an hour elaborately planning a fight sequence. When they finally went upstairs to act it out in real time, the fight lasted maybe a minute.

For her part, Margaret Olivier spent a lot of time scheming with her gay bestie and arguing with her would-be boyfriend, who had his hands up the skirt of another woman. She did a few lines of coke (powdered sugar) and danced a lot. Eventually she was introduced to a very tall guy who said he was a Russian mobster. He hinted he was part of a secret society and kept showing off a signet ring he was wearing. He was clearly hitting on Margaret. I realized that this was my chance.

The Russian invited Margaret into a dark corner at the top of a rickety metal staircase overlooking the main party room. Regarding the scene below, the two of them could see a couple humping against a wall and a vampire sinking her teeth into a consenting victim, blood spraying everywhere. The Russian and Margaret chatted about their lives and got to know each other. Then he told her that he had valuable information about what was really going on at the party that night, about a secret group running the show, and asked if she would give him a blow job in exchange for the information.

In the workshop, we had been told that women should wait five to ten seconds before deciding whether to say yes or no to any invitation, because our impulse would be to say yes right away. I counted fifteen seconds after the blow job question before saying no. To my surprise, the other player did not question or pressure me. He wasn't supposed to; we had been told that if a person says they don't want to do something, not to take it personally or ask why—because as soon as you ask why, you're opening the door to coercion. The guy simply nodded and continued the script for negotiating sex/violence. Even four hours into the party, the plan was working in action.

We entered the negotiation as players rather than characters. This was a complex moment, because I did not want to give this guy a blow job, but Margaret also did not want to give the Russian a blow job, and the other player needed to know that both were the case (meaning I would not simulate a blow job, either). As a player, I said that Margaret did not trade sex for favors, but that she would be willing to debase herself in another way if this would give him a sense of power in exchange for his information. He (the player) asked what Margaret would be up for and I said she would, for instance, let him hit her. He asked what level of reality I (the player) would be up for and I said he could hit my face with his hand open. He asked whether I wanted him to remove the leather glove and rings he was wearing and I said yes please. At one point in this process his English failed him, I realized he was a German speaker, and we switched to German.

Then we went in-game again. The motives for the slap and its role in the plot were totally unclear to me by then—I'm sure Margaret had her reasons. Margaret knelt and clasped her hands in front of her. The Russian towered over her and smacked her hard on the cheek, so hard that she fell to the side. It hurt Margaret a lot; it also hurt me a lot. We were in the same body.

At that moment I grasped the revelatory potential of all this artifice and performative negotiation. I was allowed to do whatever the fuck I wanted because I was under the cover of the game, and under the cover of consent-as-law. I had plausible deniability for my actions, because I was Margaret—and I also had an out at any moment. It was an experience profoundly different from any other kind of sociality or intimacy I was familiar with. The whole ridiculous vampire-club premise was, I think, in service of this weird bifurcation: an experience of being yourself and not-yourself, in which you and your character coexist but remain distinct from each other. In that moment I went from larping a larper to larping.

Safe emergency

Anyone who's seen *Fifty Shades of Grey* knows that BDSM play involves scripting regulatory mechanisms for negotiating boundaries. In the movie, the fifty-page contract Christian Grey slaps on the table and asks his clueless submissive to sign is shorthand for consent negotiation. Obviously this is a very bad example of proper mechanics: in good BDSM you don't sign all your rights to your body away in advance. Consent cannot be total or permanent. The line between coercion and consent must be continually redefined, and, as I learned in the larp, often the act of defining it is the sum total of the excitement. (Is larping a subset of BDSM? Is larping BDSM a form of BDSM? What *isn't* a larp?)

Whenever pleasure and pain are explicitly combined, or when power discrepancy is the source of the pleasure, the membrane around the magic circle has to be explicit: contracts, safe words, aftercare. Power roles can diverge widely from reality—witness the pervasive cliché of the CEO crushed beneath the dominatrix's heel—but in the game space you get to choose your role, which means you get to consent to it. There is a well-known therapeutic aspect to roleplay, sexual, vampiric, or otherwise. Acting out fear or fantasy in a safe space can be cathartic—some forms of trauma therapy rely on these tactics. Gestalt therapy manufactures scenarios called safe emergencies in which frightening or traumatic events can be (re)enacted without the genuine threat of mortal harm, and new outcomes can be tested.

The concept of the safe emergency, a suspended period of time in which to risk oneself, could be extrapolated to describe a much wider realm of experience. Intimacy of all kinds requires risk for the reward—and feeling safe enough to test one's boundaries is a precondition for erotic intimacy in particular. In *The Body Keeps the Score*, trauma therapist Bessel van der Kolk writes that "achieving any sort of deep intimacy—a close embrace, sleeping with a mate, and sex—requires allowing oneself to experience immobilization without fear. It is especially challenging for traumatized people to discern when they are actually safe . . . This requires having experiences that can restore the sense of physical safety." How jarring it was for me to experience a sense of safety while kneeling on the floor and being violently slapped by a stranger.

Worlds in worlds

The day after the larp I went to the WoD convention to continue my "research." I was tired and hungover, not too unlike a typical morning after a night out in Berlin, and my hair was still crusted with fake blood. The convention took place in a huge hotel in the city center and the gamers had taken over the whole building. I had arranged an hour-long interview with Johanna Koljonen, a longtime larp designer who was responsible for building the consent mechanics for *End of the Line*. I told her about my night and about my revelatory experience of being both player and character, and she smiled as if she'd heard it a thousand times from other noobs before.

I asked Koljonen about the political stakes of designing game worlds today. She explained what it means to design experiences that "suit the participant" in a humane way. "The minute you're creating a world to suit the participant," she said, "you have to treat the participants as humans, and there has to be a social contract." In most games, this contract is left "implicit," but the aim of her work is to "demand a negotiation of social contract" on the explicit level. Her goal is to slowly transform the toxicity that often results from anonymity and a lack of constraints into mutual accountability, by making obvious the connections between real world and game world. She said she believes narrative games—"whether digital, analog, or board games"—that explicitly take on "agency and power dynamics and complexity" are "extremely suitable for our age."

Koljonen is not shy about the potential here. "We realized that designing a fictional culture is the exact same skill set as designing a functioning real-world community." If you know the basics of how consent feels in your body, for example, it might help you navigate a global economy reliant on mass coercion. Seen in this way, larping is basic training not just for particular kinds of intimacy, but for civic engagement.

I asked her about how this kind of engagement could be imported into, say, the art world. Koljonen pointed out that traditions of participatory practice in gaming and art have been entwined since the happenings and new age sensory experiments of the 1960s, and continued to cross over and mingle since the advent of the internet. In her view, relational art and participatory gaming express a similar need to modulate the feedback loop between simulated and real sociality that contemporary power structures make so opaque. Fictional worlds *are* worlds that can either reproduce or alter the real world that's there once you leave the game, take off the headset. But in the worlds of art this reciprocal, causal relationship between the work produced and the well-being of the people producing it is typically disregarded or ignored.

Larp designers, with their megatools for social engineering, are in demand for everything from mass-market entertainment endeavors to corporate and military training. The U.S. military has, by some reports, spent hundreds of millions of dollars on what can only be called highly advanced larps to simulate combat scenarios. Koljonen admitted that there may be a rift emerging between the larpers who want to lend their skills to, say, the military or to Disney's ambitious new *Star Wars*–themed larp park and those who feel they should keep their hard-earned knowledge away from arenas where interaction design is focused on profit. Indeed, it is unlikely that the principles of consent-based engagement can scale up. Creating safety mechanisms, training players with scripts—this is not easily made a commercially viable endeavor. Trying to mass-market it will probably produce Fifty Shades of middlebrow larp lite.

After talking with Koljonen, I watched a vampire-tooth fitting take place and then wandered into a hall where Mark Rein-Hagen, the creator of the original Vampire: The Masquerade game, was answering questions from adoring fans. And who did I see sitting in the last row nearest the door but the Russian.

He gestured for me to sit next to him and politely struck up a conversation. He said he had enjoyed his scene with me the night before and asked me about myself in real life. My face got hot and I started to sweat. I could still feel the mark he'd left on my cheek, a raised welt. I felt ashamed, and then angry at him. I didn't *know* him. That wasn't *me*. I did not want to be seen in the light of day by this person. The only reason I'd been able to submit to the game (to him) was my reasonable certainty that the magic circle would remain sealed off from my real life. I was not a person who faked BDSM in a costume.

So I told him the version of the truth that kept me safe: that I was a writer hoping to publish something about the convention. He looked puzzled. Then he looked upset. So you aren't a gamer? I shook my head. No. I never do this, I've never done this before. I won't be going to any of the other larps this weekend, either. Actually, I'd better go right now.

Later, when I described the conversation to Susan, she laughed and said that I had broken up with my larp boyfriend. Classic, she said. I hadn't learned to manage my bleed.

Bleed

Bleed is the name given by larpers to the crossover between player and character. Your real-life experience bleeds into the game, and what happens in the game likewise bleeds back into your real life. Players will inject themselves into their characters, and the experience of being in character will inform their senses of self. This is one reason the pregame workshop and the postgame debrief time are important, to ease the transition from one role to another, to remind you that they are separate while respecting the validity of both.

Even outside of vampire games, there is something erotic about the concept of bleed. Trying on different roles is one of love's "tactics of imagination," to borrow a phrase from Anne Carson: tactics aimed at resolving the "edge between two images that cannot merge into a single focus because they do not derive from the same level of reality—one is actual, one is possible. To know both, keeping the difference visible, is the subterfuge called eros." To know that you are both a player and character is to know that others are, too; to negotiate between these selves, allowing the actual and possible to coexist while not merging into a single focus, is an act of bravery, if not an act of love. Acknowledging bleed is acknowledging the possibility of taking on infinite roles, without fearing loss of self among them.

Every larper knows that bleed is inevitable. The game happens in life, not outside of life. And while game bleed can cause problems when unmanaged, the experience of bleed—the blurring of the line between the narrative of your life and the narrative of the game—is the most exciting part. I return often to that moment on my knees, waiting for an intimate stranger to slap me hard enough to leave a mark. I imagine all the weird things that were happening to the other seventy people in that space at that very moment, and the many small but concentric magic circles that encompass all the roles I'll play in my whole life. I am still painfully embarrassed; I have written many versions of this essay that leave out the slap, but without the slap there is no story.

That the self bleeds is a particular kind of realization, something you can know abstractly but which I, anyway, have had few opportunities to feel. I have otherwise felt it only when mortally terrified or in love or both. When held for too long, this state of multiplicity becomes quickly unbearable, and if so, pathologized; suddenly you have dissociative identity disorder or belong to some other DSM category. And beyond pathology, contemporary systems of capture and control have a vested interest in making sure your character is pinned to your player. Your real name is fixed to your social media profile; your phone reports your whereabouts to the credit card company; once you're on a flight watch list you probably won't be removed. In mass society you are constituted by your identifying characteristics and your target demographic. For this reason games may be a condition for resisting the imperative to be singular. Games are also a condition for learning forms of intimacy outside prescribed social roles.

The intimacy required for love is often thought of as mutual recognition: I see you for who you are and you see me back. But recognition is also inevitably a naming, a fixing, a pinning down. In order to recognize, you have to categorize. The writer Jan Verwoert describes the slippage between love-as-recognition and love-as-control in an essay called "Masters and Servants or Lovers: On Love as a Way to *Not* Recognize the Other." Verwoert explains that intimacy cuts both ways:

> To love the other, we believe, is the most intimate way to recognize the other, to get to know and understand who he or she really is ... But this is what power is about as well when it

manifests itself in structures of domination. Modern regimes of power are built on the intimate knowledge of who the people are they dominate. Surveillance, espionage and market research are techniques of recognition that help to identify, understand and control the other—be that the citizen, the enemy or the consumer . . . Consequently, [a] radical love would be a love that goes *beyond recognition*, that is a love in which the lovers would renounce their desire to fully grasp the identity of the other and no longer insist on understanding who the other is.

You can die in a larp. From my *End of the Line* notes I find that "a couple of characters died during the game, with one person playing a corpse in the closet for at least thirty minutes at the end of the night." To sink into death in a closet and then be reborn into a room full of blood-smeared strangers who are thrilled to see you again. We should all be so lucky.

A Book Explodes

The best reading is an uncertain reading . . . We are educated to think that we should be able to know the meaning of a piece of writing, but what if the intention of the writing is to throw us into confusion, induce a state of wonder, and unravel the basic tenets of our experience?

—ROBERT GLÜCK

Hate: a romance

A breakup caused my novel. The relationship was a short, relatively unserious one in the scheme of things, but my heartbreak when it suddenly collapsed was way out of proportion with that unseriousness and brevity. I could not manage to explain what had happened between us—even the simple fact of who had done the breaking up—and, most upsettingly, I could not figure out how to assign blame. The heartbreak felt uncannily inevitable, as if there had been no way for us to act besides our prescribed roles, as though we were playing bit parts in a story we had not chosen to write. For this reason the failure of the relationship stank of much bigger failures on the level of society. I was determined to solve the mystery of what had happened and why. Could we have done things differently?

I set about to solve the mystery through puppetry. I started to write a story. I arranged two characters a little like us in a city like ours in a reality that resembled the reality we were in: mid-2010s Berlin. I exaggerated or embellished the details of our lives, swapped our biographical details, invented a cast around us—a mash-up of friends and acquaintances—and tweaked some aspects of the cityscape. My main intervention into reality was the installation of an artificial mountain on the airfield of Berlin's well-known Tempelhof Airport (a proposal some real architects had dreamed up years before). I installed the couple in a house in an ecovillage on the side of the mountain. These divergences from the factual world helped me look at the constellation askance, from an angle.

The only fact I stole wholesale from my ex's life was the sudden death of his mother. This tragedy had, in life, been the catalyst for the breakup, if not exactly the cause. When I started writing, I didn't expect the story to be published, so I tried not to feel guilty about stealing this fact, which was after all crucial to my investigation. More to the point, I assured myself that there was nothing wrong with stealing for art. During our relationship, my ex and I had once argued about whether or not taking someone's life as fodder for a book was an OK thing to do. He had given me a book by Tristan Garcia called *Hate: A Romance* (strangely translated from the original French title *La meilleure part des hommes*, or The

Best Part of Men). One character in the novel is reportedly based nearly exactly on a person who explicitly requested that Garcia *not* novelize his life. Although he loved the book, my ex thought that Garcia was in the wrong. I also loved the book, and I disagreed. I did not think stealing was inherently immoral, and plus, it was validated by how good the book was. (Secretly, I hoped that someday my career would consist of stealing life for books, too.)

Anyway. The more I tried to get the characters in the story to enact the behavior that would lead to their relationship's demise, the more I found myself spiraling outward to describe their entire world. How else could I show how death had infiltrated their lives and ruined their capacity to connect with each other? How else could I dissect the woman's overempathizing and intense projection of her own fears onto the man's grief? How else could I find out how to distribute fault? To get there I surely needed to first describe a whole society where, for instance, there are no grief rituals to handle death; everyone is in their twenties and thirties and has no intergenerational ties; awareness of climate change forecloses the future imaginary; gentrification is destroying the capacity for creative freedom (which extends to the creativity required for love); everyone feels like they are subversive while role-playing the gender dynamics and social hierarchies they've inherited; charity is the only clear expression of empathy; and so on.

I got carried away by the world-building. I told myself that the relationship was still the nexus of the story, its reason for being, but each time I got close to the lovers I found myself zooming out and inventing some new corporate scheme or technological development or subplot. Eventually a friend suggested that, the validity of world-building aside, I was maybe trying to distract myself from the thing I still didn't want to look at: that wound at the center of it all. I had started writing the story to make myself deal with the inexplicable sadness of death and heartbreak, and still hadn't dealt with it. Worse, two years into writing a full-length novel, I hadn't allowed myself any closure for those old feelings, because I was still picking at the wound.

Anyone who's experienced any kind of grief knows that closure is a dumb myth. Pain might diminish, forgiveness and forgetfulness might be achieved, but there is no explanation, justification, or solution for loss. The more I wrote the novel the more I approached the realization that it would not lead me out of the traps I was investigating. I could only expect it to help me articulate the nature of entrapment. In the articulation, though, I found that I gained the company of my characters, who became private allies—trapped in the same way as I was. In the event that my articulation were to be published, I might gain the company of readers, too. We would all be trapped together. This might sound grim, but to me it felt utopian.

I started over. This time I followed the couple and gave them the autonomy to grieve and suffer and struggle and argue, although it hurt me to do this to them. I pretended I didn't know what was going to happen in their lives and tried to discover it along with them. To some extent I *didn't* know what was going to happen, and I stumbled upon several surprises. But the lovers in the book still broke up in the end. When I got to the last page I did not feel anything like closure. Unexpectedly, it felt more like an opening. A separate world now existed where many things might go the same way, but other things might go differently.

Xenogenesis

The main character of the novel, unlike me, is a scientist. She is employed by a biotech think tank, where she studies self-replicating cells that are programmed to multiply in particular patterns on command. But she does not work with the real, organic cells; she examines how they behave in a computer simulation. She runs the simulation again and again to predict how the cells will behave. She has no reason to believe the simulation will not accurately predict the real behavior of the cells—but there is always that infinitesimal chance that they will not follow their preprogrammed course, that the simulation will turn out to have been faulty. She can't help but suspect that there is a mysterious element that cannot be accounted for in advance.

This might be a decent metaphor for writing a novel. Even for those writers who have every paragraph outlined before they begin (not me), there remains a tiny element of the unknown when you set the simulation in motion. You can only create the conditions for something to happen, and plan for that thing to happen, but you can't ever be completely sure—unless you write the whole fucking book. You have to carry out the experiment.

In the process of running my experiment, I wrote a lot of plotlines and backstories that never made it into the final version of the novel. I still have trouble remembering which were included in the published book, because they're all equally real to me. This is to say I am aware there are infinite possible versions of the book. In my mind—or somewhere?—the simulation keeps running.

Around the time I finished a draft and was working on edits, my friend Susan Ploetz invited me take part in a larp she was developing. Her larp was based on some elements of Octavia E. Butler's Xenogenesis novel trilogy, which explores human-alien interspecies sex and breeding, in an allegory for the power dynamics of colonialism. I had only read the first book, and most of the players hadn't read any of the Butler trilogy, so the larp could not be strictly based on the novels. Susan had plucked a few strands from the novels and spun them into a new scenario entirely of her—our—own making.

We started early on a cold morning in an empty artist studio in the north of Berlin. There were around ten of us, some friends and some strangers. Susan told us the basics and sketched in parts of the books: we lived in a world where humans were slowly being hybridized with aliens who wanted to overtake the Earth, and we had to decide whether we would fight against or consent to interbreeding, which would mean losing the "purity" of our humanness. She let us invent our own characters, get to know one another, and debate the issue for the first couple hours. But the second phase of the larp was mostly nonverbal. We enacted a touching ritual in groups of threes, practicing a form of non-human, nonsexual intercourse.

Not only was I uncomfortable and embarrassed by much of the experience, especially the part where I was touching strangers,

I was initially unsettled by how far we were straying from the plotlines of Butler's stories. As a person in the process of writing a novel, I had taken for granted that novels were supposed to be manufactured inside one's head, sealed and delivered to a reader to receive and swallow whole. But when I thought about it in terms of my own story, it seemed entirely logical to enter the simulation Butler had set in motion and take it somewhere new. On one hand, according to my own philosophy, once books are in the world they are part of life—which means they are available for stealing, just like everything else. On the other hand, I acknowledge that there are different kinds of stealing: for instance, stealing with attribution versus without attribution, stealing for play versus stealing for profit, stealing from above versus stealing from below. Appropriation is tricky work.

But what about stealing from myself? Immediately I had the urge to try to steal from my own story. The more I considered the possibilities, the more endless the options became. I could have players invent their own characters within the world of the story. I could have people swap all my characters' identity markers; I could have players larp the story before reading the book and then again after reading it; I could run a larp to come up with an idea for a new book; I could record the characters' dialogue and then import that material into the book; I could write a book about real people and then have them play themselves, or one another. I could make an unknown, independent version of the book by handing it over as raw material to a group and leaving. The book could mutate beyond the wildest dreams of its author.

Static objects

Like a larp, a book is supposed to be a kind of magic circle, a covenant that requires mutual suspension of disbelief, but in its standard form it has only two participants. Author and reader. The author's thought process might be elaborated through interviews and paratexts, and turned into serials or adapted for other media; there is also a tradition of books being cowritten, or anonymously written, or sourced from oral histories. Fan fiction is one clear counterexample to single authorship, with fandom producing its own crowdsourced multiverses. Some authors revise and rewrite forever, republishing updated versions. And translation between languages is an act of rewriting. But in general, and even in most of these cases, the book has a writer with an implied reader, consumption goes in one direction, and everything that happens in the book happens *in the book*. It is hermetic; it contains itself.

The author Francesco Pacifico describes a ten-year period in which, through "a mix of chance, poor luck, and my utter boredom with the workings of book publishing" he ended up translating his own novel *Class* (2014) from Italian to English, and then reverse-translating the English back into a revised version of the original Italian. He says this process was cumbersome and excruciating, but also enlightening and revitalizing. It forced him to confront his own characters and story again and again—also, his own attitude toward the book, and what novels can and should do. For instance, after round three of revision he says he found at the heart of the book an unresolvable tension between empathy and satire—the first version was satirical to the point of cruelty, the second version was injected with too much empathy to try to temper the satire, and the third was somewhere in between. He does not claim to have found a balance, but instead an acceptance of the elusiveness of the balance. Treating the book as a malleable object offered him a wealth of insight into the lives of the characters, and pointed him toward the kinds of stories he wanted, or felt responsible, to write.

Pacifico: "I asked myself why what I was doing was such a rare occurrence. If all that bounty can be found inside one's own book, why isn't self-revision a more common practice?" Directors make director's cuts. Bands remaster old albums. Visual artists can endlessly modify, reinstall, and recontextualize their artworks. "I'm overwhelmed," Pacifico says in reference to visual artists, "by the sense of kinship I feel wandering around these artists' exploded inner landscapes." Yet once a novel is done it presents itself as the only way it could have been.

Pacifico suggests that this is primarily due to the mechanics of the publishing industry with its roots in the industrial revolution. The conventional novel provides a microcosmic view of everyday life that can conceivably be replicated on a mass scale through industrial uniformity. A commercial novel can feel uniquely tailored to you while reassuring you that you are a recognizable member of a group or a generation. New books are constantly being produced to match the pace of change. Pacifico believes that "this is what explains the desperation in publishing to move on to a new and different product, to the next thing. There is no possibility of reworking one's own work because there is new work that must be produced." Each novel should be a world-containing entity that stands for the rest of the world, and each new book must immediately be made historic by adding another new book to the top of the pile. Like other art forms, books could be explosions with fragments and shrapnel and detritus, but the explosion has been tamped down by the commercial production of discrete objects.

The drug

When I had finished the first draft of my book, I applied for a monthlong residency in Vilnius, Lithuania, with the proposal that I run a larp based on the novel while there. Susan offered to join me for a week and design the explosion with me. I considered that the larp might be useful for the editorial process—maybe the players would show me unexpected ways that the characters could act, or inspire some new dialogue. Maybe they would even reroute the story and give me a better ending. A happy ending! But more than any functional goal, I simply desired to give the novel a life outside myself, an unruly form. Rather than fan fiction or translation or any other method of revivifying my text, a larp explicitly distributes authorship among multiple players. The story could become rhizomatic and multiple and simultaneous in a way I could never conjure alone.

Stories are not games, and after two weeks of trying by myself I realized that a direct translation from book to larp would be impossible. We weren't going to be able to get people to act out the plot—that was not the point. Susan arrived and together we decided that all the world-building would take place during the workshop before the game: I would first explain the setting of the book, the ideas that were important to me, and the questions I had asked myself while writing it. We would give each player—eight people signed up—a simplified character description approximating the book's characters, with a set of motives and desires. Then we would pretty much let them take it from there.

We decided to utilize the two separate spaces of the game area (a café/bar/art space/restaurant in central Vilnius called Autarkia) to simulate two different life modes of the book: day and night. Upstairs would be work life; downstairs would be nightlife. Susan and I were the game masters (GMs)—a somewhat outdated term that nonetheless gets across the basic idea that we were in charge of running the workshops and game and making sure play kept moving.

We also decided to both take on non-player characters (NPCs). An NPC is like a film extra: a person whose presence is needed in the game but who is not a fully fledged character with a crucial role. As NPCs, our roles were to be corporate representatives of the notorious Finster Corporation, whose dealings were responsible for everything happening in the game/city. We intervened in gameplay regularly by sending emails (passing notes) to characters, giving them secret information or assigning them tasks from their employers. Players were told they could interact with us if they needed information but were instructed not to pull us into the story. It made sense that corporate overlords would be both GMs and non-player participants, like the corporate overlords of the real world, who are typically exempt from the rules of the world they create.

In this particular fiction, one central aspect of the plot is the invention of a drug that induces generosity in the user. The drug is meant to unlock the empathic potential of the selfish creative class by giving them a rewarding feeling upon giving away money or possessions, eventually spreading to a broader scale, with the aim of mass wealth redistribution. In the book, this has unforeseen consequences—as it did in the larp.

In the book, one character is responsible for the invention and distribution of the pill. In the larp, several characters got together to communally decide what to do with the newly invented drug (which Susan and I had introduced in the form of Tic Tacs partway through the game). About two hours into the play, we were in the midst of a nighttime party sequence. An authentic soundtrack of music that Susan and I had gleaned from many memorable Berlin club nights was pounding. We had rigged up some colored lights and a makeshift bar. As GM/NPC, I was working undercover as a bartender, spying for the Finster Corporation to see how the drug was acting on the crowd. Two of my characters leaned across the bar and started a casual conversation with me; they offered me a drink, which seemed harmless enough to accept.

When I took a sip, I saw the Tic Tac at the bottom of the red plastic cup.

I suppose I could have declined to participate, or claimed that in my role I was immune to the influence of the substance. I could have refused to break the fourth wall and stayed on the edge of the game. But where's the fun in that? They had given me, the author of a story about a cruel world they were inhabiting, the pill that I had invented. It was perfect.

In accordance with the rules of the game, I became compelled to empathize with the subjects formerly under my control. By drugging me the characters overthrew not only the corporate overlords of the story but the game itself. Soon after, I lost the reins of the gameplay and the "night" spiraled into a dance party. The experience of being folded into a game that I was supposed to be the master of pushed me to consider the possibility that writing a story in which a nefarious shadowy corporation is authoring reality is to re-create a system of control. It made me consider that single authorship might often risk replicating the top-down systems that make the real world so unbearable—unbearable to the point that we often treat writing and reading novels as catharsis.

Hyperstition

During the Q&A at my first book launch, after the book was packaged and published, a friend of mine said that she found my book to be an odd hybrid of nineteenth-century social comedy centered on a woman's romantic drama and masculine systems novel. In retrospect, I have come to understand it in exactly this way: as an attempt at androgynous storytelling that forces individual human feelings into narrative collision with those "background" systems bigger than them. I wanted the thoughts, feelings, and bodies of the characters to mingle, coalesce, and reciprocally influence the financial, political, and climate elements of their world. I wanted the people and corporations and weather to function as an ecosystem, where sometimes individuals were driving the action, sometimes the systems were the protagonists, and sometimes the cause and effect were impossible to discern. I wanted figure and ground to merge or flip, with the goal being neither to exacerbate nor to diminish the importance of the characters' feelings.

I did not drastically alter the structure of the book when editing the manuscript after the larp. The story still seemed like a world-machine that I could not intervene in so much as decide how to portray. And the most crucial event that occurred in the book occurred in the larp, too. The couple split up, and for similar reasons. She could not handle the way he could not handle his feelings, and she gave him no room to do so on his own.

In the larp, I watched the couple fight and break up on the dance floor of the nightclub. There I was; there we were. It was me through a double distortion, fictionalized and then brought to life in another body. In the breakup they confirmed, again, the inevitability of something. Throughout the larp I consistently felt the presence of infinite possible scenarios—the multiverse—but at that moment when the universes coincided, when the couple succumbed to the same forces as my ex and I had, I felt an incredible synchrony and sense of time collapsing. In that moment I also realized the extent to which a desire for atonement had driven my urge to write a book. Like Pacifico, I found neither absolution nor indictment in reliving my own story. Just as there would be no closure, there would be no moral resolution.

In order to illustrate the ways that novels can't help but explode, however people might want to contain them, Pacifico explains an instance of spillover from his fiction into his own life. The couple at the center of his endlessly revised novel in question was based on two acquaintances from his life who were not dating. Years after writing the book, he ran into the two of them in a bar together—and saw that they were now a couple. He had somehow manifested their relationship, or presaged it, or simply recognized it in the making. "This is what writing books is about!" he exclaims. "This is the black magic that is going on."

Once my own book was published I, too, experienced a proliferation of magic. People whose personalities had seeped into character identities began to do things the characters did; I read about an iPhone app for calculating social capital nearly identical to a satirical app I had described in the book; I heard a rumor (which I never followed up on) that a pharmaceutical company in Portugal was manufacturing a pill that made users more financially generous. I met the architects who designed that fake mountain proposal in Berlin and learned that their initial design sketches had included many of the elements I had invented for the version in the book.

Perhaps strangest of all, I somehow conjured a job for myself. I was invited to be a researcher at a think tank, just as my main character was, and the language of my contract held many similarities to hers. The way the think tank functioned was at times indistinguishable from the way my simulated version did. In the first chapters of the book, the main character is fired from being a researcher and rehired as a corporate consultant; a similar thing happened to most of the researchers at the real think tank where I worked. I can only agree with Pacifico when he writes that "writing books is so much creepier than readers know."

Just as games bleed into life as life bleeds into games, novels exist as part of the world that they pretend to encapsulate and then hermetically travel within. In terms of science fiction or speculative fiction, much has been said about the ability for fiction to predict reality, or in some instances for reality to steal and implement ideas from fiction—even fiction that was meant to critique said reality. I try not to dwell on the mechanisms by which a story (my story) seeps into reality because I know they are not likely straightforward or directional. They are creepier than I can ever know.

Biodiversity

I had been thinking of books as ecosystems in themselves, but it was not until mine was circulating in the world that I understood how books enter into and alter existing ecosystems, too. Wai Chee Dimock writes that

> literary history has yet to be seen as a mediating network of this sort: imperfect and incessant. Seen that way, as a nonsovereign field weakly durable because continually crowdsourced, it offers one of the best examples of redress as an incremental process, never finished because never without new input. Mindful that the world isn't what it should be and rarely able to effect a definitive cure, it always has room for one more try.

Dimock describes the inevitable explosion of books in terms of contagion, an especially appropriate concept for the pandemic era. In her book *Weak Planet*, she proposes that literature creates "contagious sites in globalized ecosystems" that can turn "shared vulnerabilities into shared plenitude." Literary history and the existing body of literature could be "taken as an ecosystem with weakly defended borders, and with adaptive variants." This "turns literary history into a history of nonsolitary acts. Discrete texts give way here to input-bearing networks, collective DNA culled across space and time. Such collective DNA, still under threat but newly connected and recombined, does seem to have a shot at the future." The literary canon that depends on books sold as prepackaged goods is only one history, after all.

Dimock likens the comingling of literary works (beyond the preserved and canonized and historicized kinds) to the maintenance of biodiversity. And if you look at literary history in another way you'll find exploded books all over the place. Books that are stolen and translated and bootlegged and gamified. This is a much more resilient and extinction-proof model for thinking about how literature lives in the world than the dominant one in which a novel sits passively on a bookshelf, opened and closed. The writer J. R. Carpenter, whose practice includes making books, digital poetry, and zines, told me she thinks of the zine as "the cockroach of the medium"—cockroaches being the species that is most likely to survive nuclear fallout.

I'm not delusional enough to claim that a novel is going to explode the value systems, politics, economics, and forms of knowledge that have produced the extinction era, nor that literature will not go extinct if humans do. But on good days I do think that fiction—which might not come in the form of a novel at all—works:

as in, it performs a type of labor in service of change, for better or for worse. Its effects are not linear, one-to-one, or necessarily calculable, and should not be measured as such. No cause-and-effect equation can account for them. Fictions are myriad small explosions with far-reaching fragments.

Explosion is one way to think about what can happen to books. But I often think about it in other terms: as a process of composting. The essays contained in this book have been decomposed again and again, recycled and used as soil for new seeds, new ideas. Some of them started as talks or pieces of journalism. Others started as midnight emails to friends. I wrote and rewrote them over the course of two years, often starting from scratch after reading a new book or having a new conversation. Most of the texts have become recombinant, with related ideas cropping up like sprouts across them. Nothing here is static or dead. Long after this becomes a book they will continue to dissolve and evolve, with or without me.

EPILOGUE

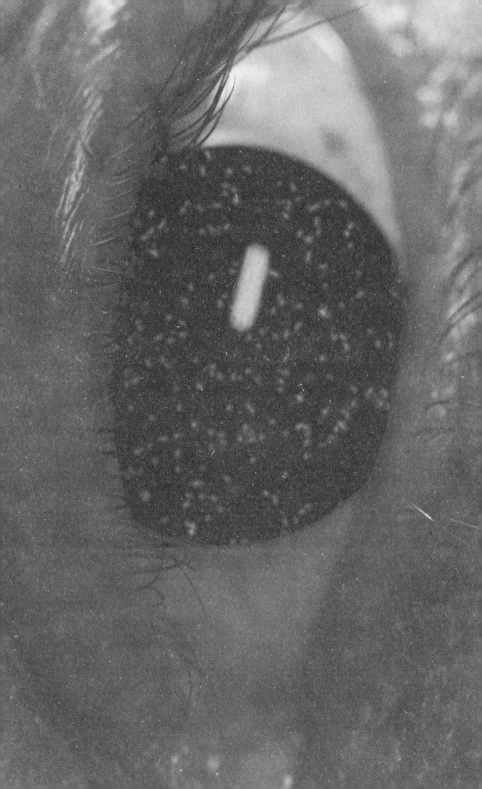

The Queen of Reps

On Spaceship Earth

AN INFLUENCER I FOLLOW on Instagram posts female-focused self-help content about boundaries and expectations during lockdown. She says it's OK not to be productive during this unprecedented time. She says we should be kind and forgiving to our bodies. She says we should be wary of wasting our energy. She posts up to thirty times a day. I look at every single upload, clinging to the reassurance even as I loathe the basicness. I eat it up like butter—butter, a formerly unhealthy ingredient that scientists recently deemed healthy after all. I'm jealous of this influencer, this person who seems to have a definitive idea of what life's healthy ingredients are.

Day 50-something or 60-something of lockdown in Brooklyn. I wake up and look at Instagram. I hardly notice the sound of constant sirens outside anymore. My partner, A, is probably in the kitchen chopping or cleaning, or maybe he's having coffee and reading a book on the fire escape. I roll out of bed and head straight to my computer, where I spend several hours trying to concentrate on pumping out words. Eventually there is lunch, after which there is the dishes, after which I do a workout video in front of my computer.

Remember your breath, yogis, the on-screen instructor with calves like onion bulbs says. He's talking to the group of people doing the workout with him in the prerecorded video but he's also talking to me, implicitly. Which makes me a yogi, too, implicitly. My fellow yogis in the video are a diverse bunch, "all shapes and sizes."

This isn't really yoga. It's some yoga postures as a preamble to three circuits of crunches and squats. As a grand finale we go through the asanas while holding five-pound weights. I watch the yogis in the video wincing and grunting. *Just four more! You got this.* I notice one of the yogis cheating; she's only doing every other rep. I wonder when this video was recorded. It must have been in a time and place where people were allowed to be in the same room together. This makes me wistful, but then I remember that I prefer to work out alone anyway. I don't want anyone to see me wincing and grunting or skipping reps. I don't want a witness to my work.

My work ethic is a major problem. This is the big lesson of quarantine. I have no structuring principle for how to spend my time besides work. Without any life events outside the domestic vacuum, the problem has become unavoidable. The issue is not simply that I've filled the hole left by social and professional routine with extreme working hours instead of something nice. It's not even that work is the only way I know how to cope. It's that my productivity itself has lost its telos. I can no longer figure out what I'm working *toward*. The future is a blank space; it always has been; once you understand this, your ordering principle falls apart.

I have no muscles that have developed through play or the immediate need to survive—just countable reps. I write a certain number of words today; I answer a certain number of emails today; I do a certain number of lunges. I lunge—"a sudden thrust forward of the body," as if to seize prey—and then I retract without grasping anything in my jaws. Just the lunge and the act of lunging. A certain number of lunges. A certain number of calories. A certain number of recreation hours. And then the day is over.

A is very productive, too. He gets work done. Only he doesn't seem to exalt it as his ordering principle for being alive. Taking a day off can be nice for him; the meaning of life does not disintegrate as soon as the disciplinary structure is removed. He doesn't panic as I do when interrupted at the desk, because you can't interrupt something that isn't sacred. Free time does not provoke an existential spiral. For me, anything that isn't quantifiable productivity can only be construed as procrastination. There's no "life" that is not a means to an end of —?

Over dinner, which we have tacitly decided is a meal I do not eat while sitting at the computer, A and I have conversations about the meaning of work and why we do it. Lockdown has given us all this time to talk about how we spend our time. I maintain that there is work and then there is *work*—there is the thing capitalism makes me do to feed myself, and then there is the thing I do because it gives my life meaning. I'm a writer; my work is meaning-making, so often these overlap. But I have to believe I'd do the latter kind of work no matter what. Of course, as soon as I say these things, the distinction between types of work dissolves into a sea of reality-TV-style Right Reasons questions.

Would you truly work if you didn't have to? How do you differentiate between the work that is sacred and the work that is profane? Is any work sacred under neoliberal capitalism? Is there such a thing as a labor of love that has not been recuperated? Where did you get this Protestant work ethic?—you're a Jew. What's really the driving factor, artistic expression or desperation for recognition? Couldn't you find meaning in something less excruciating? What would happen if you took a day off? Why, and what, are you always counting? Where is pleasure? Are you squashing all the pleasure out of something that you really do want to do, just by dint of counting it in the form of reps? If it's what you want to be doing, why does it feel and look so much like punishment?

One night after dinner we watch my favorite childhood movie, *The Princess Bride*. In one scene, the princess's true love, Westley, is being tortured by the princess's evil husband in a dedicated underground chamber. Westley is laid out on a rack called the Machine, a device with special suction cups that suck out future years of the victim's life, causing excruciating pain. The Machine whirs and Westley writhes on the table, while the torturer observes his responses dispassionately and takes notes. "I've just sucked one year of your life away," the torturer informs Westley after the first bout is over. "What did this do to you?" he asks earnestly. "Tell me. And remember, this is for posterity."

I've always identified with the torturer as much as Westley. The torturer is a sadist, but he is also a scientist who has spent his entire life inventing this evil device, and he genuinely wants to quantify what it does. Posterity is an inside joke with myself: When I'm really struggling to get something done, I tell myself, "Remember, this is for posterity." So I take a quick look at Instagram and then I prostrate myself upon the Machine.

———

One way to make sure I've done my reps for the day is to keep lists of all my tasks. Everything goes on the same list because everything has to get done. Shower, eat, write a friend, write a colleague, talk about my feelings, call my dad, write an email, write an essay, write a diary, write a new list of tasks.

Something on my list that is not work, but that is on the same list and so has become ontologically flattened into work, is to record a video message for my friend's birthday. Given the quarantine situation, her kind husband has invited almost a hundred people to upload pictures and videos to an app where she'll be able to watch them on her birthday. It's possible to see what other people have uploaded so far. Before recording a video, I watch some of the other video messages. One of our mutual friends has made a lovely one: she's sitting in a bathtub and extolling the virtues of the birthday girl, whom she dubs the Queen of Pleasure. I smile. It's true! This friend is wonderfully adept at enjoying life. She knows how to live in a body in time, how to maximize joy as its own end, and I dearly love this about her. I get emotional thinking about friends I haven't seen in so long, who are all Queens of something. The Queen of Finding the Hilarious. The Queen of

Even Keel. The Queen of Gathering Us Together. The Queen of Optimism and Ambition. I must be a Queen of some kind, too, I think. What Queen am I? The Queen of Time Management. The Queen of Third Draft of an Essay. It is I, the Queen of Reps.

Joy in a certain type of work must be a timeless thing. At least it was timeless, before work was stolen from us, so maybe it's not timeless after all. I mean the kind of work that is about the perpetuation of life. Reaping the hay, feeding the family, reproducing ourselves and one another. Tending the garden. Taking care. That is not the kind of work that is easily countable as reps, although people—such as my influencer—have found many ways to commodify it. Women were made to do most of the labor of life for the last few centuries, so maybe there is a reason I dislike uncountable care work, favoring the numerable kind with accolades.

My mom, a professor at a big Midwestern university, says that her greatest challenge is teaching undergraduates that learning doesn't have to be a miserable chore. She wants them to understand that work is not the opposite of entertainment. She wants them to experience joy in reading, writing, and thinking instead of feeling like that's what you have to get done so you can go to the movies or a kegger. But then, my mom also complains that she puts so much energy into teaching, unlike her male colleagues, and that her teaching work is never fully appreciated.

———

I take a break from writing this to look at Instagram. My influencer has just made a video where she describes herself proudly as "really crushing it" during lockdown. She says we need to give ourselves credit when we're doing well. I tap through to a series where she asks people to post their "smallest wins" of the day. *Think of your smallest win today, then think of something even smaller.*

What does it mean to win? She doesn't say. The implication, I assume, is that life might be a rat race but that we're only truly in competition with ourselves. Winning at life is nothing glamorous—it's just about getting better in small ways every day. Getting better means being healthier and less miserable? Still, the concept of winning seems to counter what it describes, since you can't actually beat yourself unless you are also beaten.

My small win today is my only win today, because I don't know any other concept of winning: I worked and then I worked out, even though I didn't want to. But then I see that lots of the small wins people are posting in response to the influencer's story are things like taking a shower and eating a healthy bowl of organic grain. So winning, or at least small winning, is about not working? It's about self-care? I'm confused.

Instagram-style self-care is for the rich and white, and even the influencer is woke enough to know that. Self-care is something you pay for. It's reproductive labor you do for yourself, because you don't have to do reproductive labor for anyone else instead. But if I stopped looking at Instagram I *would* have time to take a shower. I'm a well-off white woman and my boyfriend is making me dinner in our nice apartment from the groceries we paid to have delivered. Maybe I could construe *not* taking care of myself as an act of resistance?

I used to fantasize that I was Kurt Vonnegut whenever I worked on fiction. He was my favorite author, whose strict writing schedule is well-known. He took reps very seriously because he was concerned with posterity. But then I read his biography and I had a hard time maintaining the fantasy. Turns out the reason he was able to lock himself in the study and clack away on his typewriter for several hours every morning is that his wife was making food and taking care of his children and answering his letters. During his sanctified writing hours, nobody, not his wife, not his three biological children, nor his three adopted children—whom *he* chose to adopt—was allowed to knock on the door.

A often brings me snacks while I'm at the computer. He might kiss my cheek, but he doesn't say anything because he knows I get agitated when interrupted. I reach blindly for the carrot stick he's placed beside me. I realize he's done the dishes and swept the house while I've been emailing. I worry that I'm winning at being Kurt Vonnegut.

———

One of my friends used to have a shitty boyfriend who always insinuated that she was lazy for not working enough. "It's true," she told me. "It's not like I work very much. But I'm making enough money to live on. So what's the problem? I don't get it. I thought *not* working was *what we were working for.*"

———

I've had an undefined autoimmune issue for at least ten years. A few weeks before the pandemic hit I got yet another diagnosis. The verdict: I have lazy lungs and I haven't been getting enough oxygen this whole time. In January a doctor gave me an asthma inhaler, an allergy pill, and a few nasal sprays, and within weeks my debilitating pain and fatigue became miraculously, infuriatingly, confusingly, suddenly manageable. Ironic: while the world is ailing and my city is dying, I have more energy than ever before. I marvel at the extent of my newfound ability, my changing limits. My max five reps become ten become twenty. I always wondered what I'd do if I were suddenly able, and here I am, #blessed with this energy and this privilege, this time . . .

———

When I was in my final year of art school, depressed and trying to finish my thesis exhibition, I called my dad to complain about how everyone seemed to be doing less work than I was but making better art. I spent most of my time in my windowless studio agonizing and doodling; outside, the Good Artists were chain-smoking and chatting. I'd make a hundred drawings or whatever, but invariably their work would be cleverer and much cooler. "Well, honey," my dad told me, "some people are geniuses, and the rest of us just have to work harder."

One of my teachers required all her students to spend forty hours in the studio each week. She'd clearly read that Malcolm Gladwell book. Just show up, she impressed upon us, even if you don't have any ideas, because that's the only way something will happen. You have to be there when the inspiration hits. The more you sit there trying to work, the more you'll eventually get done—a variant of the classic "ass-in-chair" writing advice. Or a variant of the motivational gym poster: "10% inspiration, 90% perspiration."

Some of my classmates were probably geniuses. Others managed to parlay the genius myth to their advantage. Others were just rich or from famous families, so it didn't matter. Others were ahead of me in a different way: they understood that creative work also happens when your ass is not in the chair and they saw no purpose in self-punishment. And others were probably working as hard as I was and just not making such a big deal out of it. They realized that artists are not supposed to *look* like we're toiling this hard. Our labor is supposed to be mysterious exceptional labor, in service of making exceptional timeless objects, etc.

In retrospect, I'm guessing we all felt bad about how much we were working or not working. In retrospect, it's obvious that the ten-thousand-hours rule is just another weapon for individualizing our pain. We're millennials and artists; we always knew meritocracy is a farce. But we never figured out how to redeem ourselves beyond work, and we experience our feelings of failure in isolation. We don't know how much we're supposed to work, how much we're supposed to *seem* like we work, how much we're supposed to enjoy work. "Do what you love" is an even more insidious farce than meritocracy. We experience our small wins and our big losses alone. Hoarding them, then belittling them. Nothing we can do is enough but trying this hard is both pointless and embarrassing.

———

I read a report about the climate. It says even now, in the midst of COVID, when travel is at a record low, the results are not nearly enough to make a dent in the catastrophically upward-sloping temperature trajectory graph. And in fact, in some freak turn of events, the global temperature is maybe going to rise this year, because of a decrease in the layer of pollution surrounding the planet, which, despite its toxicity, has actually been helping Earth cool off.

A asks if I want to go with him to the community garden to drop off some compost. We have to take it to the garden now because the city has suspended organic waste collection in order to spend more money paying police to harass unhoused people sleeping on the subway. I shake my head and tell A I want to stay home to write. I tell him I'm writing in my diary, so it sounds like a healthy activity, but actually it's an article about climate change that I hope gets published and I get paid for. After he leaves the house, I spend an hour wondering whether going to the community garden is a better use of time than sitting inside and writing about the importance of community gardens. My ordering principle short-circuits. I take another shower and have a glass of wine. I win.

———

The documentary *Spaceship Earth* comes out two months into quarantine. It's about one of my favorite historical utopias,

Biosphere 2. In the 1960s, a group of performance artists and counterculture enthusiasts got together and started the Theater of All Possibilities, an art-theater-business venture that would last decades. Funded by a billionaire oil magnate, they first built a ship and traveled the world, buying land, constructing a hotel, holding performances, and documenting themselves. Their collective work culminated in the 1987–1991 creation of Biosphere 2, a giant glass structure in the Arizona desert. The biosphere contained a closed-loop life-support system, which eight people lived inside for two years.

Biosphere 2, resembling a geodesic dome crossed with a Victorian greenhouse, was equal parts performance art, science fiction, and science project. To create its internal ecosystem, the Biosphereans first traveled the world collecting plant and animal species they chose to populate their world in captivity. Once inside the biosphere they subsisted (almost) off farmed food and recycled air and water, a feat intended as the first-ever dress rehearsal for a sustainable human habitat in space. They also intended it as a consciousness-raising stunt to spread awareness about the environmental devastation that might someday force humanity off-world—Biosphere 1 being the original planet Earth.

I am guest teaching a master's class on Zoom about storytelling in times of crisis. The students have seen *Spaceship Earth*, so we talk about Biosphere 2. I ask leading questions about whether the documentary gives a balanced portrait of the project and its political flaws—for instance, its colonial and biblical undertones. I ask whether anyone feels nostalgic for an imaginary past when utopian thinking seemed possible, at least for some. One of the students points out that it's hard to have nostalgia for a past where the future was eight white people in a dome filled with exotic species they stole from around the world.

As an assignment, I've asked the students to briefly describe a future scenario where the world is still in quarantine, but things are different. Not better or worse, just different. A basic science fiction exercise to think beyond the utopia/dystopia binary. It seems like most of them have not done the assignment. They have reacted negatively to its implications. The gist of the reaction is: *How could you ask us to imagine a future? Who do you think has access to the future? You think we get to decide what's going to happen? Why should we lend our imaginations to the people in command?* I can see their faces frowning in the little boxes on the screen. I can't blame them.

I think about my yoga workout videos, about the pointedly diverse bunch of yogis selected to be in each class. I imagine a yoga class in a biosphere. I imagine my living room is full of the plant and animal species of the world, ones I specially handpicked for my quarantine zone. I imagine there are no plant or animal species left in the world except for the ones I have preserved. I wonder whether there could be an anti-colonial/decolonial biosphere. I wonder whether imagination can be totally uncoupled from prediction, and whether future thinking is always going to be in the service of power, or whether it's possible to imagine a future in a way that can't be instrumentalized. *Welcome, yogis.*

One person brings up her favorite moment from the *Spaceship Earth* documentary: when one of the Biosphereans calls her therapist from inside the dome. Frozen inside her insular, fake-natural world, she casts a line outside—she makes contact with Biosphere 1, to ask for psychiatric support. It's funny, because I've also described that same scene to my own therapist. I've told my therapist that ever since she and I have had to stop meeting in person, I feel like we're living in different biodomes. I've spent several sessions with her talking about the pandemic and climate change and Biosphere 2.

In one session, I ask her whether I talk about politics too much in therapy. She says that in classical psychology, too much talk of politics is supposed to be interpreted as an avoidance tactic. But she has come to believe that *not* mentioning politics in therapy is the real avoidance tactic, especially right now. How could we pretend there is an inside without an outside? How could the global not be the personal, the geopolitical not be the psychological? How could the pandemic that has changed time and the future not change my time and my future and vice versa?

After they survived for two years, the Biosphereans left their habitat. Steve Bannon bought the whole complex in the interest of profit-driven research. The Theater of All Possibilities was never allowed back.

———

Sometimes I take a tiny break from work and go into the other room, the only other room, and say hi to A. A little visit. One day I ask him if he's sick of his room. Maybe he wants to switch rooms with me?

Of course I'm sick of this room, he says. Are you sick of your room, too? Yes, I say, but I'm sick of both rooms. I'm sick of *room*.

We know we need to get out of the house. We rent a car and drive to the beach, to the Rockaways. The shore is cold and windy on the day we've chosen, but it's gloriously empty. The sunlight is yellow in the early afternoon and the pale water dissolves into pale sky where there should be a horizon line. A reads a book and I sit a few feet away, scooping sand with my feet and chatting on the phone with a friend in California (even though I feel like I should be reading, too, because reading a certain number of pages counts as a certain number of reps).

My friend in California tells me that he started quarantining even earlier than most of us, because he had a normal flu and didn't want anyone else to catch it—a concept that seems like it should be the norm now that we know it's possible to just stay home rather than go to work when sick—and he's feeling pretty good about isolation. He attributes his decent mental health to the fact that he limits his computer time each day, holding back his urge for constant updates.

"I was treating my desk like a command center," he says. "Every few hours I would feel the need to sit down, buckle in, and get all the news. Like I could get some control if I knew what was going on. But *I'm* not in command of *anything*."

I laugh, because I know exactly what he means. But then as soon as we hang up, I pull out my phone and look up the most recent death statistics.

Spaceship Earth was a concept made popular in the 1960s by Buckminster Fuller. It encompasses the idea that Earth is our only survival system and that we are all its crew. We have to work together to pilot the thing—to stay alive. If the metaphor holds today, who is in the command center? It is certainly not I, the Queen of Reps. But if work is not my ordering principle, how will I manage to stay in command of anything at all?

Today, some of the Biosphereans still work together on a farm in New Mexico called Synergia Ranch. The last shot of the documentary *Spaceship Earth* shows them drinking wine together around a table on the ranch at twilight, laughing and maybe reminiscing. I'm jealous of their ability to reminisce about something. I wonder how they're doing now.

———

What a luxury it is to live in this apartment and have all this time to toil with my mind. I wouldn't be able to spend my time this way had I not had that costly education, the network based on privilege. Posterity is an incentive, but so is the obligation I feel to maximize this silly luck. I keep looking for "good" things to spend my work ethic on.

Because of the autoimmune factor, less on the surface now but still underlying as far as conditions go, I'm not supposed to go places full of people or touch surfaces, even with a mask on. That means that any *work* I can do with altruism in mind involves more time on the Machine. I accept that the only way we're going to abolish a system where people are forced to risk their lives to go to work is for people like me to do work, so here we go.

Some evenings I join a Zoom meeting run by an organization that assists asylum seekers in filling out immigration applications, and I spend a few hours doing reps on behalf of someone else. I

listen to the testimony of an asylum seeker who's endured un-
speakable things and I wonder what she thinks of the concept of
the future.

Another day I make a countable number of phone calls to elderly people in my neighborhood to ask if they need help and not
a single person says yes; I donate a hundred dollars to a bail fund;
I sign a petition for canceling rent. A and I volunteer to teach a
Zoom class to kids who are stuck at home and need edutainment.
We plan a forty-minute class about climate change, waste, and
composting and teach it repeatedly to groups of K–5 kids. Most
sessions are full of ten or fifteen students, but due to some glitch
in the sign-up system, our final class is attended by only one student. She's a six-year-old named Dorothy and she's very shy.

Dorothy's dad keeps trying to get her to sit still in front of
the screen, plying her with snacks and promises of playtime afterward, but he seems harried. While we're teaching, we can see
him in the background doing the dishes with another small child
slung around his hip. We feel like keeping Dorothy occupied for
a little while is the least we can do. But when we get to the part
of the lesson on composting, we ask Dorothy whether she knows
what global warming is. She bursts into tears and ducks under the
table. I can't blame her.

———

A magazine asks me to write a short piece in response to Italo
Calvino's *Six Memos for the New Millennium*, a series of texts
Calvino wrote in the 1980s about the qualities he believes are

unique to literature and which will carry us through the next millennium. My assignment is to write about his first memo on "Lightness," in which he says you can't write about this heavy world with a heavy hand; you have to treat the gnarly stuff with delicacy and wit.

I find this six-hundred-word assignment excruciatingly difficult to write. I try to explain the importance of lightness, but every word is an anvil. I want to learn this lesson from Calvino, I really do. But I've never known how to do anything besides to try harder, hit harder, keep lunging. I sit and stare at the Machine and tell myself to unclench my teeth.

I used to live with a certified genius writer who would come home after a party and stay up late to write an essay flashing with brilliance that would be published within a few weeks to great acclaim, all while I was working 8:00 a.m. to 8:00 p.m. in the next room on a single infuriating text that went nowhere. We all know someone like this, but no one thinks of oneself as that kind of person. Is that person "lightness"?

Sometimes I get angry with myself for not being able to produce words and A gets frustrated with me, too. He asks whether I really have to work until I have nothing left. He lists my accomplishments. He says he loves my writing but that I can't be reduced to what I produce. He says I have intrinsic value as a human being.

I nod, but I don't know what the hell he's talking about. I don't have low self-worth. I'm just not sure I exist. I have to do some mark-making as evidence. But you *have* evidence, he tells me, and points to himself.

A friend sends me a quote from Ingeborg Bachmann's book *Malina*. "I don't think about growing old, just about one unknown woman who follows another unknown woman . . . I don't know myself any better at all, I have not grown any closer to myself. I have only watched one unknown woman slide further and further into another."

Of course, from the perspective of posterity, Ingeborg Bachmann is not an unknown woman. She wrote that book.

———

I try to take a rest when I start to feel overwhelmed. That's what the influencer recommends: *You don't have to be burned out to take care of your body.* But when I pause the reps an old problem starts up again. I get incredibly drowsy and fall into a deep sleep. It feels like I have no choice, like I'm drugged and dragged under consciousness level. It doesn't matter how much I've slept the night before or how tired I feel. Whenever I decide to stop working, I pass out.

My therapist says this sounds like a traumatic stress response. She suggests I listen to a radio interview with Laurie Anderson, in which Anderson talks about being in a terrible plane crash. I listen to the interview. Anderson says she didn't stop flying after the crash, but when she gets on a plane now, she becomes catatonic. She'll get in her seat and be fine before takeoff, but as soon as the engine revs up her whole body goes slack and she sinks into a coma-like trance. "My mind shut down," she says of the last time this happened. "My mind protected me from being there anymore."

After I listen to the radio interview, I ask my therapist what the meaning of life is. She says she is not going to give me an answer, not because she doesn't have some ideas, but because I'm so desperate for someone to tell me that I'll lunge at whatever she gives me and never let go.

———

When I was sick I had an excuse for needing to rest; when I had a social life I had an excuse to take a break; without these premises I realize the flimsiness of those stopgaps, and the ridiculous impoverishment of a life in which everything not work is a procrastination tactic or an excuse.

I return to my influencer, who I need to believe really does want the best for me. She agrees that I have to put my ass in the chair if I'm going to be really crushing it during quarantine. But if I *really* want to crush it, I also have to get my ass *out* of the chair and do five hundred reps and then drink a gallon of water, set healthy boundaries for my relationships, and forgive myself for everything I've ever done.

———

My parents are competitive people. They have the same job as each other—they're academics in similar fields—which means there is always a measuring stick handy. Work is undoubtedly the family ordering principle and we do not give much credence to small wins. Technically my dad is retired now but he still writes an article or reads someone's dissertation or gives a lecture every day. Once I asked him what the meaning of life is and he told me *learning and curiosity*, which I think is laudable and true but which I think is only part of the truth, given the family emphasis on recognition and accomplishments. Life is about the work of meaning-making itself but it's also about someone noticing that we're doing all this work.

When I call my mom at a given moment and ask how she's doing, the first thing she usually says is a variant of "Oh, you know, buried under work." Buried is how she's doing. It's the only way to do. She and my dad are often working on topics related to ethics and social justice, so there is a moral imperative justifying this work being done. But for my mom, there is an extra moral component because she's a woman and it was a battle to get where she is, so her success is its own justification. I inherited the em-battled feeling of that second wave, even though the battle itself isn't exactly mine.

The belief that work will be there for me even if all else falls apart is also part of my inheritance. After every breakup or rejec-tion I call my mom in tears in order to receive her reliable instruc-tion to *work through it*. She tells me to write about my feelings and to channel my energy into other projects. I must not give up, I must process and parse the mess, I must harvest meaning from it, I must find my way back to myself through laboring by myself. I must gain recognition elsewhere to remind me that I exist, even when there is no lover to assure me. And she's right: work always works. Work will always take me back.

———

I write half a short story about a group of office workers living in outer space. There's nothing glorious about their situation; they're just working way more remotely than the rest of us remote workers. They're employed by a software company that has sent a portion of its workforce to space in perpetuity, basically as a publicity stunt. The employees-cum-astronauts have agreed to the arrangement just because having an office in space is more interesting than a regular office.

I send the story to my writing group, which meets weekly instead of monthly now, because we're all stuck at home, so we have time to show up. The group seems unsure whether the premise of the story is sound. They are not convinced whether it's plausible that people would sacrifice their whole lives to live in space with their colleagues without a very good reason. The group has a point. There's a reason I haven't been able to finish the story. Characters are supposed to have motives: as Vonnegut says, "Every character should want something, even if it is only a glass of water." One person in the group says the story is an interesting take on quarantine, but that she doesn't think millennials are interested in outer space. Why would they be, when we're all living in Biosphere 3?

———

One of my art teachers in college sympathized with my inability to leave the studio until I made something *good* (with no criteria for what that would be). He said the problem was that I couldn't get out of my own head enough to let things flow. He said I was too worried about what *people would think*. He passed on a piece of advice, advice that John Cage once gave to Philip Guston:

> When you start working, everybody is in your studio—the past, your friends, enemies, the art world, and above all, your own ideas—all are there. But as you continue, they start leaving one by one, and you are left completely alone. Then, if you're lucky, even you leave.

I get the lesson: it takes a lot of time to learn to rid oneself of other people's opinions and voices and create something that isn't about pleasing anyone or getting attention. The lesson is that a true artist makes work for no one else but—no one? Posterity? The lesson is that good work comes from within. I used to find this a helpful image, but now it creeps me out. Who is this person with no body behind her? One unknown woman slides further and further into another . . .

I don't think the influencer has the same goal as John Cage or Philip Guston. She wants someone to be looking over her shoulder at all times. And here I am, hungrily looking over her shoulder. One day she posts a quote that says: *We don't need to come out of quarantine skinny, we just need to come out alive.* I nod. I'm grateful for this post. I really do not feel like doing any lunges or squats right now. I should rest and unplug . . . I should step away from the Machine . . . I should indulge in some organic grains . . . This is me, listening to my body and being kind to myself . . . This is what it must be like to know what the ingredients for a good life are ... the right way to cope ... Then I flip to her next post. It says: *There's no right way to cope.*

What is *cope*? Is it the same as *exist*? To exist, you need an ordering principle, similar to what the influencer calls priorities. Here are some priorities—work, money, posterity, love, self-care, saving the world, fun. However: If I don't have time to do all these priorities before dinner, I'm going to have to figure out how to rank them, that is, how to prioritize. But this is impossible because all of them are necessary to be a person who exists.

Incredibly, some days I feel like I almost get the balance right. Giddy: I've done enough work of all kinds, real and recreational. I've attended to all the priorities. This is what winning feels like! The healthy butter! On those days of success, I fantasize about going on vacation. Maybe I've earned a holiday!

The allure of vacation is slightly different during the pandemic; it might also be a misplaced desire for a time when everything around us wasn't dying. But when the fantasy hits, it hits hard. I just have to say the word *vacation* to A to get us going.

Sunburn, he says.

Fruit, I say.

Hot, overripe, fruit.

Fruit that we eat from each other's hands.

Swimming.

Reading all day and falling asleep in the sun.

Lemon trees. Sweat.

We smile. Then one of us points out that we have everything

we need and that missing vacation because of the pandemic is really a very pathetic thing to complain about.

For me, the fantasy has always been the point anyway. The possibility of exit. In truth vacation scares me, because on vacation, time slides toward death without any notches to help a person keep a grip. One feels a moral imperative to not work on vacation that can be very oppressive. What if one gets an idea? What if one feels the need to make a mark on life while everyone else is playing boccie? What if one wants to play boccie and realizes one never wants to go back to work? One gets so drowsy in the heat.

———

An artist friend of mine is having difficulty being productive. We talk on the phone about how stagnated we feel, no matter how much time we put in. She also has the added distraction of motherhood, because she had a baby last year. Do you think you could ever be happy if you stopped doing work completely to just be a mom? I ask her. Of course, she says, and I'd love it. But I'd have to kill myself.

———

When I was very young, I believed that all my thoughts were being recorded somewhere in a giant book, and that when I died the book would be given to me to read in the afterlife. For this reason I tried to think in third person, past tense: *She looked across the yard and saw the dog lying under the tree* . . . *She didn't want to eat dinner but Dad said it was time to eat* . . . *She was sleepy that day* . . . *It seemed fun to her* . . . so that it would read like a story when it was all put together someday. I don't know where I got this idea, but I know I was very afraid of dying and that I could only imagine my own death if I knew my whole life would be safely preserved in a book.

At some point I realized nobody was going to write this book for me, and that any evidence of my existence is going to be of my own making. I realized I have no choice but to try to make it, even though it is never going to be as sublime as the book of all thoughts.

I, the Queen of Reps, sit at my desk cranking out words, take a break to kneel on the floor next to my desk and lift my leg a hundred times, then back to the desk to eat some calories that A lovingly puts within my reach. I take a shower and tell myself it is a small win. I walk from one room into the other room and back again. I search for a new ordering principle. I find none. I'm on a spaceship but I'm not in the command center. Is there a command center? Just another room. This very room. Luckily, *when I entered the room, A was there, backlit by sunshine with a book in one hand, his uncut quarantine hair spiraling into fresh curls, watering the plants* . . .

NOTES

Earlier versions of these essays appeared as:

"Death by Landscape," talk at the Serpentine Galleries, 2019, published as "Toward a Theory of the New Weird," *Literary Hub*, 2019

"This Compost," *Granta*, 2020

"The Word Made Fresh," *e-flux journal*, 2018

"What's Happening?" *Bookforum*, 2020

"Future Looks," published as "Is Ornamenting Solar Panels a Crime?" *Positions, e-flux architecture*, 2018

"Trauma Machine," *Popula*, 2018

"Ask Before You Bite," *e-flux journal*, 2019

"The Queen of Reps," *Los Angeles Review of Books*, 2020

Some ideas have been borrowed from:

"More than a Game," *frieze*, 2017

"The World of Yesterday," *The Baffler*, 2020

"All Systems Go," *Artforum*, 2021

SOURCES

Epigraphs

Dimock, Wai Chee. *Weak Planet: Literature and Assisted Survival.* Chicago: The University of Chicago Press, 2020.

Glück, Robert. *Communal Nude: Collected Essays.* South Pasadena, CA: Semiotext(e)/Active Agents, 2016.

1. Plants

DEATH BY LANDSCAPE

Atwood, Margaret. "Death by Landscape." *Harper's Magazine,* August 1990.

Baldwin, James. "Nothing Personal." *Contributions in Black Studies* 6 ([1964] 2008).

Coccia, Emanuele. *The Life of Plants: A Metaphysics of Mixture.* Cambridge, U.K.: Polity, 2018.

Davis, Erik. "The Digital Weird talks: Sanneke Huisman, Jan Robert Leegte and Rebecca Edwards in conversation with Erik Davis." arebyte X LIMA, July 14, 2021. Video.

Davis, Erik. *High Weirdness: Drugs, Esoterica, and Visionary Experience in the Seventies.* Cambridge, MA: The MIT Press, 2019.

Fisher, Mark. *The Weird and the Eerie.* London: Repeater Books, 2016.

Ghosh, Amitav. *The Great Derangement: Climate Change and the Unthinkable.* Chicago: The University of Chicago Press, 2016.

Hildyard, Daisy. *The Second Body.* London: Fitzcarraldo Editions, 2018.

Kang, Han. "The Fruit of My Woman." Translated by Deborah Smith. *Granta*, January 19, 2016.

Kang, Han. *The Vegetarian.* London: Hogarth, 2016.

Koja, Kathe. "The Neglected Garden." *The Magazine of Fantasy & Science Fiction* 80, no. 4 (April 1991).

LeClair, Tom. *In the Loop: Don DeLillo and the Systems Novel.* Champaign: University of Illinois Press, 1987.

Lovecraft, H. P. "The Call of Cthulhu." *Weird Tales* 11, no. 2 (February 1928).

Naimon, David. "Marlon James: Black Leopard, Red Wolf." *Between the Covers*, March 4, 2019. Podcast.

Phillips, Helen. *The Need.* New York: Simon & Schuster, 2019.

Powers, Richard. *The Overstory.* New York: W. W. Norton & Company, 2018.

Richter, Anne. "The Sleep of Plants." In *Sisters of the Revolution: A Feminist Speculative Fiction Anthology,* edited by Ann and Jeff VanderMeer. Oakland: PM Press, 2015.

Shaviro, Steven. "Hyperbolic Futures: Speculative Finance and Speculative Fiction." *The Cascadia Subduction Zone* 1, no. 2 (April 2011).

Sperling, Alison. "Towards a 'Weird Modernism': Lovecraft's Embodied Temporalities." Paper presented at Weird Fiction, Weird Methods panel at the Modern Language Association Convention, Vancouver, British Columbia, January 11, 2015.

Sullivan, Tricia. *Occupy Me*. London: Gollancz, 2017.

VanderMeer, Ann, and Jeff VanderMeer, eds. *The New Weird*. San Francisco: Tachyon Publications, 2008.

VanderMeer, Jeff. *Annihilation*. Southern Reach trilogy. New York: Farrar, Straus and Giroux, 2014.

Wark, McKenzie. "On the Obsolescence of the Bourgeois Novel in the Anthropocene." *Verso* (blog), August 16, 2017.

THIS COMPOST

Badiou, Alain, and Nicolas Truong. *In Praise of Love*. Translated by Peter Bush. New York: The New Press, 2012.

Boyle, Alan. "Study says pollution makes birds gay." NBC News, December 2, 2010.

Carson, Anne. *Eros the Bittersweet*. London: Dalkey Archive Press, 1998.

Coccia, Emanuele. *The Life of Plants: A Metaphysics of Mixture*. Cambridge, U.K.: Polity, 2018.

Edelman, Lee. *No Future: Queer Theory and the Death Drive*. Series Q. Durham, NC: Duke University Press, 2004.

Ehrenreich, Barbara, and Deirdre English. *Witches, Midwives & Nurses: A History of Women Healers*. New York: The Feminist Press, 1973.

Federici, Silvia. *Caliban and the Witch: Women, the Body, and Primitive Accumulation*. New York: Autonomedia, 2004.

Haraway, Donna. "Situated Knowledges: The Science Question in Feminism and the Privilege of Partial Perspective." *Feminist Studies* 14, no. 3 (Autumn 1988).

Ho, Rosemarie. "Want to Dismantle Capitalism? Abolish the Family." Interview with Sophie Lewis. *The Nation*, May 16, 2019.

Hval, Jenny. *Paradise Rot*. Translated by Marjam Idriss. London: Verso, 2018.

Hyde, Lewis. *The Gift: How the Creative Spirit Transforms the World*. New York: Vintage Books, 2019.

Laboria Cuboniks. *The Xenofeminist Manifesto: A Politics for Alienation*. London: Verso, 2018.

Lagalisse, Erica. *Occult Features of Anarchism: With Attention to the Conspiracy of Kings and the Conspiracy of the Peoples*. Oakland: PM Press, 2019.

Lewis, Sophie. *Full Surrogacy Now: Feminism Against Family*. London: Verso, 2019.

Moshfegh, Ottessa. "How to Shit." *The Masters Review Blog*, October 19, 2015.

Pollock, Anne. "Queering Endocrine Disruption." In *Object-Oriented Feminism*, edited by Katherine Behar. Minneapolis: University of Minnesota Press, 2016.

Preciado, Paul B. "Anal Terror: Notes on the First Days of the Sexual Revolution." Epilogue to *El deseo homosexual* (Melusina, 2009), Geoffroy Huard de la Marre's Spanish translation of Guy Hocquenghem's *Homosexual Desire*. Translated and published by the editors of *Bædan 3—journal of queer time travel*. Seattle: Contagion Press, 2015.

Preciado, Paul B. *Testo Junkie: Sex, Drugs, and Biopolitics in the Pharmacopornographic Era*. Translated by Bruce Benderson. New York: The Feminist Press, 2013.

Russell, Karen. "The Bad Graft." In *Orange World and Other Stories*. New York: Alfred A. Knopf, 2019.

Sappho. Fragment 130. In *Eros the Bittersweet*, by Anne Carson. London: Dalkey Archive Press, 1998.

Singh, Pooja. "Gay by mercury: Water contamination may alter white ibises' hormones." *Down to Earth*, January 15, 2011.

Whitman, Walt. "This Compost!" In *Leaves of Grass: Comprehensive Reader's Edition*. Edited by Harold W. Blodgett and Sculley Bradley. New York: New York University Press, 1965.

THE PLANTS ARE WATCHING

Allado-McDowell, K. *Pharmako-AI*. London: Ignota Books, 2021.

Backster, Cleve. *Primary Perception: Biocommunication with Plants, Living Foods, and Human Cells*. Anza, CA: White Rose Millennium Press, 2003.

Butcher, Daisy, ed. *Evil Roots: Killer Tales of the Botanical Gothic*. British Library Tales of the Weird series. London: British Library Publishing, 2020.

Castro, Teresa. "The Mediated Plant." *e-flux journal* 102 (September 2019).

Coccia, Emanuele. *The Life of Plants: A Metaphysics of Mixture*. Cambridge, U.K.: Polity, 2018.

Janisse, Kier-La. "Murder Season: The Strange World of Vegetal Detecting." *byNWR*, vol. 5, June–August 2019.

Kapil, Bhanu. "Pinky Agarwalia: Biography of a Child Saint in Ten Parts." Introduction to *Unknown Language*. London: Ignota Books, 2020.

McNeile, H. C. "The Green Death." *The Strand Magazine* 60 (July–December 1920).

Merritt, Abraham. "The Woman of the Wood." *Weird Tales* 8, no. 2 (August 1926).

Moshfegh, Ottessa. *Death in Her Hands*. New York: Penguin Press, 2020.

Power, Kevin. "Ottessa Moshfegh's 'Death in Her Hands' Is a New Kind of Murder Mystery." *The New Yorker*, June 23, 2020.

Pryce, Charlotte. *Pwdre Ser: the rot of stars*. 2018. 16mm film transferred to digital, sound.

Sarno, Jonathan, dir. *The Kirlian Witness*. Hollywood: Paramount Pictures, 1979.

Tompkins, Peter, and Christopher Bird. *The Secret Life of Plants*. New York: Harper & Row, 1973.

Tsing, Anna. "More-than-Human Sociality: A Call for Critical Description." In *Anthropology and Nature*, edited by Kirsten Hastrup. Routledge Studies in Anthropology. London: Routledge, 2014.

THE WORD MADE FRESH

Allison, Leslie. "The Ecstasy and the Empathy." *BLOCK*, no. 4, 2018.

Angela of Foligno. *The Book of Divine Consolation of the Blessed Angela of Foligno*. Translated by Mary G. Steegmann. London: Chatto and Windus; New York: Duffield & Co., 1909.

Bennett, Jane. *Vibrant Matter: A Political Ecology of Things.* Durham, NC: Duke University Press, 2010.

Bucke, Richard Maurice. *Cosmic Consciousness: A Study in the Evolution of the Human Mind.* Philadelphia: Innes & Sons, 1901.

Bynum, Caroline Walker. *Fragmentation and Redemption: Essays on Gender and the Human Body in Medieval Religion.* New York: Zone Books, 1992.

Carson, Anne. *Decreation: Poetry, Essays, Opera.* New York: Alfred A. Knopf, 2005.

Chun, Wendy Hui Kyong. "Algorithmic Authenticity." Lecture at The Proxy and Its Politics—On Evasive Objects in a Networked Age, Berlin, Germany, June 24, 2017.

Crichton-Browne, Sir James. *Cavendish Lectures on Dreamy Mental States.* London: Ballière, 1895.

de Beauvoir, Simone. *The Second Sex.* Translated by H. M. Parshley. New York: Vintage Books, 1989.

Dionysius the Areopagite. *Dionysius the Areopagite: The Mystical Theology and the Celestial Hierarchies.* Translated by the editors of The Shrine of Wisdom. Surrey, U.K.: Nr. Godalming, 1923.

Eckhart, Meister. *Meister Eckhart: The Essential Sermons, Commentaries, Treatises, and Defense.* Translated by Edmund Colledge, O.S.A., and Bernard McGinn. Classics of Western Spirituality. Mahwah, NJ: Paulist Press, 1981.

Haraway, Donna. "Situated Knowledges: The Science Question in Feminism and the Privilege of Partial Perspective." *Feminist Studies* 14, no. 3 (Autumn 1988).

Hartsock, Nancy C. M. "The Feminist Standpoint: Developing the Ground for a Specifically Feminist Historical Materialism." In *Feminism and Methodology*, edited by Sandra Harding. Bloomington: Indiana University Press, 1987.

Hollywood, Amy. *Acute Melancholia and Other Essays: Mysticism, History, and the Study of Religion*. New York: Columbia University Press, 2016.

Hollywood, Amy. Introduction to *The Cambridge Companion to Christian Mysticism*. Edited by Amy Hollywood and Patricia Z. Beckman. Cambridge Companions to Religion. New York: Cambridge University Press, 2012.

Hyde, Lewis. *The Gift: How the Creative Spirit Transforms the World*. New York: Vintage Books, 2019.

James, William. *The Varieties of Religious Experience*. New York: Modern Library, 1902.

Julian of Norwich. *Revelations of Divine Love*. Translated by Elizabeth Spearing. New York: Penguin Classics, 1998.

Julian of Norwich. *The Showings of Julian of Norwich*. Edited by Denise N. Baker. New York: W. W. Norton & Company, 2004.

Kraus, Chris. *Aliens & Anorexia*. Los Angeles: Smart Art Press, vol. VII, no. 66, 2000.

Laing, R. D. *The Divided Self: An Existential Study in Sanity and Madness*. London: Penguin Books, [1959] 1990.

McGinn, Bernard, ed. *The Essential Writings of Christian Mysticism*. New York: Modern Library, 2006.

Porete, Marguerite. *The Mirror of Simple Souls*. Translated by Edmund Colledge, O.S.A., J. C. Marler, and Judith Grant. Notre Dame, IN: Notre Dame Press, 1999.

Statt, Nick. "How Annihilation changed Jeff VanderMeer's weird novel into a new life-form." *The Verge*, February 28, 2018.

Thacker, Eugene. Lecture at the New School for Social Research, New York, January 30, 2018.

Thacker, Eugene. "Wayless Abyss: Mysticism, mediation and divine nothingness." *postmedieval* 3, no. 1 (Spring 2012).

Tompkins, David. "Weird Ecology: On the Southern Reach Trilogy." *Los Angeles Review of Books*, September 30, 2014.

VanderMeer, Jeff. *Annihilation*. Southern Reach trilogy. New York: Farrar, Straus and Giroux, 2014.

Weil, Simone. *Gravity and Grace*. Translated by Emma Crawford and Mario von der Ruhr. London and New York: Routledge, [1952] 2002.

2. Planets

WHAT'S HAPPENING?

Butler, Octavia E. *Parable of the Sower*. New York: Four Walls Eight Windows, 1993.

Dick, Philip K. *Do Androids Dream of Electric Sheep?* New York: Del Rey Books, 1996.

Easterling, Keller. *Extrastatecraft: The Power of Infrastructure Space*. London: Verso, 2014.

Gibson, William. *Agency*. Jackpot Trilogy. New York: Berkley Books, 2020.

Gibson, William. *The Peripheral*. Jackpot Trilogy. New York: Berkley Books, 2014.

Haraway, Donna. "Anthropocene, Capitalocene, Plantationo-cene, Chthulucene: Making Kin." *Environmental Humanities* 6, no. 1 (2015).

Hoban, Russell. *Riddley Walker: Expanded Edition*. Bloomington: Indiana University Press, [1980] 1998.

James, P. D. *The Children of Men*. New York: Alfred A. Knopf, 1993.

Jensen, Liz. *The Rapture*. New York: Doubleday, 2009.

Lessing, Doris. *The Memoirs of a Survivor*. London: Octagon Press, 1974.

Ma, Ling. *Severance*. New York: Farrar, Straus and Giroux, 2018.

Mandel, Emily St. John. *Station Eleven*. New York: Vintage Books, 2015.

McCarthy, Cormac. *The Road*. New York: Vintage Books, 2006.

Nixon, Rob. *Slow Violence and the Environmentalism of the Poor*. Cambridge, MA: Harvard University Press, 2011.

Riesman, Abraham. "William Gibson Has a Theory About Our Cultural Obsession With Dystopias." *Vulture*, August 1, 2017.

Robinson, Kim Stanley. *New York 2140*. New York: Orbit, 2018.

Russell, Karen. "How the Coronavirus Has Infected Our Vocabulary." *The New Yorker*, April 6, 2020.

Stephenson, Neal. *Seveneves*. New York: William Morrow, 2015.

Suvin, Darko. *Metamorphoses of Science Fiction: On the Poetics and History of a Literary Genre*. New Haven: Yale University Press, 1979.

FUTURE LOOKS

Ballard, J. G. Introduction to *Crash*. New York: Pinnacle Books, 1974.

Barber, Daniel Colucciello. "On Black Negativity, Or the Affirmation of Nothing: Jared Sexton, interviewed by Daniel Barber." *Society and Space*, September 18, 2017.

Blomkamp, Neill, dir. *District 9*. Culver City, CA: Sony Pictures, 2009.

Blomkamp, Neill, dir. *Elysium*. Culver City, CA: Sony Pictures, 2013.

Butti, Ken, and John Perlin. *A Golden Thread: 2500 Years of Solar Architecture and Technology*. New York: Van Nostrand Reinhold Company, 1980.

Clarke, Arthur C. "Peacetime Uses for V2." *Wireless World* 51, no. 2 (February 1945).

Dick, Philip K. *The Minority Report*. New York: Fantastic Universe, 1956.

Dunne, Anthony, and Fiona Raby. *Speculative Everything: Design, Fiction, and Social Dreaming*. Cambridge, MA: The MIT Press, 2013.

El Akkad, Omar. *American War*. New York: Alfred A. Knopf, 2017.

Evans, Claire L. "Interface Prophecies: Does Future Fact Depend on Present Fiction?" *uncube*, March 11, 2014.

Fezzioui, Naïma, et al. "The Traditional House with Horizontal Opening: A Trend towards Zero-energy House in the Hot, Dry Climates." *Energy Procedia* 96 (September 2016).

Fisher, Mark. *Capitalist Realism: Is There No Alternative?* Winchester, U.K.: Zer0 Books, 2009.

Fisher, Mark. *k-punk: The Collected and Unpublished Writings of Mark Fisher*. Edited by Darren Ambrose. London: Repeater Books, 2018.

Flynn, Adam. "Solarpunk: Notes toward a manifesto." *Hieroglyph*, September 4, 2014.

Ginsberg, Alexandra Daisy, James King, and University of Cambridge iGEM 2009 team. *E. chromi.* 2009. Embossed aluminum briefcase, foam, acrylic, printed vinyl, plastic models.

Graeber, David. "Of Flying Cars and the Declining Rate of Profit." *The Baffler*, no. 19 (March 2012).

Hudson, Andrew Dana. "On the Political Dimensions of Solarpunk." *Solarpunks*, October 14, 2015.

Kehe, Jason. "'Sci-Fi,' Dystopia, and Hope in the Age of Trump: A Fiction Roundtable." *Wired*, July 4, 2017.

Korody, Nicholas. "Mere Decorating." *e-flux architecture*, November 2017.

Lepore, Jill. "A Golden Age for Dystopian Fiction." *The New Yorker*, May 29, 2017.

Lodi-Ribeiro, Gerson, ed. *Solarpunk: Histórias Ecológicas e Fantásticas em um Mundo Sustentável*. São Paulo: Editora Draco, 2012.

missolivialouise. "Here's a thing I've had around in my head for a while!" Tumblr, 2014.

Owens, Connor. "What is Solarpunk?" *Solarpunk Anarchist*, May 27, 2016.

Pho, Diana M. "Politics in Steampunk—A Sampling (aka 'Why it Matters')." *Beyond Victoriana*, April 6, 2013.

Perschon, Mike Dieter. "The Steampunk Aesthetic: Technofantasies in a Neo-Victorian Retrofuture." PhD diss., University of Alberta, 2012.

Springett, Jay. "Solarpunk: A reference guide." *Solarpunks*, February 26, 2017.

Stephenson, Neal. "Innovation Starvation." *World Policy Journal* 28, no. 3 (Fall 2011).

Vale, V. Interview with Elvia Wilk. April 2017.

Valentine, Ben. "Solarpunk wants to save the world." *Hopes&Fears*, August 28, 2015.

Wallace-Wells, David. "William Gibson, The Art of Fiction No. 211." *The Paris Review*, no. 197 (Summer 2011).

Wilk, Elvia. "Unreality by Design: Interview with Dunne & Raby." *Afterall* 50 (Autumn/Winter 2020).

Woodbury, Mary. "Interview with Adam Flynn on Solarpunk." *Dragonfly.eco*, July 2, 2015.

A PLANET OF FEELING

Berlant, Lauren. "Feel Tank." *Counterpoints* 367 (2012).

Crimp, Douglas. "Mourning and Militancy." *October*, no. 51 (1989).

Freud, Sigmund. "Mourning and Melancholia." In Vol. XIV of *The Standard Edition of the Complete Psychological Works of Sigmund Freud*. Translated by James Strachey with Anna Freud, Alix Strachey, and Alan Tyson. London: The Hogarth Press, 1953–1974.

Fisher, Mark. *Capitalist Realism: Is There No Alternative?* Winchester, U.K.: Zer0 Books, 2009.

James, Robin. *Resilience & Melancholy: Pop Music, Feminism, Neoliberalism.* Winchester, U.K.: Zer0 Books, 2015.

Laing, Olivia. "*Black Wave* by Michelle Tea review—a rollicking apocalypse fantasy." *The Guardian*, February 11, 2017.

Robinson, Kim Stanley. "The Coronavirus Is Rewriting Our Imaginations." *The New Yorker*, May 1, 2020.

Ryan, Hugh. "The Apocalypse of Adulthood." *Los Angeles Review of Books*, October 13, 2016.

Taubin, Amy. "Lars von Trier's *Melancholia*." *Artforum* 50, no. 2 (October 2011).

Tea, Michelle. *Black Wave*. New York: The Feminist Press, 2016.

von Trier, Lars, dir. *Melancholia*. New York: Magnolia Pictures, 2011.

FUNHOLE

Bidart, Frank. "The Arc." In *The Book of the Body*. New York: Farrar, Straus and Giroux, 1977.

Carson, Anne. *Eros the Bittersweet*. London: Dalkey Archive Press, 1998.

Carson, Anne. "Variations on the Right to Remain Silent." *A Public Space*, no. 7 (2008).

Clarke, Jim. *Science Fiction and Catholicism: The Rise and Fall of the Robot Papacy*. Canterbury: Gylphi Limited, 2019.

Duras, Marguerite. *Practicalities*. New York: Grove Press, 1993.

Faulkner, William. *As I Lay Dying*. New York: Random House, 1964.

Fisher, Mark. *The Weird and the Eerie*. London: Repeater Books, 2016.

Fleischmann, T Clutch, and Torrey Peters. "T Clutch Fleischmann and Torrey Peters on trans essays." *Essay Daily*, January 4, 2016.

Koja, Kathe. *The Cipher*. New York: Dell, 1991.

Lethem, Jonathan. *As She Climbed Across the Table*. New York: Doubleday, 1997.

McCarthy, Tom. *Recessional—Or, the Time of the Hammer*. Zurich: Diaphanes, 2016.

McCarthy, Tom. *Typewriters, Bombs, Jellyfish: Essays*. New York: New York Review Books, 2017.

Sontag, Susan. *Against Interpretation and Other Essays*. New York: Farrar, Straus and Giroux, 1966.

Sontag, Susan. *Illness as Metaphor and AIDS and Its Metaphors*. New York: Anchor Books, [1978, 1989] 2001.

Wallace, Michele. "Variations on Negation and the Heresy of Black Feminist Creativity." *Heresies* 24 (1989).

3. Bleed

EXTINCTION BURST

Agrippa von Nettesheim, Heinrich Cornelius. *Three Books of Occult Philosophy*. London: Printed by R.W. for Gregory Moule, 1651.

Berlant, Lauren. *Cruel Optimism*. Durham, NC: Duke University Press, 2011.

Bernard of Clairvaux. *Bernard of Clairvaux: Selected Works*. Edited and translated by G. R. Evans. Classics of Western Spirituality. Mahwah, NJ: Paulist Press, 1987.

del Cossa, Francesco. *Griffoni Polyptych*. c. 1473/1474. Tempera on poplar panel. *The Rediscovery of a Masterpiece* at Palazzo Fava, May 18, 2020–February 15, 2021.

Ficino, Marsilio. *Platonic Theology*. Edited by James Hankins and William Bowen. Translated by Michael J. B. Allen and John Warden. Cambridge, MA: Harvard University Press, 2001.

Hollywood, Amy. *Acute Melancholia and Other Essays: Mysticism, History, and the Study of Religion*. New York: Columbia University Press, 2016.

Julian of Norwich. *Revelations of Divine Love*. Translated by Elizabeth Spearing. New York: Penguin Classics, 1998. As quoted in McGinn, *The Essential Writings of Christian Mysticism*.

Sedgwick, Eve Kosofsky. *Touching Feeling: Affect, Pedagogy, Performativity*. Series Q. Durham, NC: Duke University Press, 2003.

Thebaut, Nancy. "Bleeding Pages, Bleeding Bodies: A Gendered Reading of British Library MS Egerton 1821." *Medieval Feminist Forum* 45, no. 2 (2009).

van der Kolk, Bessel. *The Body Keeps the Score: Brain, Mind, and Body in the Healing of Trauma*. New York: Penguin Books, 2015.

von Bingen, Hildegard. "Hildegard von Bingen to St. Bernard of Clairvaux, 1147." In *The Personal Correspondence of Hildegard of Bingen*. Edited by Joseph L. Baird. Oxford: Oxford University Press, 2006.

von Bingen, Hildegard. *Scivias* I, i. In *Selected Writings*, translated by Mark Atherton. London: Penguin Classics, 2001.

TRAUMA MACHINE

Cioffi, Sandy. Interview with Elvia Wilk. December 11, 2017.

Cioffi, Sandy, dir. *Sweet Crude*. New York: Cinema Guild, 2009.

Conners, Daryle. Interview with Elvia Wilk. December 1, 2017.

Garling, Caleb. "Virtual Reality, Empathy and the Next Journalism." Interview with Nonny de la Peña. *Wired*, November 3, 2015.

Jamison, Leslie. "Authors of injustice." *Times Literary Supplement*, October 6, 2017.

Jamison, Leslie. *The Empathy Exams: Essays*. Minneapolis: Graywolf Press, 2014.

Kristof, Nicholas. "Refugees Who Could Be Us." *The New York Times*, September 4, 2015.

Lanier, Jaron. *Dawn of the New Everything : Encounters with Reality and Virtual Reality*. New York: Henry Holt & Company, 2017.

Milk, Chris. "How virtual reality can create the ultimate empathy machine." Filmed March 2015. TED Talk.

Smith, Stephen D. Interview with Elvia Wilk. December 6, 2017.

Sontag, Susan. *On Photography*. New York: Farrar, Straus and Giroux, 1977.

Sontag, Susan. *Regarding the Pain of Others*. New York: Farrar, Straus and Giroux, 2003.

Streep, Abe. "Crisis and Opportunity: How One VR Startup Is Capturing the 360-Degree Reality of the World's Most Vulnerable People." *Wired*, July 15, 2016.

Ticktin, Miriam. *Casualties of Care: Immigration and the Politics of Humanitarianism in France*. Berkeley: University of California Press, 2011.

Wilk, Elvia. "Rebel Architecture 3: Eyal Weizman: The Architecture of Violence." *uncube*, September 2, 2014.

ASK BEFORE YOU BITE

Alderson, Giles, dir. *World of Darkness*. 2017.

Carson, Anne. *Eros the Bittersweet*. London: Dalkey Archive Press, 1998.

Castronova, Edward. *Synthetic Worlds: The Business and Culture of Online Games*. Chicago: The University of Chicago Press, 2005.

Davis, Heather, and Paige Sarlin. "On the Risk of a New Relationality: An Interview with Lauren Berlant and Michael Hardt." *Reviews in Cultural Theory* 2.3 (2011).

Edland, Tor Kjetil, Margrete Raaum, and Trine Lise Lindahl. *Mad About the Boy*. Larp, first run in Norway, 2010.

Fatland, Erik, Irene Tanke, Jannicke Krogh, Attila Evang, Heidimarie Evensen, Cath Røsseland, Annika Evensen, Britta Bergersen. *Europa*. Larp, first run in Norway, 2001.

Grins, Aigars, Martin Ericsson, Gabriel Walldén, Christian Angerbjörn, Alexander Graff, Gabriel Sandberg, Joakim Skog, Christopher Sandberg. *Trenne Byar* (Three Villages). Larp, first run in Sweden, 1994.

Koljonen, Johanna. Interview with Elvia Wilk. Berlin. May 14, 2017.

"LARPing Saved My Life." *Vice*. Vice Media LLC, 2015.

Mustafa, Riad, Ureib Samad, and Mohamad Rabah. *So You Think You Can Dance?* Larp, first run in Palestine, 2013.

Pedersen, Bjarke, Juhana Pettersson, Martin Elricsson. *End of the Line*. White Wolf Publishing and Odyssé with Solmukohta and Inside Job Agency. Larp, first run in Finland, 2016.

Pettersson, Juhana, Mike Pohjola, Mikko Pervilä. *Luminescence*. Larp, first run in Finland, 2004.

Rydland, Asbjørn, Anne Isene, Margrete Raaum, Geir Carl-ström, Thomas Nes, Kristian Spilhaug, Espen Nodeland. *Once Upon a Time.* Larp, first run in Norway, 2005.

Sonne-Jørgensen, Michael. *We Are One.* Larp, first run at Black-box Cph VII in Denmark, 2018.

Stenros, Jaakko, and Markus Montola, eds. *Nordic Larp.* Stock-holm: Fëa Livia, 2010.

Tanke, Irene, Jared Elgvin, Erik Fatland, Kaisa Lindahl, Cath Røsseland, Espen Nodeland, Rune Haugen, Trine Lise Lindahl, and Erling Rognli. *PanoptiCorp.* Larp, first run in Norway, 2003.

van der Kolk, Bessel. *The Body Keeps the Score: Brain, Mind, and Body in the Healing of Trauma.* New York: Penguin Books, 2015.

Verwoert, Jan. "Masters and Servants or Lovers: On Love as a Way to *Not* Recognize the Other." In *Tell Me What You Want, What You Really, Really Want.* Berlin: Sternberg Press and Piet Zwart Institute, 2010.

A BOOK EXPLODES

Butler, Octavia E. *Xenogenesis.* New York: Guild America Books, 1989.

Dimock, Wai Chee. *Weak Planet: Literature and Assisted Survival.* Chicago: The University of Chicago Press, 2020.

Garcia, Tristan. *Hate : A Romance.* Translated by Marion Du-vert and Lorin Stein. New York: Farrar, Straus and Giroux, 2010.

Leuzzi, Tony. "Interview with Robert Glück." *EOAGH*, Spring 2009.

Mila Architects. "The Berg." Proposal for Tempelhof Airport, 2009.

Pacifico, Francesco. "American Dream." *n+1*, no. 37 (Spring 2020).

Pacifico, Francesco. *Class.* New York: Melville House, 2017.

Wilk, Elvia. *Oval.* New York: Soft Skull Press, 2019.

Epilogue

THE QUEEN OF REPS

Anderson, Laurie. *Fresh Air.* Interview by Terry Gross. November 19, 2015.

Bachmann, Ingeborg. *Malina.* Translated by Philip Boehm. New York: Holmes & Meier, [1971] 1990.

Calvino, Italo. *Six Memos for the Next Millennium.* Translated by Patrick Creagh. Cambridge, MA: Harvard University Press, 1988.

Guston, Philip. *It Is*, no. 5, (Spring 1960).

Fuller, Buckminster. *Operating Manual for Spaceship Earth.* Carbondale: Southern Illinois University Press, 1969.

Reiner, Rob, dir. *The Princess Bride.* Act III Communications, 1987.

Vonnegut, Kurt. "8 Rules for Writing." Preface to *Bagombo Snuff Box: Uncollected Short Fiction.* New York: G.P. Putnam's Sons, 1999.

Wolf, Matt, dir. *Spaceship Earth.* New York: RadicalMedia, 2020.

IMAGE PERMISSIONS

1. Plants: Raffard-Roussel, *Lives of grass*, 2010. Soil, wheat seeds, recycled metal, fabric, thread. Exhibition at the Invisible Dog Art Center. Courtesy of the artists.
2. Planets: Rachel Rose, still from *Enclosure*, 2019. Video installation presented on a holographic screen. Courtesy of the artist; Gladstone Gallery, New York and Brussels; and Pilar Corrias, London.
3. Bleed: Francesco del Cossa, *Saint Lucy*, c. 1473/1474. Tempera on poplar panel. Courtesy of the National Gallery of Art.
4. Epilogue: Jenna Sutela, still from *Holobiont*, 2018. Courtesy of the artist.

ACKNOWLEDGMENTS

Thanks to Yuka Igarashi for the incredible insight and care in shaping this project from start to finish. Thanks to Cynthia Cannell for supporting my writing life in its many forms.

Thanks to the wonderful Sarah Lyn Rogers for saving the day many times and, along with tracy danes, Samm Saxby, and everyone at Soft Skull, transforming an armful of essays into a book.

Thanks to Mathias Zeiske and the Haus der Kulturen der Welt for inviting me to hold an event about the new weird in 2019, during which several ideas were hatched. Thanks to the Young Girl Reading Group for finding weird stories to read with me.

Thanks to Lucia Pietroiusti, Filipa Ramos, and the Serpentine Galleries for asking me to give a talk in 2019 that evolved into the themes of this book. Thanks to Ben Vickers for telling me about solarpunk.

Thanks to McKenzie Wark for advising me in all things, and thanks to Eugene Thacker and Simon Critchley for their class on mysticism at The New School in 2018.

Thanks to Susan Ploetz for bringing me to larp, and to Erik Martinson for the wealth of material on plants and larps.

ACKNOWLEDGMENTS

Thanks to the editors who worked with me on earlier versions of these essays: Kaye Cain-Nielsen, Nick Axel, Josie Mitchell, Emily Firetog, Michael Miller, Medaya Ocher, and others.

Thanks to Jess, Sasha, Beny, Theresia, Vincenzo, Kristen, Domenick, Laura, Tania, William, Vijay, Madeleine, Emily, and Daisy for thinking with me and keeping me afloat.

Thanks to Andreas for reading every draft, watering our plants, and creating a world I want to live in.

ELVIA WILK is a writer living in New York. Her work has appeared in publications like *Frieze, Artforum, Bookforum, Granta, The Atlantic, n+1, The White Review, BOMB, Mousse, Flash Art,* and *art-agenda.* She is currently a contributing editor at *e-flux journal.* She is a recipient of the 2019 Andy Warhol Foundation Arts Writers Grant and a 2020 fellowship at the Berggruen Institute. Her first novel, *Oval,* was published by Soft Skull in 2019.